"*The* DEVIL
Made Me Do It!"

And yet all this severity of punishment could not suppress the breaking out of sundry notorious sins, especially drunkenness and uncleanness; not only incontinence between persons unmarried, for which many both men & women have been punished sharply, but some married persons also . . . The Devil should take some blame, being determined to cast a blemish and stain upon us . . . by tempting Saints into sin.

—WILLIAM BRADFORD, GOVERNOR OF PLYMOUTH COLONY, 1642

"*The* DEVIL Made Me Do It!"

CRIME AND PUNISHMENT
in
EARLY NEW ENGLAND

JULIET HAINES MOFFORD

Guilford, Connecticut

To buy books in quantity for corporate use
or incentives, call **(800) 962-0973**
or e-mail **premiums@GlobePequot.com.**

Library of Congress Cataloging-in-Publication Data

Mofford, Juliet Haines.
  The devil made me do it! : crime and punishment in early New England / Juliet Haines Mofford.
    p. cm.
  Includes bibliographical references and index.
  ISBN 978-0-7627-7165-3
  1. Crime—New England—History—17th century. 2. Trials—New England—History—17th
century. 3. Punishment—New England—History—17th century. 4. New England—History—
17th century. I. Title.
  HV6793.N295M64 2012
  364.97409'03—dc23

                                                                                    2011038537

Printed in the United States of America

10 9 8 7 6 5 4 3 2 1

Note to the reader: the Georgian Calendar that we all use today, with the year beginning on January
1, has been in use since 1582. The English however continued to use the earlier Julian Calendar
with the first day of each new year being observed on March 25. New Englanders, following British tradition, did not adopt the Georgian Calendar until 1752. Many dates presented throughout
the text will appear for example as 1692/3 since this is how dates from the first of January through
March are designated in history books, court records, and other primary sources.

Contents

PREFACE

IT WAS THE FIRST DAY OF SEPTEMBER IN THE YEAR 1640, AND NEARLY every man, woman, and child in the village was gathered outside the meetinghouse to witness the whipping of Thomas Pinson. His new wife, Joan, would not be flogged, but there she was, locked in the stocks. Tears streamed down the young woman's face as the small group of laughing boys took turns pelting her with rotten fruit and raw eggs.

"They need not suffer such punishment," a woman said, "had they paid the fine."

"Too poor to pay," commented an older man.

"'Tis a pity, for the two be husband and wife now," another villager remarked.

"Fornication before marriage, that be their crime," the town minister announced. "It is God's will they are punished for such a sin."

Court records reveal that early New Englanders were more apt to be lusty swains and loving maids than what is portrayed by those dour images traditionally associated with Puritans. Their earthiness and "wanton dalliance" hardly fits stereotypes from Hawthorne's historical fiction and the traditions found in the poetry of Longfellow. Examples of cases brought before the bench on grounds of fornication and illegitimacy provide proof that Puritans and Pilgrims participated wholeheartedly in earthly delights. Indeed, the attitude prevailing among seventeenth-century ministers and magistrates was that pleasures of the flesh were to be thoroughly and frequently enjoyed within the confines of marriage, so long as they took second place to honoring the glory of God through daily prayers. There were penalties for those who broke colonial moral rules and enjoyed such delights outside of matrimony, and for breaking numerous other laws that seem humorously quaint to us today.

Crime needs to be examined within its cultural context and punishment, viewed in terms of its social, religious, and political background. Today, Joan Andrews would not be forced to wear a "T" for Theft upon her bodice for placing stones in the firkin of butter she sold a client. A husband and wife experiencing marital discord would never be locked side by side in the village square beneath a sign reading QUARRELSOME COUPLE. And Lydea Abbot would certainly not be made to suffer in the stocks for "uttering ten profain curses."

Whether it was Sabbath-breaking, blasphemy, or drunkenness, colonial laws were frequently broken, and those who broke them could expect swift punishment. Laws were designed to reflect Puritan ideas of ensuring God's blessings upon the community, as well as to tightly maintain order in ways that would benefit the entire colony. Some of the ways that seventeenth- and early-eighteenth-century New England communities dealt with murder and mayhem seem brutal to us today. The use of public humiliation to deal with offenders and modify community behavior at the same time has become a staple in period movies and seems an amusing custom, but it was a grave matter for colonists. Each neighbor had a role in preserving family values and keeping the community safe from "railing scolds," vagabonds, malefactors, and malefic witches.

As we look at these laws and customs in relation to colonial crime, many questions arise. How did gender, race, and social status impact the punishments that were doled out? Who made the rules and passed judgment? Did the punishment fit the crime? Why were hangings considered public entertainment and attended by enthusiastic crowds? Modern technology and recent scholarship offer new and innovative methods of reexamining history so we are now better equipped to reevaluate the past and recognize many long-treasured myths as folklore or, simply, false.

Drawing from seventeenth- and eighteenth-century trial records, official documents, sermons, contemporary accounts recorded in personal diaries and journals, prison-keepers' records, broadsides, and even the dying words of condemned convicts, this book investigates selected court cases. Citizens on trial for their lives, witnesses, alleged witches, and judges offer allegations and testimonies in their own words, providing modern readers with a unique glimpse into the colonial justice system and the daily lives of our ancestors. *The DEVIL Made Me Do It!* provides an opportunity to understand how the people we have come to call Pilgrims and Puritans dealt with the challenges presented by deviant behavior at a time when accused felons frequently pleaded in their own defense, "The Devil made me do it!"

Part I

The Puritan Way

Massachusetts Bay Colony, as well as Plymouth and the New Haven and Connecticut colonies, represented a determined attempt to establish a theocracy where every person was expected to live according to a sacred covenant made with Almighty God to establish Christian settlements in the New World. Known first as Non-Conformists, and later as Puritans, these believers were intent upon reforming the Church of England—that is, to purify it by eliminating crosses, religious statues, clerical vestments, bishops, and all ecclesiastical rituals that were, in their view, "papist." Going a step further, the Separatists, now known as Pilgrims, wished to sever ties with the Anglican Church altogether.

More than simply a preferred way of worship, the Puritan faith provided a guidebook for how they preferred to live their daily lives. For them, worldly existence was not divided into secular and religious realms. They had no concept of a personal pursuit of happiness. It was godliness they aimed to achieve, and they read His Divine Plan into every aspect of earthly existence. Most early New England settlers considered life a contest between good and evil, with each individual on a pilgrimage toward eternal salvation or damnation. This world presented continual challenges and obstacles that were to be considered tests of one's faith. Satan placed endless temptations along the path to righteousness in hopes of thwarting each individual's commitment to God. Should a community suffer an epidemic or crop failure, it signaled a warning from the Lord that the congregation had grown lax about attending worship services or tolerating sin.

Crime represented a threat to the colonies' very survival. Thus, local authorities could not abide immoral or idle behavior, nor could they permit any disrespect for ministers and magistrates, whose responsibility it was to protect God's chosen people from Satan and sin. Pilgrims and Puritans believed that God had given mankind the Bible as the legal guide for life on Earth. Along with traditional English law, the Scriptures also contained rules to live by, and therefore formed the basis of New England's social and political structure. It was the duty of clergy and courts, as the earthly administrators of morality, to maintain harmony and stability within each family, and to oversee orderly and peaceful communities.

Prior to 1690, only male church members who were freeholders or owned land had the right to vote or hold public office. Attending meetings and contributing minister's rates to help pay the minister's salary and provide him with wheat, Indian corn, and firewood were required of every household. Refusing to pay this tax might mean having some of your property seized.

Women were considered "the Weaker Vessel"—not only because they were weaker in terms of physical strength, but also because they were considered weaker in intelligence and ability to reason. In fact, since it was Eve who tempted Adam in the Garden of Eden, females were viewed as morally weak by nature. God demanded obedience from women and wives, and, in turn, it was the duty of husbands to provide and protect. A wife was her husband's legal property and as such, had few rights of her own.

A husband was responsible for his wife's transgressions. If she neglected to attend Sabbathday services or Thursday Lecture Days at the local meetinghouse, he was held accountable and required to forfeit a fine. If a wife shouted rude remarks at a neighbor, both she and her spouse became defendants in any suit that might result.[1] Wives were expected to be subservient to husbands, as servants and slaves were required to obey their masters. Children were expected to be obedient to their parents, just as each citizen had to be subservient to ministers and magistrates. The entire structure of seventeenth century New England life depended upon maintaining this tight hierarchy.

Both Puritans and Pilgrims were Calvinists who, as followers of John Calvin's theology, believed in predestination. Because Adam and Eve dared to disobey the Creator, every human being was doomed to be born into original sin. However, because He was a loving God, some of His people would be rewarded with eternal salvation. No one knew who numbered among the Saints, but there *were* certain clues along the way. If one achieved wealth, health, and material success in this world, that was considered a significant sign that you could expect to be rewarded in the afterlife. Wealth was one indication that you were among God's Elect. On the other hand, poverty revealed that you were certainly not in God's favor.

The First Execution

It did not take long for Pilgrims and Puritans to realize that many who had immigrated to New England and now lived among them had not come to establish a new society based upon religious convictions and strict moral codes. The English settlers were forced to deal with crime and punishment from the beginning. Massachusetts's first murder forced New England's earliest leaders to quickly focus on developing a workable body of laws.

New England's first execution took place at Plymouth on September 30, 1630, when John Billington, an original *Mayflower* passenger, was hanged for killing John Newcomen with a blunderbuss. According to William Bradford, governor of Plymouth Colony, the men quarreled and Billington "waylaid a young man about a former quarrel and shot him with a gun, whereof he dyed." Billington was found "guilty of wilfull murder, by plaine & notorious evidence . . . This was the first execution among them, so it was a matter of great sadness unto them."

Since Plymouth Colony had been established without a formal charter, there was some question as to whether or not they had a legal right to enact the death penalty. So the colony leaders consulted with Governor Winthrop and other Massachusetts Bay Colony leaders as to "whether the perpetrator ought to dye, and the land be purged from blood . . ." According to these authorities at Boston, God demanded the death penalty for murder.

Governor Bradford wrote that Billington was "a knave and so shall he live and die." This troublemaker had "previously been punished for miscarriages of justice, his being one of the profanest families." Bradford was referring to an earlier offense committed by Billington when he had defied a direct order from Captain Miles Standish, "with opprobrious speeches." His punishment for this offense was to have "neck and heels tied together." Five years after Billington was hanged, his widow was found guilty of slander, fined £5 sterling, whipped, and locked in the stocks.

Beginning with the Billington case, the colonists viewed capital punishment not only as a triumph of justice but also as a means of social control and a deterrent to future crime.

LAWS CRAFTED FROM ENGLISH PRECEDENTS AND HOLY SCRIPTURE

Colonial leaders labored to maintain political stability in their new settlements, enacting strict rules to keep their people on the path of righteousness. New England's first immigrants brought with them experience and knowledge of the British justice system. Indeed, some of the earliest colonial leaders, including Governor John Winthrop and Chief Justice William Stoughton, were formally trained in English Common Law.

As early as 1634, twelve-man juries were appointed by local magistrates and convened to hear capital cases in Massachusetts Bay Colony, as was customary under English law. Trials were generally swift, throughout which the accused was hammered with questions regarding the charges against him or her, and detailing the deviant behavior that brought them before the bench. "Speak to the prisoner fair to the end that you may get him to confess," advised one judge, since to the Puritans, confession meant the promise of Christian redemption.

County courts generally gathered for five or six days, four times a year, in different towns. If the magistrates agreed there was sufficient evidence, a trial was scheduled, and jurymen, with several judges, heard the case and brought in a verdict. New Haven, the strictest of all New England colonies, was the only one lacking trial by jury in the seventeenth century. Although defense lawyers were unknown prior to the mid-eighteenth century, accused persons did have the right to hear details of the charges against them and were generally permitted to speak in their own defense.[2]

Trials were typically conducted in the town's largest venue in order to accommodate curious crowds. Since Court Day was considered a community event, a local tavern or inn usually doubled as the courtroom. Everyone was eager to learn about new cases on the docket, to see the malefactors, to listen to the evidence and testimonies, and to hear the final verdicts, as well as to witness any subsequent punishments administered.

After 1740, Massachusetts juries were no longer appointed as they had been in England, nor elected, but were selected by lot. Judges and jurymen did not listen to both sides as they presented evidence in order to make a decision, as they do now.

The first formal body of laws in British North America was the *Plymouth Code of 1636*. Closely based on English precedents, it provided a governor and seven assistants with annual elections of court clerks, coroners, and constables. The *Massachusetts Bay Colony's 1641 Body of Liberties,* drafted by retired Ipswich minister, Nathaniel Ward, offered the populace a set of rules to live by, as well as a basic explanation of their new government. Its tenets remained pretty much in force until the Provincial Charter was enacted after 1692.

In 1630, when the Puritans sailed for Massachusetts, some 223 crimes still carried the death penalty in England. New Englanders reduced these to a mere 14, all of which were crimes in the Bible, demanding the death penalty.

Cursing and striking one's parents was made a capital crime. The *Body of Liberties* stated, however, that a wife could not be struck by her husband unless she hit him first. That code also included the first legislation against cruelty toward animals: "No man shall exercise any tyranny nor cruelty towards any brute creatures which are ordinarily kept for man's use." Killing wolves, however, was encouraged and rewarded with bounties, since wolves threatened the livestock upon which settlers depended, and prior to 1700, Windham County in Connecticut sponsored an annual winter wolf hunt.

Although the Old Testament and English Common Law remained the major legal sources, the *1648 Laws and Liberties of Massachusetts* was more detailed, basing criminal law upon Mosaic code, and even citing chapter and verse from the Bible, relevant to each. This legislation specifically prohibited "cruel and barbarous punishment," and limited the number of whiplashes permissible at one time to thirty-nine. Conviction for any capital crime under the *1648 Laws and Liberties* required the testimony of two witnesses and included the Right of Appeal. A defendant in a capital case could complain to the General Court of an injustice suffered in another court, and the General Court had the power to pardon a condemned criminal. Should this higher court not be in session, the governor and deputy governor, or any three assistants, in joint consent, could grant a reprieve. These laws represented a determined effort to govern the lives of citizens in accordance with the religious and moral ideals of Puritanism.[3]

The *1648 Laws and Liberties of Massachusetts* also attempted to keep married couples in line:

> *Every married woman shall be free from bodily correction or stripes by her husband, unless it be in his defense upon her assault. If therebe any just cause of correction complaint shall be made to Authoritie assembled in some Court, from which only she shall receive it.*
>
> *No man shall strike his Wife, nor any Woman her Husband, on penalty of such fine not exceeding ten pounds for one offense, or such Corporal punishment as the County Court shall determine.*

Like Massachusetts Bay, the New Haven and Connecticut colonies established by the Reverends John Davenport and Thomas Hooker, Edward Hopkins and Theophilus Eaton, was an attempt to create a society made up of persons who believed themselves living instruments of God's Holy Purpose. Thus, Connecticut's *Plantation Covenant,* also defined by Scripture, seemed to leaders "the perfect rule for direction and government of church, family, and commonwealth . . . Churches, public offices, magistrates, the making and repealing of laws . . ." adhered to biblical codes. All who came to the settlement were expected to come with the purpose of being church members. And "only church members should choose magistrates among themselves and transact public business and decide difficulties."

When Roger Ludlow shaped Connecticut's laws between 1646 and 1650, he adopted fourteen articles from the *1641 Massachusetts Body of Liberties,* and then added sixty-three new ones. In New Haven in 1650, Thomas Langden was charged with the "disorderly Intertaining of young men in his House at unseasonable times in the nights to drinke wine, strong water, and take Tobacco." Goodman Langden was also accused of leading the "company in filthy corrupting songs." His defense in court was that he "thought he was but Hospitable as if they were in Old England where they could sing and be merry." The host's fine was 20 shillings on the first offense.[4]

By 1706, perjury was added as a crime, and if the offender was unable to pay the £67 fine, he or she was locked in the pillory for an hour with both ears nailed to the frame. This was also the manner by which Connecticut "trained" the Native Americans living among them, "to honor and observe the Christian Sabbath."[5]

PUBLIC RIDICULE AS PUNISHMENT

Those who broke moral, religious, and political laws were forced to undergo public humiliation and endure ridicule from the entire community. Punishments were not only designed for the chastisement of offenders, but were also meant to provide valuable lessons for all. Not only were the malefactors admonished and hopefully deterred from subsequent crimes, but punishment also served as a warning to every citizen. Those watching were expected to empathize with the lawbreaker's fair punishment and share in his or her pain and shame.

Stocks, pillories, and whipping posts erected in the center of town, usually near the meetinghouse, were a highly visible means of social control. Stocks—used more frequently than pillories—consisted of two heavy timbers with half circles cut into each frame, which, when lowered and locked, held the seated prisoner's head, legs, and arms. A pillory was a wooden frame with a central hole large enough for the lawbreaker's head and smaller holes at each side to secure the hands.

Nineteenth century illustration (originally Culver Service) of a man locked in stocks for his punishment. COLLECTION OF THE AUTHOR

The offender was forced to stand in the pillory for the duration of his or her sentence. A placard with a capital letter was customarily tacked above each prisoner, designating the crime, such as "B" for Blasphemy, "T" for Theft, or "F" for Fornication. Hopefully, every culprit on public display would suffer guilt and remorse. Anyone locked in the stocks or pillory could expect to be taunted by townspeople. Most parents considered witnessing punishments as significant learning experiences for their children, so boys and girls were encouraged to throw rotten eggs, apples, and garbage, and even to toss stones or snowballs at any prisoner on public display.

This style of punishment was required by colony law. The Massachusetts Bay towns of Newbury and Concord were fined for "want of stocks" as early as 1638, and the following year, Dedham and Watertown were similarly charged. The Town of Haverhill paid a fine to the Quarterly Court of Essex County in 1679, "for not having stocks." Thirty years before, this same court had ordered Haverhill to "erect stocks immediately." Rhode Island rules required "good sufficient stocks" for every town, while Strawbery Banke (now Portsmouth, New Hampshire) not only erected stocks but also boasted a cage to hold offenders. By 1706, a Connecticut statute compelled all towns to build and maintain "a good pair of stocks with lock and key. The policy of the stocks being to make the disgrace of the criminal as conspicuous as possible."[6]

Military punishments were somewhat different. "Riding the wooden horse," also known as "the Timber Mare," was the most common humiliation for colonial soldiers and often continued until the soldier bled. The offender, hands tied behind his back, was perched atop two planks about eight foot in length that had been nailed together to form a triangular ridge. Supported by four posts or legs, the contraption resembled a horse and rider and was often embellished with a horse's tail and makeshift head. As the delinquent soldier straddled this instrument of torture, 25- to 50-pound weights were often tied to both his feet.

In 1670, Richard Gibson, a Maine militiaman, was "complayned of for his dangerous carriage to his commander and the multiplying of oaths." He was sentenced "to be laid neck and heels tied together for two hours or to ride the Wooden Horse at the head of the company next training day at Kittery."[7]

Whipping with the leather cat-o'-nine-tails, another means of public humiliation, was the most common punishment doled out by the courts for any crime not severe enough to warrant the death sentence. Judges usually specified the number of lashes to be administered for each particular case. Even for the most heinous miscreants, flogging ceased at "forty stripes save one," as the Bible advised. Nor were those charged with doling out such punishments immune to the law. According to the *Ipswich Quarterly Court Records* of September 1677, Jonas Gregory, the town whipper, was derelict in his duty, and, "for abusing the court in not performing the duty of his office upon Lawrence Clenton of Rowley: Himself sentenced to be whipped."

Twenty years later in New Haven, a man employed to whip lawbreakers got fined and fired for refusing to flog a woman. However, the court could not find anyone else willing to fill his position. Whipping women had been discontinued throughout New England by the 1750s, except as punishment for the crime of adultery and for the repeated bearing of bastards.[8]

The way Puritans and Pilgrims saw it, those who broke laws in this new land were punished fairly. They might be forced to suffer the personal torment of public humiliation, but this was nothing in comparison to the eternal torture awaiting them in hell should they not reform their ways. This is one reason magistrates and ministers worked tirelessly to get prisoners to confess to their crimes and seek repentance.

CLASS AND SOCIAL STATUS

Class and social status had a definite bearing upon who got arrested and what punishments were meted out. Members of the gentry were usually exempt from such demeaning punishments as public whipping or being locked in the stocks or pillories. For example, the *York County Court of Quarter Sessions* only fined Nathaniel Cane £5 for beating his slave, Rachel, to death. Had she been white, he likely would have gone to the gallows.

Wealthy persons and those of high rank were generally required to simply forfeit fines, which were frequently canceled by colleagues who sat on the bench. In 1648, all Massachusetts "gentlemen of property" were made legally exempt from whipping. In addition to receiving the prescribed number of lashes upon the bare back, an indentured servant unable to pay the imposed fine usually saw his or her term of servitude extended by years.

There were limits to punishments. The flogging of pregnant women was always postponed until after the child had arrived. Parents were permitted to whip rebellious children, and teachers could beat their pupils, just as masters were permitted to chastise servants and slaves with whips or sticks, but corporal punishment applied in excess was illegal. The *1641 Massachusetts Body of Liberties* was clear on the subject, "For bodilie punishments we allow amongst us none that are inhumane, barbarous or cruel."

Quakers and prostitutes, however, were evidently exempt from this pronouncement. Their usual penalty was to be stripped to the waist and tied to the end of a cart, where they were whipped from town to town, through lines of jeering spectators. The *Plymouth Court Records of 1665* tell the tale of a woman named Sarah Ensigne, who, "for committing whoredom aggravated with divers circumstances, was sentenced by the Court to be whipt at the carts taile; and that it be left to the discretion of such of the magistrates as shall see the said punishment inflicted for the number of stripes, but not to exceed twenty."

TREATMENT OF NATIVE AMERICANS

In the view of most Puritan authorities, "heathen" Native Americans did not deserve the same legal respect as Christians. Indians considered idle or troublesome were either sold or bartered to other New England and New York tribes, or exiled to the British West Indies. Many colonists believed what clergy in both Old and New England often preached: that God cleared the way for the Christian settlement of "His New Zion in the American Wilderness" by sending plagues that decimated approximately two-thirds of New England's Native American population. Some ministers went so far as to preach and publish the idea that Indians, with their face paint, near nakedness, and shamanistic rituals, were but "Agents of the Devil."

In 1646, the Reverend John Eliot, the Puritan minister who dreamed of converting all "savages" to Christianity, prepared a set of rules for "Praying Towns," or settlements of Native Americans who had converted to Christianity. These strict new codes of behavior prohibited such Native American customs as the plurality of wives, gambling, the greasing of bodies, and the picking and eating of lice (the penalty was a penny due for every louse). Orders also decreed "there be no more pawwowing amongst Indians and if so, both he that shall pawwow and he that shall procure him to pawwow, shall pay 20 shillings apiece." (*Pawwow* was defined as "witches or sorcerers that cure by help of the devil.") Indians were also "to desire they may understand the wiles of Satan, and grow out of love with the Devil's suggestions and temptations." Anything stolen was to be restored fourfold (though Massachusetts law stated but threefold restitution for everyone else). They should also "wear their hair comely, as the English do, and whosoever shall offend herein shall pay 5 shillings."[9]

The majority of Puritans and Pilgrims seemed to consider Native Americans simply as "unfortunate heathens who deserved the Saving Grace of the Gospel," and so, yearned to "civilize and educate Indians to Christianity." Thus, John Eliot's regulations for *Praying Indians,* or Christian converts, also required "they do observe the Lord's Day, and whosoever shall prophane it shall pay 20 shillings." And "they do all resolve to set up prayer in their wigwams and to seek to God both before and after their meats [or meals]…"[10]

Most judges did attempt to be fair in dealing with Native American issues and seemed to consider both sides of a sticky situation. The *Essex County Court Records* of 1651 reported on one case:

> *Benjamin Muzye of Rowley, for bartering a gun to the Indians, and denying it, fined 50 shillings, and to sit four hours in the stocks; also to pay the Indian his beaver again, or 50 shillings, if in other pay.*

Still, prejudice was nearly impossible to overcome. After King Philip's War of 1675–76, the Massachusetts General Court decreed that no one could buy or keep as slaves any Indians over the age of twelve, "as Indians cause much trouble and fear to Inhabitants where they reside and could be dangerous to towns."

In 1711, three Indians and a Frenchman were caught stealing a sloop in York Harbor. They were put on trial, found guilty, and quickly hanged at Stage Neck. Following execution, their scalps were removed and their bodies tossed into the sea. Presented to authorities in Boston, each scalp received a bounty of £40 each. Enmity continued to increase. Five years later, in 1716, Samuel Sewall, soon to be chief justice of the Massachusetts Superior Court, noted in his diary, "I essayed to present Indians and Negroes being rated with horses and hogs, but could not prevail."

Nightwalking was against the law for all citizens, but blacks and Native Americans were required to be inside before dark unless accompanied by their masters, or else receive ten whiplashes.

In fact, hatred against Native Americans in Maine was so strong that in 1750, no white man could be convicted for killing one. Most Englishmen protested killing an Indian could not be considered murder.[11]

At Wiscasset, in 1749, six white men allegedly attacked a group of sleeping Indians, killing one and wounding two. The perpetrators were captured, then escaped with their leader, Obadiah Albee. Though five of the men were soon caught and incarcerated in York Gaol, Albee remained at large for some time, but with a reward offered, was recaptured.

This unhappy affair produced a strong sensation throughout the eastern country, and although the government did everything in their power, with gifts and kind treatment of the Indians, to appease their anger and to conciliate their friendship, they did not succeed in allaying the spirit of revenge that governed these people . . . Albee went on trial at York in June 1750, and after a four month trial, was found Not Guilty, though later convicted of felonious assault. Fearing reprisals from Indians seeking revenge, two of the prisoners were taken to Middlesex in Massachusetts Bay for their trials, but "since Indian friends of the deceased were present," the men were not tried at the time appointed and were subsequently remanded to York for trial, which does not appear to have taken place.

The acquittal of Albee produced dissatisfaction . . . [S]o strongly seated was the feeling of resentment against the Indians in the hearts of the people who had long contended with them for their very existence, that a jury could not be impaneled to convict a white person of murder for killing one of them.[12]

"Ordeal by Touch"

In a secret murder, if the dead body be at any time thereafter han-
dled by the murderer, it will gush out blood, as if crying to heaven for
revenge . . . God having appointed that secret supernatural sign for the
trial of that secret, unnatural crime.

—James Stuart, *Demonology*, Scotland, 1597

One of the most curious methods for a murder conviction was brought
to New England from Europe. This concept of *Ordeal by Touch* was based
upon God's judgment against Cain in the book of Genesis, when the
voice of his slain brother, Abel, "crieth from the ground: *Truth Will Out.*"
It was believed that a murderer's guilt could be determined for certain
when the criminal suspect, ordered to touch the victim, caused the corpse
to bleed anew, thus immediately identifying the murderer and proving
certain guilt. Also known as *Ordeal by Blood* and *Trial by Ordeal,* this
method was used to obtain the most difficult confessions.

England's King James the First, formerly James IV of Scotland,
made certain that *Ordeal by Blood* was included in all legal manifests in
the kingdom.

The Convictions of Mary Martin and Katherine Cornish

When prosperous merchant Richard Martin returned to England on
business, he left his two daughters, "proper maidens of modest behavior," behind with the Mitton family, friends who lived at Casco Bay (now
Portland, Maine). Although Mr. Mitton had a wife and children, he was
quite taken with twenty-two-year-old Mary. According to the account
in Governor Winthrop's journal, he "solicit[ed] her chastity, obtained his
desire, and diverse times over three months, committed the sin of adultery
with her." When Mary realized she was pregnant, she moved to Boston,
where she found a job as a servant and a room to rent at Widow Borne's.

In December of 1646, Mary Martin gave birth to a daughter in
Goody Borne's back room, and, "not able to bear the shame kneeled upon
the head till she thought it dead." She then "hid the body in a chest and
cleaned the room." When Mary found a position in another household

the following week, she carried the chest containing the infant's body along with her.

A midwife soon confronted Mary with her suspicions, although Widow Borne insisted that "Maid Mary's behavior was so modest and her service so faithful that she would not give ear to any such report." However, authorities were summoned, and to prove innocence or guilt, Mary was ordered to undergo the test of *Ordeal by Blood.* According to eyewitnesses and Mary's jury, "when the chest was opened and the young woman put her hand upon the face of her dead infant, the blood came forth fresh to it," causing the terrified Mary to immediately confess to infanticide.

Mary Martin was executed on March 18, 1647, although "after she was turned off and had hung in space, she asked the hangmen what they did mean to do. Someone then stepped forward from the crowd to turn the knot of the rope backward," and Mary soon died.[13]

The idea that guilt could be legally determined by having a murder suspect touch the corpse of a victim had been applied the previous year at Agamenticus, where Katherine Cornish was accused of killing her husband. Goody Cornish had appeared in court several times before for "lewd behavior." Then, in 1644, the bruised body of her husband, Richard Cornish, was discovered floating in the York River with a pole sticking out of his side. The mayor of Agamenticus presided at her trial, during which the defendant accused him of having enjoyed carnal relations with her.

According to early *York Records,* when confronted with her husband's dead body, it "bled abundantly." Katherine still refused to confess to murder, although she did admit to "having lived in adultery with divers." She even named Mayor Roger Garde, who, although he did have a reputation of being "a carnal man," flatly denied having ever had any sexual liaison with Goodwife Cornish. She was marched to the gallows solely on the conclusive evidence of *Ordeal by Touch.*

The Spark That Ignited a War

John Sassamon was a Praying Indian who attended Harvard College and served as translator and scribe for the Reverend John Eliot. In March of 1674–75, soon after informing Plymouth Colony governor Josiah

Winslow of rumors he'd heard that Metacom (whom the English called King Philip) was planning to join his Wampanoag forces with the Narragansett and other Native American tribes to launch an attack against the English, Sassamon's body was discovered underneath the ice in a frozen pond. His hat and rifle had been placed on top to make it seem as if Sassamon had fallen through. Bruises discovered on his body quickly led to suspicion of murder. Considered a traitor by many Wampanoag for warning the English authorities—and Governor Winslow in particular—Sassamon had indeed feared for his life.

Then an eyewitness stepped forward, a Native American who told the English he had been standing on a hilltop when he saw three men "lay violent hands" upon Sassamon, "twisting his neck." Although Metacom angrily protested English authorities interfering in what he considered to be solely Indian business, Governor Winslow arrested the three Native American suspects. They were subsequently tried before a jury of twelve Englishmen and six Indians.

When one suspect, ordered to touch Sassamon's body, approached the alleged victim, it "fell a-bleeding afresh as if newly slain." This *Ordeal by Touch* became the final spark that ignited Metacom's Rebellion, or King Philip's War, in 1675–76. All three Indians received the guilty verdict and two were quickly hanged, while the third was shot. Metacom was incensed, and claimed "the English had no right to execute any Indians for killing other Indians."[14]

Twelve days later, the English settlement of Swansea was attacked and the bloody and tragic King Philip's War was under way. By the end of the year 1675, out of ninety English settlements, fifty-two had been attacked and twelve completed destroyed.[15]

The End of Ordeal by Touch

The last known example of any court's use of Ordeal by Touch or Ordeal by Blood used to indict any accused person was in Connecticut in 1680, but its final employment as judicial evidence in New England is believed to have been the 1769 Ames case in West Boxford, Massachusetts. Ruth Perley wed Jonathan Ames and died a year later under mysterious circumstances.

At the coroner's inquest held in the local meetinghouse, it was ascertained that Ruth Ames "came to her death by Felony (that is to say, by poison)." Her husband and mother-in-law, Elizabeth Ames, were suspected. Five weeks after burial, the body of Ruth Ames was exhumed and laid upon a table under a sheet. Jonathan and his mother were invited to touch the neck of the deceased with the index finger of their left hands, but both refused to undergo the *Ordeal by Blood* test. Both were arrested and sent to Salem Prison to await trial for murder. Future U.S. president John Adams served as defense attorney, winning their acquittal and release.

PART II

Governing the Family

Thomas Chubb presented for misspending his time idly to the prejudice of his family.
> —ESSEX COUNTY COURT OF QUARTERLY SESSIONS,
> DECEMBER 1643

Goodwife Andrews admonished for cursing and reviling her son-in-law, Humphry Griffin.
> —ESSEX COUNTY COURT OF QUARTERLY SESSIONS,
> MARCH 1647

MAINTAINING HARMONY IN THE HOME PRESENTED A NEVER-ENDING challenge for ministers and magistrates. The family was expected to be a model of piety and mutual respect, since religious faith, education, and deference to authority began in the home. The family and the community that kept God's rules and lived in faith and goodness would be rewarded with peace and prosperity. Otherwise, Almighty God might decide to punish the disorderly household with misery. A man known as a *tything-man* was appointed by local selectmen to keep watch over every ten families and report any signs of marital strife, disobedient and stubborn children, or Sabbath-breakers, *common tipplers* (habitual drunks), and *nightwalkers* (persons out in the streets after nine o'clock curfew, without authorization), as well as any townspeople suspected of inappropriate sexual liaisons. During worship services, *tythingmen* walked the aisles of the meetinghouse carrying long poles prepared to poke any member of the congregation caught snoozing. In the early 1700s, parents of Connecticut children not easily shushed or caught giggling and playing during meeting forfeited 3 shillings per child.[16]

Tythingmen also had to make certain every member of the congregation was seated in his or her assigned place during services. People sat in the meetinghouse according to social rank. Known as "dignifying the pews," this "seating the meeting" demonstrated to everyone in the community how hierarchy governed every aspect of life. Magistrates, for example, were expected to "sit High and have a cushion." In Andover in 1680, anyone discovered out of place was required to forfeit 20 shillings.[17]

Descriptions of the *tythingman* performing his duties might seem amusing to modern readers: "It was the custom of this time, during the service, for a person to go about the meeting-house to wake the sleepers. He bore a long wand, on one end of which was a ball, and on the other, a fox tail. When he observed the men asleep, he rapped them on the head with the knob, and roused the slumbering sensibilities of the ladies by drawing the brush lightly across their faces."[18]

But the repercussions for those who failed to heed the rules of the Sabbath were serious. In 1643, Roger Scott, a citizen of Lynn, was presented at court "for common sleeping at the public exercise upon the Lord's Day, and for striking the tythingman who waked him from his godless slumber." Later that same year, "not having amended his conduct, Goodman Scott was sentenced by the court, to be severely whipped."

MINDING YOUR NEIGHBOR'S BUSINESS

Since the transgressions of a few citizens might possibly bring God's wrath upon the entire community, surveillance of neighbors was considered one's Christian duty. Being a good citizen meant bearing witness against one's neighbor. As your brother's keeper, you were expected to keep close and constant watch for discord within families. Spying and reporting infractions of moral behavior was one's personal and communal responsibility. Tattling and gossip kept most people in line.

Community concern sometimes went too far, however, as when William Clark was whipped in December of 1643, "for spying into the Haverhill chamber of his master and mistress and for reporting what he saw." In another Haverhill incident, on August 17, 1680, the Haverhill constable issued a "warrant for the appearance of Benjamin Greely at court upon the complaint of John Severns for peeping in the windows."

Neighbors' reports often resulted in due punishment for the ones being tattled on; for example, James Creeke would not have been whipped for "heinous, lascivious, and adulterous behavior" with Luke Perkins's wife, Elizabeth, had his Ipswich neighbors not gone to the authorities. Mary Brown, for one, testified to seeing "Creeke kiss Perkins' wife several times one moonlight night and saw her go into Haly's shop where he was working, pull up his hat, look into his face, tickle him and bring him drink, making a great deal more of him than she ever saw her make of her own husband." This nineteen-year-old gossip claimed she'd also seen the couple kissing on the street.

John Brown, another witness in Creeke's case, testified that he was returning from the pasture when he saw James and Elizabeth "tickling one another about the ribs." Brown said he was so ashamed that he hurried into his own house. Others reported seeing the couple enter the orchard together after church services, "handling linen with their heads close together."[19]

DRESS ACCORDING TO YOUR STATION

Seventeenth-century New Englanders believed that God preordained some persons to positions of wealth, status, and leadership, while others were meant to remain servants. Early New Englanders could get into trouble with the law simply for *excess in apparel*, or dressing above their social station.

Connecticut passed a law in 1641, and the Massachusetts General Court did the same in 1651, to keep ordinary folks from dressing in a manner "exceeding their conditions and ranks." In 1663, John Kindrick was fined "upon his wife's presentment: for excess in apparel, wearing a silk hood, scarf and French fall shoes." Those of "meane condition" could be punished for donning gentleman's garb by wearing ruffled shirts, lace cuffs, or gold and silver buttons on waistcoat cuffs or at the knees of breeches. Goodwives had best not be caught wearing silk scarves, tiffany hoods, slashed sleeves, ribbons, or embroidery, as was then all the rage in Europe. The dress code was another way to keep everyone in their designated places and maintain the colony's desired social order.[20]

Daniel Bosworth's two daughters were fined 10 shillings each in 1667 for wearing silk, "contrary to law for persons of their station." The personal worth of the girls' father was valued at less than the £200 required for donning fashionable clothing.

Among young men in the 1650s, there was "a lust for long hair worn like women's hair." Governor Endicott and his assistants made a public declaration in court against long hair: "For as much as the wearing of long hair after the manner of Ruffians and barbarous Indians has begun to invade New England."[21]

In 1692, Stephen Johnson Jr., a thirteen-year-old confessed witch from (North) Andover in Massachusetts Bay, admitted making a pact with Satan because he was promised a pair of French fall dancing shoes. Seventeen-year-old William Barker Jr., from the same town, agreed to sign the Devil's Book and serve him in exchange for a new suit of clothes.

INCORRIGIBLE AND DELINQUENT YOUTH

If parents or masters neglect training up their children in learning and labor and other employments which may be profitable to the Commonwealth, they shall be sufficiently punished by fines for the neglect thereof.
—MASSACHUSETTS BAY COLONY, EDICT OF JUNE 14, 1642

Calvinist Puritans considered it the parents' duty to break the wills of their children. They called it "ruling" the child rather than "disciplining," and favored the use of rods or switches as a punitive measure. Parents were blamed for any misbehavior of their children, and those continually unable to control their offspring might see them removed from the household by local selectmen and placed in other homes.

A Massachusetts General Court order of November 4, 1646, declared that

If a man have a rebellious son of sufficient age and understanding-viz. 16-which will not obey the voice of his father or the voice of his mother, and that, when they have chastened him, will not hearken unto them, then shall his father and mother, being his natural parents, lay hold on him, and bring him to the magistrates assembled in court, and testify unto them, by sufficient evidence, that this their son is stubborn and rebellious and will not obey their voice and chastisement but lives in sundry notorious crimes. Such a son shall be put to death.

Fortunately, no historical record has yet been found showing that this harsh and extreme measure was ever enforced. Unmanageable young people did, however, get summoned to appear before the Massachusetts General Court, as was the case with young John Downing, who was presented "for his disobedience to his father."

After 1675, wayward young people from the Bay Colony were to be whipped or fined upon their second and all subsequent convictions.

On July 4, 1679, Edward Bumpas of Plymouth was charged with striking and abusing both parents. He was whipped at the post, the *Plymouth Colony Court Records* noting leniency "in regard the youth was crasey-brained." Otherwise, he would have been executed.

In 1658, the General Court at Boston expressed deep concern over

"incorrigible and delinquent" youth keeping corrupt company without leave . . . to the great grief of their Superiors . . . the sun being sett, both every Saturday & on the Lord's Day, young people take liberty to walk and sport themselves in the streets or fields . . . to the dishonor of God and the disturbance of others in their religious exercises, and too frequently repair to publique houses of entertainment & there sitt drinking, all which tends, not only to the hindering of due preparation for the Sabbath, but as much as in them renders the ordinances of

God altogether unprofitable, & threatens rooting out of the power of
godliness, and procuring the wrath & judgment of God upon us and
our posterity . . .

Governor Bradford of Plymouth expressed concern in his journal about young people being particularly prone to sexual temptations. "All mankind possesses corrupt natures," he wrote, "so hardly bridled, subdued and mortified." In 1675, the Massachusetts General Court condemned young people who rode from town to town together upon the pretense of attending lectures, but instead, "went drinking and reveling in ordinaries and taverns." Such behavior worried adult authorities since it was considered "notable means to debauch our youth and hazard their chastity."

An Arrow Against Profane and Promiscuous Dancing: Drawn Out of the Quiver of the Scriptures, was the title of a sermon delivered in 1686 in Boston by the Reverend Increase Mather. In 1704, this same minister complained in his diary of "a profane dancing school" that was but "fitting testimony to these sad times." Twenty years before, even in small rural communities like Boxford, young people frequently gathered to dance at Moses Tyler's place.

William Harding of New Haven was whipped and fined in 1642 for his "[b]ase carriage and filthy dalliances with divers young girls at night meetings and junketing."

In 1720, the New Haven Court spoke against young people who attended "frolicks and went out junketing; those who misspend and waste time at night meetings, debauching themselves in corrupt songs and foolish jesting . . . with wanton and lascivious carriage and mixed dancing." Authorities were especially concerned about illicit goings-on during gatherings where young people were husking Indian corn.[22]

In 1679, according to *Suffolk County Records,* the Dorchester selectmen summoned Robert Stiles "to give an account how he did improve his time for himself and Children," and said he "should look out for a place for one of his Children at least, or else the Selectmen would provide a place." The same town fathers expressed concern over the "State of the

A Puritan family gathered around the table at mealtime. SEVENTEENTH-CENTURY WOODCUT, AUTHOR'S COLLECTION

Family" of Francis Bale, advising him to "put out two of his children." Goodman Bale replied that "his wife was not willing." The Dorchester selectmen "perswaded Bale to perswade his wife to it."[23]

Many parents lost control over their offspring because young people were often *bound out* to live in other households as servants, or apprentices learning trades. Rebellious teenagers such as Andover's Mary Lacey caught outside past curfew got accused of *nightwalking* and "refusing to shun bad company." Mary's father was a habitual drunk and she was sent to live with her uncle's family.

In the New Haven and Connecticut colonies, youth were fined 10 shillings, or sentenced to spend time in the stocks for nightwalking without parental consent.

"RAILING" WOMEN

Wives who "railed" against their husbands and neighbors were known as "scolds," and were seen as a threat to community stability. The Reverend Cotton Mather admonished women to tame their tongues. "Feminine virtue requires careful speech," the Boston minister preached. He instructed all females to constantly admonish themselves: "I will take heed unto my ways that I sin not with my tongue. I will keep my mouth with a Bridle."[24]

Jane Collins was summoned before the Hartford court in 1654, for calling her husband a "gurley-gutted devil." That same year, at Taunton in Massachusetts Bay, Joan, the wife of Obadiah Miller, was charged with "beating and reviling her husband, and egging her children to help her, bidding them to knock him on the head, and wishing his victuals might choke him."[25] And the following year, Isabel Pudeator received "fifteen lashes upon presentment for drinking, an unruly carriage and for abusing her husband."

"Railing women" seemed to be epidemic all over New England for much of the latter half of the eighteenth century. Joan Ford received nine lashes at the Casco whipping post in 1665, for calling the constable a "horn-headed, cowhead rogue" (this translated to "the Devil"). A few months later, this same scold was back in court for "reviling and abusing her neighbors with very evil speeches and for abusing the constable." She was given ten more lashes upon her bare back at the whipping post. Ursula, wife of Henry Edwards, was presented before the bench at Boston in 1672, "for striking her husband & abusive Carriage & Language; the presentment was Owned [confessed] & she was Sentenced to be whipt with ten Stripes or pay twenty Shillings fine."

Elizabeth Cole's unfettered tongue got her into trouble when she said of her ministers that she had "as live hear a cat meow as them preach." Foul-mouthed Joan Andrews, a resident of Kittery and York, was a repeat offender. This woman's outrageous and uncontrolled tongue got her summoned before court in 1652, 1657, 1659, and 1666, where at one hearing she informed the bench that she "cared not a turd for Edward Rishworth nor any magistrate in the world!" The jury agreed this contentious woman was a liar who drank too much. Her punishment "for heaping abuses" upon Governor Rishworth was twenty-five whiplashes upon her bare back. Goody Andrews's "reviling speech" was certainly colorful. She called Kittery merchant Shapleigh "a base knave," and labeled his wife a "peddler's trull."[26]

The *York County Court Records* reveal that Joan Andrews also attempted to cheat Nicholas Davis by placing several stones in a firkin of butter and selling it to him in a wooden tub. For this particular act of fraud, she was compelled to stand for a couple of hours at both York and Kittery town meetings with a sign on her forehead describing her dishonest deed. Ever defiant, the notorious scold threatened to sign an oath of fidelity to the Devil and become a witch so that she might wreak vengeance upon them all.[27]

The Cucking Stool

Most readers today probably associate colonial ducking, or *cucking*—suspending an offender tied onto a chair by a crane over water into which she was repeatedly plunged until her impatience and irritability were moderated—with witchcraft trials. Indeed, this method was applied in England and Scotland to test women suspected of witchcraft. The theory was that if the accused floated, it signified rejection by "water's purity," thus proving guilt. Should the body sink, the woman was deemed innocent of familiarity with the Devil, even though she sometimes drowned. The only example of this practice being used for witchcraft suspects in New England comes from Connecticut. That colony dunked its last "scold" in 1662, but put two alleged witches to this "water test" in 1692.

In Massachusetts, the use of cucking (or ducking) stools was a punishment reserved for "scolds" and "brawlers"—women unable to keep their tongues bridled. On May 15, 1672, the General Court of Massachusetts passed a new law "against exorbitancy of the tongue in rayling and scolding . . ." It ordered that "Scolds and Railers shall be gagged or sett in a ducking stool and dipt over the head and ears three times in some convenient place of fresh or salt water as the Court or Magistrate shall judge meete." In 1649, the General Court at Gorgeana (later, Agamenticus; now York, Maine) ruled that "any woman that shall abuse her husband or neighbor or any other by opprobrious vile language, being lawfully convicted: for her first offense, shall be put in the stocks two hours; for her second offense, to be ducked and if incorrigible, to be whipped."

The cucking (or ducking) stool was the preferred punishment for scolds and brawlers. The offender was tied into a chair that was attached to a movable wooden post on the bank of a river or pond, which was then plunged in and out of the water. The punishment was also used for colonists found guilty of drunkenness, slander, or disturbing the peace of a community. SEVENTEENTH-CENTURY WOODCUT, AUTHOR'S COLLECTION

York, Kittery, and other Maine towns were later fined "for providing no couckling stool." And although this particular method of punishment does not seem to appear anywhere in the *Suffolk Country Court Records,* there is evidence of wide use of ducking stools in Rhode Island.

Three married women from Reading were fined 5 shillings each for "scolding" in 1649, but in 1672, this same town decreed that "any woman convicted of railing or scolding, shall be gagged, or set in a ducking pool and dipped over head and ears three times."

Woodcuts of quarrelsome couples or fornicators sentenced to serve time together in the pillory and the stocks. SEVENTEENTH-CENTURY WOODCUTS, AUTHOR'S COLLECTION

QUARRELSOME COUPLES

"Quarrelsome couples" were regularly summoned before the entire congregation at the meetinghouse to be publicly warned to cease bickering and live in Christian charity or suffer punishment. On August 6, 1695, Judge Samuel Sewall made the following entry in his diary: "Mr. Obinson's wife comes to me and complains of her Husband's ill usage of her … Kick'd her out of bed last night; lets her have nothing but water to drink; won't let her have Clothes or victuals."

John Barrett of Wells, Maine, protested being called before York County Court for slighting and abusing his wife. "What hath any man to do with it? Have I not the power to correct my own wife?"

The Stormy Ela Marriage[28]

In one case of quarrelsome behavior, Daniel Ela, keeper of a Haverhill tavern and inn, insisted that his wife Elizabeth was "none of his wife but merely servant and slave to me."

From 1667, the Essex County Court had issued Daniel Ela an annual license to operate an ordinary or tavern and inn at Haverhill, Massachusetts, where he agreed "to give entertainment to strangers for their necessary refreshment, and sell wine and strong water." At Daniel Ela's establishment, his wife Elizabeth likely prepared meals for guests and took charge of housekeeping and providing clean linens for travelers and overnight visitors. In an attempt to resign a few years later, Goodman Ela "petitioned the court to be relieved of that trouble, [but] none appearing to take up the work, the magistrates ordered Daniel Ela to continue provid[ing] wholesome meat and drink such is of necessity for diet and lodging and entertainment for horses … and allow no inhabitant to drink in his house unless in the company of strangers as the law allowed," and according to the *Essex County Court Records,* "no one should commit disorder in his house, [which is] prohibited by law."

However, there was most certainly disorder within the Ela household, for one winter day in 1682, the tavern keeper threw his wife out the door in the midst of a snowstorm. Goodman Ela had treated his wife badly for years. Neighbors had reported hearing Elizabeth Ela "crying and sniffling in the barn," and the tavern keeper had been chastised for "reviling speeches."

One winter day when he "beat her about the head and she feared he would kill her," Elizabeth ran to magistrate Nathaniel Saltonstall's house for help. He was not at home, so the frightened woman knocked on the door of her neighbor, William White. Though Goodman White sympathized, saying, "Alas, poor woman. I am sorry for you," he did not invite her inside.

Elizabeth was desperate, saying, "If you will not entertain me and let me abide in your house, I will lie in the street in the snow, and if I perish, my blood shall be upon your head."

White persuaded another neighbor to accompany him to Daniel Ela's to plead with the innkeeper to cease abusing his wife. Goodman Ela greeted the concerned neighbors with a torrent of verbal abuse, calling them "pimping knaves and meddlers," and threatening to "get even." Ela ordered them gone, for he was "capable of managing his own family," and, "should he be called to court, [he] would denounce his wife as a scold, since it would disgrace him to have his own servant and slave whipped . . . To him, in fact, she was not even a woman, but a devil in woman's apparel."

William White then filed a legal complaint against Daniel Ela, and in court, told judge and jury how his neighbor had thrown Elizabeth out of the house into the snow. Another neighbor testified to hearing Ela call Goodman White "Old Knave," and threatening that it "would cost him plenty for coming to him about Elizabeth and meddling about that which was none of his business."

Elizabeth Ela apparently so feared her husband that she refused to testify against him in court, telling the authorities she had "nothing against her husband to charge him with." The judge fined Daniel Ela 40 shillings, which further infuriated the abusive innkeeper.

Daniel Ela was later prosecuted for wife abuse and made to forfeit another £2 when summoned to court again, making it impossible to salvage this broken marriage. Goodman Ela made it known that Elizabeth "should never come into his home again," and swore he "would never have a quiet hour until she died." Later, when she attempted to return to the inn, he chased her off with a stick.

Daniel Ela threatened to get even with anyone who harbored Elizabeth, for he was "Lord Paramount" in his own house. He "would do and say there what he would and none should control him." When this unhappy woman finally left her husband and moved in with friends, according to the *Essex County Court Records,* Goodman Ela even refused to send over his wife's Bible and spectacles, which a neighbor had requested on Elizabeth's behalf.

Hannah Hutchinson—Wayward Wife

Hannah Hutchinson of Reading and Andover in Massachusetts Bay Colony was a wayward wife. She was downright repulsed by her husband, Samuel, in fact, claiming she would "be hanged before ever having a child by him." She informed the local selectmen who intervened to mend their marriage that "though he had a pen he had no ink . . . and that it were as good to goe to bedd with a guelt dogg . . . and it was a pity for her to be married to such an old rogue," she "being a pretty woman." The court charged Hannah with "oft leaving her husband," and Sam, with "not providing necessities for her."[29]

Hannah did find some satisfaction outside of marriage, eventually naming two other men as the fathers of her children. She continued to threaten her husband, saying she "would go to the gallows soon for she vowed to kill old Sam . . ." and "if he did not die soon, she would "give him a drink to speed him." When Hannah finally went after Samuel with an ax, this violent couple was banished from town.

Goodwife Hutchinson was convicted of housebreaking one Sabbathday in 1674, and of stealing rum, sugar, and linen cloth. Yet, being whipped at the post, getting a "B" for "Burglary" burned into her forehead, and serving a stint in the Salem jail, all failed keep her in line.

As for Samuel, he was presented at court by two Andover constables in 1675, "for being an idle, slothful person who will not work nor provide for his family." Neighbors claimed Hutchinson's "manner of living made him an imprudent person." Authorities noted that "much had been said to him by townsmen to reclaim him, yet it had done no good and [he] was likely to come to extreme poverty."[30] The selectmen advised Goodman Hutchinson "to bind out some of his children in order to deliver them from much suffering." At first, Samuel agreed, but then informed the court that "the violence of his wife is such that she will not suffer it. The impudence of the woman is also a great cause of their uncomfortable living."[31]

The Andover selectman finally took charge of this sad situation by placing the seven Hutchinson children with various foster families around town.

Other wives took their violent inclinations even further. The Massachusetts Bay authorities ordered one Mary Osborne "flogged for feeding her husband quicksilver," and in 1684, the New Haven County Court sentenced Widow Sarah Jackson to forfeit £5 for her attempt on her late husband's life. A wife was hanged at Hartford in 1706, "for striking her husband in the head with a pair of scissors." However, there is no record of any Rhode Island wife even attempting to murder her husband.[32]

The Murderous Miller

Irreconcilable differences and marital miseries occasionally got so out of hand that no amount of pastoral counseling or court action could prevent disaster. On June 5, 1734, Amaziah Harding, the miller of Eastham, in Massachusetts Bay Colony, was executed at Barnstable for killing his wife, Hannah, even though he was convicted chiefly on circumstantial evidence and denied the deed to the end. Some folks testified he threw Hannah down the mill stairs in a fit of rage, breaking her neck.

When several neighbors were called in to prepare Goodwife Harding's body for burial, they immediately saw signs that the woman had suffered physical violence, even as Amaziah Harding continued to insist that his spouse of some twenty years had died of natural causes while asleep in her bed, The miller's story was that he had "noticed his wife had not been as well as she used to be and had drunk her fill of rum and sat on the doorsill as she lay on the bed and fell asleep. When he awoke he called for her but she gave him no answer. Then he rose and went into the other room and found her dead on the bed."[33]

Soon after he was accused and about to be taken into custody, the murderous miller grabbed a knife and plunged it into his stomach in a thwarted suicide attempt.

One neighbor later told the court that Goodman Harding said that he was "well-satisfied his wife was dead, since she had long been a plague to him, and that he hoped to get somebody to keep his house clean and look after his things, as Hannah was now gone to paradise among the royal breed and would be clothed in robes of glory." Neighbors agreed that the miller had seemed "disguised with drink" at the time. This is how the *Boston Weekly Newsletter* reported the case in its July 19–July 26, 1733 edition:

> *We hear from Eastham on Cape Cod that a most barbarous murder was committed there on the body of one Mrs. Harding, supposed to be done by her own husband, he having for a great while before, as 'tis said, carried it very ill toward her, to the impairing of her reason, and now being found in the room alone with her, where she laid dead near him, with her neck twisted and broke and about her mouth and throat much beat and bruised. The hard-hearted man being thus surprised and charged with the fact, by those who first discovered it, endeavored to put an end to his own life, by stabbing a knife into his bowels, which stroke not proving mortal immediately he went to repeat it, aiming at his breast, but was prevented by those about him. On Friday last he was sent to the Barnstable Gaol.*[34]

The Order for Execution reads:

> *The Juror of our Lord the King upon their oath present Maziah Harding . . . not having the fear of God before his Eyes but being Instigated by the Devil with force and arms and of his malice forethought on the Eighteenth Day of July last at Eastham aforesd, did commit assault on the Body of Hannah, his then wife and in the Kings peace did make and then and there with force Feloniously twisted the neck of said Hannah and Dislocated the same, of which the said Hannah then Instantly dyed so that the said Maziah Harding of his malice . . . murthered his said wife contrary to the peace of our sd Lord the King his Crown and Dignity, and the Law . . . upon which Indictment the said Harding being arraigned at the Barr pleaded Not Guilty . . . and the Prisoner after a full hearing of the Evidences for the King and the*

Prisoner's Defense went out to Consider thereof and returned their Verdict upon oath that the said Maziah Harding is Guilty . . . and shall suffer the pains of death.[35]

The Wife Who Would Be Hanged

Bridget Playfer was born in England about 1640. Her first husband, Samuel Wasselbee, and two of their children were dead and buried before she set sail for Boston in 1664, at the age of twenty-seven. Almost from the day she married Salem widower Thomas Oliver two years later, there was such discord in the home that the quarrelsome couple had to be chastised by the court for continual squabbling. Mary Ropes, a Salem neighbor, recalled being summoned to the Oliver house numerous times to hear complaints by one or the other. She once saw Goodwife Oliver's face bloody, and at other times, black and blue, while Goodman Oliver complained of Bridget giving him blows. The Essex County Court offered the unhappy pair the choice of paying a stiff fine or suffering ten lashes each.

Thomas Oliver had even been heard to say that he would eventually see his wife hanged, for Bridget had been in trouble with the law before. She once claimed "all ministers in the country to be bloodthirsty men." These disrespectful words got Goody Oliver tied to the whipping post with a slit-stick run through her tongue. On March 2, 1667/8, the Essex County Court fined Bridget Oliver for working on the Sabbath and for abusing the magistrate, Captain Hathorn, uttering "divers mutinous speeches" such as "you in New England are all thieves . . . ," and for telling Mr. Robert Gutch that she "hoped to tear his flesh in pieces." Refusing to pay the fine levied on her by the court, she went to jail. Thomas Oliver managed to recover 10 shillings in damages after filing a suit for "false imprisonment, their taking of her in a violent manner and putting her in the stocks."

Goodwife Oliver deserted Thomas for a time, but on November 15, 1668, was ordered by the court to return to her husband. The following February, she was back in court once more for "living apart from Thomas Oliver," who was then in England. Ordered to board the next ship and join him there, she chose to pay the fine instead. By November of 1649, the

Essex Country Court Records also reveal her in trouble a year later, this time for stealing goats, and a month later, for saying the governor was "unjust, corrupt, and a wretch," because "he forced her to pay for stealing goats when there was no proof in the world of it." Her sentence this time was "to be whipped next lecture day at Salem, if the weather be moderate, not exceeding twenty stripes."

On January 24, 1678, Bridget, wife of Thomas Oliver, according to *Essex County Court Records,*

> *was presented for calling her husband many opprobrious names, such as Old Rogue and Old Devil, is ordered to stand with her husband on a Lecture Day in the public market place, tied back to back, both gagged for an hour, with a paper fastened to each of their foreheads upon which their offense should be fairly written.*

Rumor had it that Bridget had bewitched her first husband to death back in England, so when Thomas Oliver died in 1685, she was accused of having terminated his life by means of witchcraft too. Within months, she was facing the court on capital charges. Even her new husband, Edward Bishop (with whom she dared live openly prior to marriage), suspected Bridget might be a witch. Goodman Bishop confided to a neighbor that his wife told him that "the devil came to her bodily" and that she "sometimes sat up with him all night long."[36]

The estates of the late Thomas Oliver, both in Old and New England, were found to be heavily in debt. Since he died intestate, the court ordered Widow Oliver to receive the estate and pay his debts while her two stepsons and their daughter would receive 20 shillings apiece. The enterprising Bridget Bishop eventually managed to pay Oliver's debts on both sides of the Atlantic. Advised by Salem selectmen, she sold their ten-acre lot, and chiefly made her living by operating an unlicensed tavern where she sold hard cider made from her own apple orchard, and "entertained travelers and young people . . . drinking and playing such games as shuffleboard . . . whereby discord did arise in families and made youth in danger to be corrupted."

Essex County Court Records reveal that Goody Bishop continued to break rules and defy authority. In 1687 she was accused of stealing brass from a local mill. This she vehemently denied, claiming she had merely unearthed it while weeding her garden. Bridget's daughter, Christian Oliver, got trapped in her mother's lie, for when she attempted to sell the brass, she said it had been a gift from her late father.

Because she was considered a "brawling scold" and had been previously accused of witchcraft, it came as no surprise to the residents of Salem when Bridget Bishop was the first of nineteen hanged in 1692. The enemies this woman had made over many years would later step forward at that time to blame her for the unexplained deaths of children, the loss of livestock, and strange nocturnal visits to their bedchambers by Bridget Oliver Bishop's specter. A specter was not the same as a "ghost" to people living in the seventeenth century but rather, the spirit of someone living or dead.

DIVORCE

Divorce was granted in Massachusetts on the grounds of adultery and desertion, but only after all other attempts to keep the family together had been exhausted. When a couple did obtain a divorce, the ex-husband generally kept all marital property.[37] If the court determined the wife was the injured party, she could legally claim only the equivalent of a "Widow's Dower," or one-third of her former husband's estate. Should he be judged at fault, he still retained legal access to most of his assets. Should she leave him, she walked away with no more than what she could wear or carry.

No Massachusetts Bay husband could leave his wife for foreign parts for more than two years without remitting a £20 fine. The *Essex County Court Records* report the case of Phillip Crumwell in December 1643, "for living apart from his wife: Not found / Not warned." In 1652 in York County, ne'er-do-well Cyles Parr stood before the bench "for swearing and drunkenness and for abusing people in his drink and for living [away] from his wife." In November of 1656, John Longelark of Gloucester was written up in the *Essex County Court Records* "for long absence from his wife. He was found to be out of the county."

Connecticut was the first colony to permit divorce, and this was on the grounds of adultery, fraudulent contract, willful neglect of duty, or seven years' absence "without being heard from." According to *Connecticut Court Records*, four divorces were granted there in 1653.[38]

The Hartford selectmen took legal action against John Lord in 1651 because he had "withdrawn himself from his wife and left her destitute of any bed to lodge on, and very bare in apparel, to the endangering of her health." Local authorities voted to require Lord the wearing apparel of his wife, and also a bed for her to lodge on, and to search after the same in any place within this jurisdiction, and to restore it unto her.

The Plymouth Court Records of 1668 reveal that William Tubbs divorced his wife, Marcy, then in her fifties, on grounds of desertion following her affair with one Joseph Rogers, a young bachelor from Duxbury. Goody Tubbs and Rogers were summoned to court three times on grounds of "obscene and lascivious behavior," since they had been observed lying together beneath a blanket. They were both fined and Rogers was ordered to leave town permanently. The beleaguered husband, Goodman Tubbs eventually announced that he would no longer maintain responsibility for Marcy's debts, since by 1665, she had run off to Rhode Island with another man.

Those who flouted the law faced severe penalties. On April 13, 1713, the following case appeared in the *Bristol County Court Records*:

> *Frank Townsend bound by way of recognizance to appear at this court upon complaint of his wife that he had left her and taken another woman to wife, and being convicted by his own confession, it is ordered he be whipt twenty lashes on his bare back well-laid on, and to stand committed till sentence be performed.*

New England courts also granted divorce on the grounds of impotence, or if one's marriage partner refused to regularly perform sexual obligations. Puritan wives expected their husbands to satisfy their physical needs and could publicly complain to clergy and civil authorities if they would not or could not do so.

PART III

Governing the Community

As SMALL CHILDREN, PURITANS AND PILGRIMS WERE TAUGHT THAT idle hands are the devil's tools, and local authorities were ever watchful of any citizen guilty of wasting time better put to use working. All parents were expected to instruct their children in "some honest lawful calling, labour, or imployment."[39] Idleness was considered an offense against God and community, since all hands were required to be kept busy at some useful task for the survival and success of the colony. As such, leisure activities were considered highly suspect.

Tobacco-taking was frowned upon as one habit associated with idleness. In 1656, William Rayner of Wenham forfeited a fine for smoking his clay pipe in the streets of Salem. A 1660 Massachusetts statute warned against games such as shuffleboard and bowling, for which players were liable to be fined three times the amount of their bets. A *Worcester Record of Court Proceedings* in 1761 reported a man fined simply for possessing a deck of cards.

Gaming such as dice, cockfights, wrestling, quoits, bear baiting, and gambling, though illegal, were commonly practiced. In nearly every town and village, local ministers cleared the taverns on Saturday evenings, reminding citizens to prepare for the Sabbath. "On Saturdays, even the constable goes around to all the taverns of the town for the purpose of stopping all noise and debauchery, which frequently causes him to stop his search before his search causes the debauchery to stop."[40] After 1675, Massachusetts expected the selectmen of each town to provide the county courts with names of all persons suspected of idleness. This dedicated and diligent watchfulness was expected to please God and thus prevent Him from inflicting any punishment upon the community.

VAGABONDS AND VAGRANTS

The Court being informed that John Littlehale of Haverhill liveth in a house by himself, contrary to the law of the country, whereby he is subject to much sin: which ordinarily are the companions and consequences of a solitary life; and having had information of some of his accounts which are in no way to be allowed of but disproved, do therefore order said John Littlehale forthwith within six weeks to remove himself from said place and the solitary life and settle himself in some orderly family in said towne and be subject to orderly rule of family government . . . if he shall refuse to submit and does not perform this order, this Court in his Majesty's name shall require the Constable to apprehend the person of said John Littlehale and carry him to the House of Correction in Hampton, there to be kept & set to work.
—COURT OF QUARTERLY SESSIONS, ESSEX COUNTY, HAMPTON, AUGUST 8, 1672

Everyone had a place within the tightly structured Puritan community, and no one was permitted to live alone. Bachelors, spinsters, widows, and orphans usually boarded with other families, while indentured servants and apprentices were also considered part of the extended family. Most towns required that older children of parents on public relief be put out to work at local enterprises, thus learning useful future skills. Plymouth Colony, New Haven, and Connecticut laws required unmarried males to reside with "Licensed Families, and to be fined if they did not do so."[41] And vagrancy and homelessness were crimes worthy of several hours in the stocks, generally followed by banishment.

New England towns had the legal right to determine whether or not newcomers would be permitted residency within their borders. It was the selectmen's right and duty to exclude undesirable strangers or any outsiders expected to end up as public dependents. Even single men who might have a trade but were still considered suspect were frequently denied habitation in New England towns. William Thompson's plea to dwell in Haverhill, presented at town meeting on February 27, 1676, was denied. He had requested to settle there and continue his itinerant trade of shoe-making, but the town refused to grant him "liberty or acceptance."

Henry Sherlot, a French dancing master and fencer "that Raves and scoffes at Religion and of a Tubulent spirit, no way fit to be tolerated to live in this place," was banished by the *Essex County Court of Assistants* in 1681. The fact that Monsieur Sherlot was a Roman Catholic hardly helped his cause.

Vagrants and other idle hands were by far the greatest risk to these communities, which would have to take on the responsibility of caring for any indigent residents. *The Massachusetts Bay Act of 1699 for Suppressing and Punishing Rogues, Vagabonds, and Common Beggars and for Setting the Poor to Work* decreed that "all who lived idly or in a disorderly fashion" were to be punished, then put to work in the House of Correction. This law defined a vagabond as "one who wandered about from place to place, neglecting all lawful calling and employment, and not having any home or means of support."[42] In Connecticut, no single person could even be entertained without permission of the local selectmen, since it was feared transients might become financially dependent upon the town. Vagrants and suspected vagrants were to be sent from constable to constable, back to the place from whence they had come. If they returned after being *warned out* they would be "severely whipped, not exceeding ten stripes."

In 1639, Hartford voted that "any one entertaining one not admit-ted an inhabitant in the town, was to discharge the town of any cost or trouble that might come thereby . . ." New Haven passed a law in 1656 that "no one was to entertain a stranger who came to settle or sojourn, or sell or lease to him any real estate, or to permit him to remain more than a month, without written permission of a local magistrate or a majority of the freemen, under penalty of ten pounds." Hamden, Connecticut, decreed that "any transient person without any visible means of sup-port to come within our borders, would soon be warned by Selectmen to depart town."[43]

Warned Out

After 1659, Massachusetts towns were required by law to grant public relief to persons after three months' residency. This eventually led to a system known as *warning out* being adopted in most Bay Colony towns by 1682, meaning, "to banish any indigents, undesirables or idle persons suspected of becoming financial burdens upon the community." Selectmen would issue warrants forcing the poor and indigent to get out of town, often personally escorting them to the border of the next town.[44]

In 1692, Massachusetts General Court passed an act (following a Connecticut edict of 1679), requiring persons to be warned out within three months after coming into a town, thus preventing settlement. New Hampshire had practiced warning out from its early settlement in 1638.

"DISGUISED WITH DRINK"

When drink is got into the brain, then out come filthy songs. Where there is rioting and drunkenness, there is wont to be chambering and wantonness.
—REVEREND INCREASE MATHER, *TWO SERMONS TESTIFYING AGAINST THE SIN OF DRUNKENNESS*

Disguised with drink—also known as *distempered with drink*—is the crime that appears most frequently throughout all seventeenth- and eighteenth-century court records. Being drunk was considered a deliberate act, and a drunk was legally defined as "a person that either lisps or faulters in his speech by reason of overmuch drink, or that staggers in his going or that vomits by reason of excessive drinking, or cannot follow his calling."[45]

Robert Coles was Roxbury's town drunk in 1634, and the local court records reflect the penalties he paid for his behavior:

> *. . . for drunkenness, he shalbe disfranchised, weare about his necke and so to hang upon his outwd garment a D made of redd cloth & set upon white; to continue this for a year, and not to have it off at any time he comes among company, under penalty of 10 shillings for the first offense & five pounds for the second & afterwards, to be punished by the Court as they think meete.*

Every town was required to have at least one tavern, also known as an ordinary, as well as an overnight inn to accommodate weary travelers. In 1678, the Town of York was fined by the grand jury "for not having a licensed tavern." Running an ordinary provided a steady income, and the tavern keeper was likely the best-informed man in town, since he had access to all the news from outlying districts. Broadsides advertising horses and land for sale, descriptions of runaway servants, slaves, or wives, along with the latest political happenings were posted all over the walls. Tavern keepers could run afoul of the law for not providing adequately for customers: "Mr. William Hilton was admonished for not keeping victuall and drink at all times for strangers and inhabitants," by the York County Court on October 16, 1649.

For all that they were required to do by law, however, taverns represented a male bailiwick and one that signified disorder, even mayhem. The *Essex County Quarterly Court Records* note the disturbance or breach of peace at a Wenham ordinary, where a patron named Peters threw cheese at Thomas Willet and pursued the latter, who attempted to escape until stopped by tavern keeper John Selado. Peters then abused Selado, and the local constable had to be summoned.[46]

The *Suffolk County Records* of 1639 cite "Thomas Gray, for being drunk, prophaning of the name of God, keeping a tipling house, & drawing his knife in the Court, was censured to be severely whipped and fined Five pounds."

Since taverns might quickly turn into dens of iniquity, the law required proprietors to renew their licenses annually or face charges. In April of 1738, James Donnell, a York mariner, appeared before the Court of General Sessions "to answer a presentment of the Grand Jury exhibited against him for selling strong Drink without a License."

Anyone wishing to become a licensed vintnor (an inn or tavern keeper with a liquor license, that is), had to be recommended by at least one local selectman, and was also required to present two other men for "surety," vouching the applicant to be a worthy and law-abiding citizen. In order to operate a publick house, all New England tavern keepers had to agree:

not to permit, suffer, or have any playing at Dice, Cards, Tables, Quoits, Loggets, Ninepins, Billiards or any other unlawful Game in his house, yard, Garden, or Backside; nor shall suffer to be or remain in his House any persons not being of his own family upon Saturday nights after it is Dark, nor at any time on the Sabbath Day or Evening . . . nor shall suffer any person to lodge in his House above one day and one night . . . nor sell any Wine or Liquors to any Indians or Negroes, nor suffer any servants or apprentices to remain in his house Tippling or drinking after nine of the clock . . . nor buy or take to Pawn any stolen goods, nor willingly harbor in his said House, Barn, Stable, any Rogues, Vagabonds, Thieves, nor other notorious offenders . . . [47]

Retailers of beer, ale, and "strong waters" that included West Indian rum, brandy, or wines from France and Spain were liable to fines if they sold liquor to common tipplers, whose names were regularly posted on tavern walls:

Upon complaint made to the Wenham Selectmen, Robert Symonds lived as a common tippler, misspending his time and estate at the tavern, greatly to the damage of his family. Notice is given to the tavernkeeper that he do not entertain Goodman Symonds in his house to sit tippling and misspending his time upon penalty of the law.

Ordered that no person should sell or give to John Browne, the glazier, any strong drink or strong liquor, and should any ordinaries suffer him to come or stay in any of their houses and so obtain drink, they would do it at their peril. This notice is to be posted at the meetinghouse and ordinaries. [48]

Habitual drinkers were banned from all alehouses in the area. Their usual punishment was a 5-shilling fine or several hours locked in the stocks with a "D" sign hung around the neck. Should the drunkard in question be a Native American he would receive a whipping up to ten lashes if he could not pay the fine. Known drunks in Connecticut who purchased alcohol were fined 20 shillings, and tavern keepers who operated the establishments where the alcohol was obtained were required to forfeit 10-shilling fines.

A proprietor could lose his license if he sold liquor to any known drunkard, and selling to Native Americans was forbidden. John Page was licensed to keep an ordinary at Haverhill with William White to sell cider for three years, but at the next court meeting, Goodman Page was fined 40 shillings, "for selling drink to Indians." In a warrant dated March 23, 1682, the story reveals itself: "for appearance of an Indian who assaulted the wife of Joseph Peasely in Haverhill . . . The Indian said he was overcome with drink which he had at John Page's when he did so. The *Essex County Court Records* say that he was soon sent to Ipswich Prison."

In testimony given at the Essex County Court on September 25, 1682, Thomas Fiske Jr. avowed that he saw "an Indian drinking strong beer out of a quart pot and asking Goodwife Fairefield if she gave Indians strong drink. She replied, 'And why not? We are all one man's Children!'"

Although it was considered improper for women to frequent taverns, they often worked there, usually because they were the wives and daughters of the owners. Many ordinaries and inns were run by widows, who, following a husband's death, applied for tavern licenses of their own. Many such women had young children to provide for and possessed household skills that were especially useful for inn keeping. Female indentured servants were generally on hand to assist with the preparation and serving of meals and beverages to local customers and out-of-town visitors. Sons or male servants generally took charge of watering and feeding horses and oxen belonging to travelers, leading the weary animals to stalls in the barn for the night.

Sign of the Horseshoe

Drunkenness was an ongoing problem, and one that only grew larger over time as the population increased and clerical authority weakened. Liquor laws were reinterpreted and changed to address this difficult issue. The *Essex County Court Records* reveal that partaking of "strong waters" sometimes led to double trouble, as in 1655, when Christopher Avery sued James Standish for slander and William Vincent for defamation of character at the same time. Standish and Vincent reported that Avery was in company drinking strong liquors, and that "they drank so long that they could not tell ink from liquor; also they broke bottles and that he dangled another man's wife on his knee, as ye foolish man, her husband, looked on."

In March of 1689, thirty-five Andover citizens petitioned to get The Sign of the Horseshoe tavern shut down and William Chandler's liquor license revoked. Their grievance was that this particular tavern had "grown to an epidemicall evill that overspreads and is like to corrupt the grater part of our towne if not speedily prevented." Andover historian, Sarah Loring Bailey, cites a long-lost early document that reveals how citizens complained of "excess and disorder" in Chandler's ale-house, and how through

> *his over forwardness to promote his own gaine he . . . entices persons to spend their money and time to the great wrong of themselves and family they belong to . . . Servants and children are allowed by him in his house at all times, unseasonable by night and day sometimes till midnight and past & till break of day; till they know not their way to their habitations, and gaming is freely allowed in his house by which means the loser must call for drink . . . [I]f he be not restrained from the selling of drink our town will be for the greatest part of our young generation so corrupted that we can expect little else but a course of drunkenness of them . . .* [49]

According to *Andover Selectmen's Records*, because William Chandler had kept his "house of publick entertainment" for a considerable time in the past, and had cautiously maintained order since local citizens had petitioned against him, the selectmen renewed his license. They noted that Chandler was "an infirm man incapable of hard labor," and that Andover needed a house "convenient for travelers" on the road leading from Ipswich to Billerica. Thus, Chandler paid his license fee and remained in business.

James Morgan—The Dangers of Drink

*The murderer's soul is filled with hellish horror of heart so that he is,
as it were, damned above ground and in Hell whilst he is still alive.*
—INCREASE MATHER, 1686/7

Authorities were well aware that excessive drinking could lead to violence. In 1685, James Morgan, a Boston currier who made his living soaking, scraping, and beating tanned leather, killed Joseph Johnson in a Boston boardinghouse. Morgan and his wife, both about thirty, were habitual drinkers known to quarrel outrageously when in their cups. One December night, the couple was verbally abusing each other so loudly that Goodman Johnson, the Boston butcher, found it impossible to chat with friends downstairs. Morgan shouted *Bitch!* and *Jade!* at his wife, who was hollering *Rogue!*, *Dog!*, and *Old devil!* right back at him.

Suddenly, Morgan's wife began calling for help, and determined to put an end to the noisy marital dispute, Joseph Johnson rushed upstairs, leaving his friends downstairs by the fireside. He found the couple in bed, managed to calm their fury, and returned downstairs. They were soon at it again, screeching *Whore!* and *Whoremaster!* Goody Morgan again cried for help, but when Johnson entered their room this time with his friends, James Morgan gored him in the stomach with a three-foot-long iron spit. (This kitchen utensil, commonly kept beside the hearth, was designed for spearing large chunks of meat to roast over an open fire.)

Morgan pleaded "not guilty" at his trial, but Joseph Johnson's friends had witnessed the murder. The Boston minister Joshua Moody, along with the two reverends Mather, father and son, paid numerous visits to the condemned man in prison. The accused eventually confessed to murder and accepted his death sentence as just. The currier admitted having lived a sinful life, and that he had killed Johnson "in drunken passion." Although the law provided for a period of at least four days between sentencing and execution, this condemned prisoner appealed for a stay of execution in order to receive further spiritual guidance. He even asked young Cotton Mather to preach a sermon just for him. Mr. Moody and both Mathers delivered sermons on Morgan's behalf that were heard by "a vast concourse of people" in Boston's First Church. One witness who came to watch James Morgan die on March 11, 1686, reported that some folks traveled fifty miles to attend the event.

The Reverend Increase Mather preached and later published *A Sermon Occasioned by the Execution of a Man found Guilty of Murder, Together with the Confession, Last Expressions and Solemn Warning of that Murderer, to all Persons; Especially to Young Men, to beware of those Sins which Brought him to his Miserable End.* Considered the first in what would become an immensely popular literary and theological genre, these sermons were printed in a format that would appear in many subsequent publications. Best-selling pamphlets and broadsides were often produced to mark the execution of criminals and to educate the public. Most included the attending minster's "Discourse with the Malefactor walking to his Execution," the "gallows warnings" of the condemned to the attending crowd, as well as the criminal's final apologies, expressing regret and repentance. It provided a recipe for redemption as the penitent prisoner recounted his or her wayward life that inevitably began with disobedience to parents, and continued through sins of Sabbath-breaking, lying, profanity, and drunkenness, all of which led to the crime for which the prisoner was soon to be hanged.

Execution pamphlets also offered other clergy guidelines on how to lead condemned convicts to repentance and redemption, along with ways to caution their own congregations regarding the perils of parental disobedience, idleness, debauchery, and drinking.

According to accounts of the Morgan execution, Cotton Mather walked with James Morgan along the path to his place of execution on Boston Common, explaining that he must not bear grudges against the judge and jury who convicted him. Morgan dutifully replied that he "heartily wished them all well." To the end, Cotton Mather kept reminding the prisoner of his sinfulness and guilt. The minister scolded this man about to die, telling him that "even since you have been in Prison you have done wickedly. You have even made yourself drunk several times since your imprisonment . . ." At the scaffold, Mather implored Morgan to "Repent! Do not wait until the executioner puts the cloth of death over your eyes!"

A SERMON
Occasioned by the EXECUTION of
a man found Guilty of

MURDER

Preached at Boston *in* N. E. *March* 11th 168⅚.

 Together with the *Confession*, Last *Expressions*,
& solemn *Warning* of that Murderer to all persons; *especially to* Young men, to beware of *those*
Sins which brought him to his *miserable End.*

By *INCREASE MATHER,* Teacher of
Church of CHRIST.

The *SECOND EDITION.*

Deut. 19. 20. 21. *And those which remain shall*
hear and fear, and shall henceforth commit no
more any such Evil *among you.*
⎯ 21. *And thine eye shall not pity, but* Life *shall go*
for Life, *Eye for Eye,* &c.
Prov. 28. 17. *A man that doth violence to the blood*
of any person, shall flee to the pit, let no man stay him.

Boston, Printed by *R. P.* Sold by *J. Brunning*
Book-seller, at his Shop at the Corner of the
Prison-Lane next the *Exchange.* Anno 1687.

"A Sermon Occasioned by the Execution of a Man found Guilty of Murder:
preached at Boston in N. E. March 11th, 1685/6. Together with the confession,
last expressions & solemn Warning of that murderer to all persons; especially to
young men, to beware of those sins which brought him to his miserable end," by
the Reverend Increase Mather (1639–1723), teacher of Church of Christ, Boston. Published in 1687, this is the title page of what became the first of many
pamphlets in the popular genre of gallows sermons. Preached to a multitude on
the day that James Morgan was hanged for murdering Joseph Johnson. COURTESY
OF MILNE SPECIAL COLLECTIONS, UNIVERSITY OF NEW HAMPSHIRE LIBRARY

Standing upon the ladder, "suspended between heaven and earth," and using the scaffold as a pulpit, James Morgan told the crowd, estimated at five thousand, that he had been "a most hellish sinner," and that he was "sorry for what I have been. I pray God," Morgan continued, "that I may be a warning to you all . . . Now that I am going out of this world, take solemn warning by me, and beg of God to keep you from this sin which has been my ruin." It was an awesome gallows performance, worthy of the crowd's rousing cheers and applause. Executions could always be counted on to provide popular public entertainment.

Gathering at the gallows, or executions as public entertainment. SEVENTEENTH-CENTURY WOODCUT, AUTHOR'S COLLECTION

THE POWER OF SPEECH

You had to watch what you said in seventeenth-century New England! Name-calling could land you in court. *Jade, bawd, strumpet, trull, rogue*— these colorful curses run through all the early court records. Even profane cursing of animals was punishable by law. Angry name-calling disrupted harmony among neighbors and indicated that local leaders were unable to maintain proper order within a community in which certain residents rudely expressed their hostility to authority.

Nicholas Bickeford, resident of the Isles of Shoals, off Portsmouth, New Hampshire, and the Maine coast, was, according to *Maine Provincial and Court Records,* "complained of for profaine swearing and multiplying of oaths, where being convened before the Court & by 2 evidences Convicted of his Crime, for which sd Bickeford was sentenced to pay 20 shillings in money and 2s 6d for Costs of Court, or to receive 13 lashes well layd on upon the bare skine."

Slander and Defamation

Litigation over libel was common in early New England. In fact, records verify that the populace became increasingly litigious as time went on. Slander and libel were considered serious matters by colonial courts because such crimes and misdemeanors demonstrated hostility among neighbors, and thus threatened community harmony. Citizens regularly looked to the courts to settle disputes over land and livestock, to deal with domestic quarrels, drunken behavior, and cases of assault and battery. Many complaints brought to the bench focused on disgruntled and rebellious indentured servants or runaway apprentices. Cases involving debt could often be settled by allotments of firewood, Indian corn, or bushels of wheat and rye. The majority of cases had to do with land disputes, arguments over who owned which cow, and what to do with a neighbor's pesky pig that kept routing your crops.

Hassles between neighbors appear frequently in the *Connecticut Colony Records,* as in this example of December 7, 1642:

Forasmuch as John Owen hath had some damage done in his corne by hogs, occasioned through the neglect of Mr. Lamberton, and Will

Preston, in not making up their fence in season, it is ordered that the said Lamberton and Preston shall make satisfaction to John Owen for damage done: 8 days work and two pecks of corn, which is to be paid according to the several apportions of fence unset up respectively.

Name-Calling in the Courts

Job Tyler's name shows up seventeen times in the *Essex County Court Records*—ten as defendant and seven as plaintiff. In 1658 Goodman Tyler apprenticed his son, Hopestill, to faithfully serve Andover blacksmith Thomas Chandler for nine and a half years. According to their legal agreement, young Hopestill would work beside Chandler to learn his trade, and in turn, the blacksmith would teach his apprentice to read the Bible and to write. Hopestill would also be provided with room and board and sufficient clothing. However, Goodman Chandler proved an unkind taskmaster, and three years later, Hopestill's concerned brother, Moses Tyler, went to Nathan Parker's house, where the agreement paper had been placed between the joists and boards for safekeeping. Moses tossed this document that had been cosigned by his father, Job, and Thomas Chandler, into the fireplace, where it quickly burned to ashes.

The tiresome controversy that ensued was dragged through the courts for nearly a decade until Tyler finally lost his case to Chandler, who was one of Andover's wealthiest citizens, even serving as local deputy to the General Court at Boston.

In 1665, the two men were back before the bar in another defamation case, although according to *Essex County Court Records*, Job Tyler, "being poor, should not be fined above six pounds." Tyler lost and was ordered to nail or fasten upon the doors of the Andover and Roxbury meetinghouses, "in a plain legible hand," the following words:

I have shamefully reproached Thomas Chandler by saying he is a base, lying, cozening, cheating knave and that he hath got his estate by cozening in a base reviling manner and that he was recorded for a liar and was a cheating, lying, whoring knave fit for all manner of bawdery, wishing the devil had him . . . Therefore, I, Job Tyler, do acknowledge that I in these expressions most wickedly slandered the said Chandler . . . that without any just ground can do no less but express myself to be sorry for my cursing of him.

Two years later, Job Tyler filed another complaint against Thomas Chandler, this time for seizing two of the plaintiff's oxen for a debt owed.

The Cranky Carpenter

Timothy Yeales, a York, Maine, carpenter, appears as a repeat offender in *Maine's Province and Court Records.* As a plaintiff, he frequently made allegations over debts owed him, and made accusations against trespassers whom he was convinced were harvesting hay and felling timber on his land. On May 29, 1682, Goodman Yeales sold rum without a license and had to pay £5 for breach of law.

An individual locked in the pillory for committing libel.
SEVENTEENTH-CENTURY WOOD-CUT, AUTHOR'S COLLECTION

On January 31, 1682, the York County Court finally filed a formal complaint against Timothy Yeales, "for Instigating people to go to law [sue in court], an evill practice . . . very hurtful to Civill Society and contrary to the Law of God and His Majesty."

That same year, the Court of Common Pleas ordered Yeales to pay a £5 fine for selling rum by retail without a license, and two years later, he was fined again, this time for "not attending publique meeting upon the Lord's Day and for slighting and abusing authority."

On May 27, 1684, Mrs. Mary Sayward, a judge's wife, sued Yeales for slander and defamation before the *County Court of Pleas*. And in July, Yeales was "committed to the custody of His Majesty's Gaol Keeper at York until he could provide surety, for curseing & sweareing, multiplying of oaths and abuseing of his Majesty's authority."

This cranky carpenter's careless tongue saw him back before the *York County Court of Pleas* May 26, 1685, "for curseing and swearing severall oaths, and rendering the name of God in a profane manner."

On June 8, 1687, Timothy Yeales took his bondservant Issack Parker before the *Court of Quarter Sessions,* "for striking, beating and evil Entreating his Master, Yeales, contrary to the peace of Our Sovereign Lord the King." Parker's punishment was "twenty-one stripes on the bare skin" and another year of service to Yeales following completion of his original indenture period, "as his master paid the court and York Gaol its charges of 45 shillings."

Carpenter Yeales was involved in several defamation and slander suits against William Hilton. On March 13, 1689, Hilton "was bound over to this Court in Recognizance of twenty pounds to answer Timothy Yeales for diverse Scurrilous Speeches by him uttered, & Upon Suspicion of firing a Barn belonging to the said Yeales."

By the end of that same month, Hilton became plaintiff in an action of slanderous defamation against Yeales on behalf of his wife. The court ruled for the plaintiff, declaring that Timothy Yeales, on behalf of Naiomie Yeales, was to pay £10 to Hilton. If Yeales refused, his wife was to receive thirteen stripes on the bare skin, plus pay court costs.

CRIME ON THE RISE

Indeed, it seemed to some colonial leaders that no amount of flogging or fines could put a stop to the propensity of certain citizens to commit crimes. As early as 1641, Governor Winthrop noted in his journal that: "as people increased, so sin abounded." The majority of immigrants pouring into New England were hardly committed to living and worshipping according to the Covenant with God upon which Massachusetts and the New Haven and Connecticut colonies had been founded. As economic success became increasingly important in the daily lives and goals of the general population, Puritanism lost its previous hold. In 1679, the leading ministers of Massachusetts Bay gathered in Boston to voice their concerns, later summed up in several sermons entitled, "What Are the Evils That Have Provoked the Lord to Bring These Remarkable Judgments Upon New England?" Their conclusion was that the Cities of God they had so lovingly and faithfully established would not survive if New Englanders did not improve their behavior and promise to live according to Divine Will.

The Immoral Ironmongers [50]

Governor William Bradford of Plymouth, for one, clearly understood that not every New England immigrant numbered among God's Elect. He realized early on that the "colony represented a mixed multitude due to the need for labor and service in planting and building here." He realized that the need for special skills and practical expertise might, of necessity, sometimes outweigh New England's treasured moral codes.

The Leonards were a troublesome lot. This family of skilled ironmongers was, singularly or together, prosecuted for profanity, robbery, assault, and seemingly endless "brash and bawdy behavior." In 1674, several Leonard brothers went on trial for suspected arson in a fire that nearly destroyed the iron works they ran and where they worked. Had their particular skills and experience not been so desperately needed by the Massachusetts Bay Colony, they surely would have been banished back to England. This family's repeated deviant behavior hardly paralleled the ideals of the covenanted community. Authorities could only hope that various members of this rude family would be cured of immorality by good example and discipline.

Henry Leonard and his sons were highly skilled ironmongers from England. By 1668, Henry was manufacturing iron in Lynn and Rowley Village (now Boxford, Massachusetts), although he was never able to make a great success of the Rowley enterprise. According to the *Essex County Court Records* of March 20, 1674/5 Henry's sons, Samuel, Nathaniel, and Thomas Leonard, all "skilled hammers-men, bloomers and refiners of iron," signed a contract with Robert Lord, the Ipswich marshal and the owners of the Rowley Ironworks to manufacture iron there by the ton. They were also to take charge of repairing the chimneys and plugging the leak in the dam, and then, to deliver house, works, and all utensils, with wood and coal to their managers. Their father continued making iron at Lynn and Taunton, eventually moving to Spotswood Village, New Jersey, to establish another foundry.

The Essex County Court admonished mother Mary Leonard and her sons for "uncivil, immodest, and beastly acting." Mary was accused of getting dressed while several men were in the room, as well as using foul language and singing indecent songs. All the Leonards "used very bad words such as Devil and Damn ye . . . Expressions have been very Frequent with them."

On other occasions, Goody Leonard sat by the pond while her sons and other young men were swimming and washing themselves, even "though some of the men, more modest than the rest, were forced to creep up into the bushes while others put on their shirts in the water, letting them fall down by degrees as they came out of the pond." Several of Mary's grown sons "came out the water naked and ran races." John Gould testified to seeing Samuel and Nathaniel Leonard come naked upon the dam, and when Goodwife Blake came over the dam, Samuel spoke and acted indecently.

Two Leonard brothers were put on trial for attempted rape in 1674, but Samuel turned the tables on his accuser, Hannah Downing, claiming she had no cause, and that her "complaint was made out of malice and not conscience." Samuel Leonard told the court that Maid Downing was "a person of very scandalous carriage," whom he had "told often of the evil that would come of her habit of night-walking." He pleaded "not guilty," claiming that his "manner to Hannah was always very austere, and that she'd made this complaint against him to save her own reputation." Sarah Bixby testified on Hannah Downing's behalf at Salem Quarterly Court on June 23, 1674, saying she was "a good maid and would make a poor man a good wife, for she could spin wool and cotton and linen and could sew very well. Her dame took great care to prevent sin and often arose in the night to chide Hannah for her carriage. Samuel Leonard told her that he marveled any man would want her."

Elizabeth Looke deposed that "Thomas Leonard came to the bedside where she and Hannah lodged," and Sarah Bates testified "seeing the Leonards abuse Hannah and pull off her head-cloth."

Another witness, Elizabeth Symonds, said Samuel Leonard was "surely fuddled" when he came to her house asking for beer. When she went into the cellar to draw it, he followed her, attempting to kiss her. "There are maids enough for you to kiss," Elizabeth told him. "You do need not come here to kiss married women!" And Sam Leonard had then "struck a blow on the small of her back."

Nathaniel Leonard represented the owners of the ironworks before the Quarterly Court of Essex County on March 30, 1675, regarding the burning of the iron works at Rowley Village. The Leonards had agreed "to make into good merchantable bar iron with due care and diligence, with as little loss of coal or mine as may be . . . and were to have use of two fires . . . Their contract required them to keep a true account of every week's product of iron . . . [and] to take care to prevent danger or damage by fire or water . . ." Nathaniel was supposed to be in charge when "the forge either willfully or through extreme carelessness and negligence, was burned and all in it to the value of between 200 and 300li on September 14."

Nathaniel Leonard claimed he "arose about break of day, looked out at the chamber window and saw the works on fire." Henry Leonard testified that his brother called him: "Come hither and see how the forge do burn." And the brothers stood together at the window and watched the forge burn.

The owners wanted their money back, while some ironmongers expressed dissatisfaction in court about working with the Leonard men. Several workers blamed Nathaniel for the damage, while another claimed that he was there the evening before the fire and observed Nathaniel Leonard leaving work, and that he "never saw so much care taken to put out the fire." Nathaniel Leonard was apparently cleared of suspected arson and negligence at the Rowley Village Ironworks.

PART IV

The First Colonial Crime Wave:
Crimes against Religion

THROUGHOUT MASSACHUSETTS AND CONNECTICUT, ALL WORK CEASED
from midday Saturday through Sunday evening. Even cooking was done the
day before, since, according to early Plymouth records, "the smell of food
was an abomination to the nostrils of the Lord." An ordinance adopted by
Plymouth Colony on June 10, 1650, decreed "whoever shall prophane the
Lord's Day by doeing any servill worke should be fined or whipped."

Court records are filled with the names and petty crimes of countless
citizens who dared "profane the Sabbath." In 1630, in Boston, John Baker
was whipped "for shooting at fowle on the Sabbath day," while Humfry
Griffin got caught unloading barley before the sun set on Sunday.

The Connecticut and New Haven colonies had particularly strict
Sabbathday codes. A 1639 Connecticut ruling made it illegal to sail any
boat on Sundays. In 1670, John Lewis and Sarah Chapman were presented at Connecticut Colony Court "for sitting together beneath the
apple tree on the Lord's Day."

In 1647, the Wenham constable was called before Essex County
Court for delivering a prisoner to Salem on the Lord's Day. Captain
Kemble spent several hours locked in the Boston stocks in 1656 "for lewd
and unseemly behavior on the Sabbath." Upon returning home after three
years at sea, Captain Kemble had kissed his wife! The *Boston Court Records*
of 1675 note that a local butcher named Thomas Platts got in trouble "for

keeping open his Shop and selling meate after darke upon Saturdays in the Evening, thereby profaning the Sabbath."

In 1721, Connecticut levied a 40-shilling fine plus incarceration in the house of correction "for any persons who ignored fines imposed for rude or unlawful behavior on the Lord's Day, such as clamorous discourse, or by shouting, hollowing, screaming, running, riding, singing, dancing, jumping, winding horns in any place near to any meetinghouse for divine worship, that those who went there may be disturbed."

As late as 1750, according to Connecticut records, one clergyman was fined for walking from church too fast and for combing his wig on a Sunday.

"Railing and uttering profaine curses" and breaking the Sabbath were sins and misdemeanors, while blasphemy represented a much more serious issue, and one that was originally a capital crime in New England (though there is no record of anyone ever being hanged for it). Since specific penalties were determined by individual courts, they varied considerably. Blasphemy might result in six months of prison time, whipping, two hours in the stocks, sitting at the foot of the gallows with a noose around the neck, or getting a hot spike bored through the tongue. Punishments were particularly severe for Quakers, who continually abused members of the Puritan clergy verbally.

In his journal, Governor John Winthrop noted that Philip Ratcliffe of Medford received a whipping and got both ears cropped in 1631 "for uttering most foul and scandalous invectives against church and government." This marked the first case on record of someone losing both ears in the name of justice. Ratcliffe no doubt counted himself lucky to lose his ears rather than his life, since blasphemy carried the death sentence. Before "banishment out of the limits of this jurisdiction," Ratcliffe was also required to forfeit a £40 fine.[51]

Oaths that alluded to the crucifixion of Christ were considered the most heinous. Peter Wallis was presented at the York Court in 1652 for "swearing by God & by the Blood of God." The *Maine Court Records* of 1671 note that John Puddington was charged with "swearing by God's wounds," and "for the multiplying of oaths." If swearing by God could earn a stiff fine, whipping, and time in the pillory, denying the existence of God represented a capital offense.

John Winthrop noted in his journal that in 1640, the Massachusetts Court of Assistants found Hugh Bewett (or Buet) "guilty of heresy and his person and errors dangerous for infection of others." The villain's blasphemy was in publicly claiming himself "free of sin, because there was no such thing as original sin." Goodman Bewett was not executed, but merely banished to Rhode Island "where he was well received." Had he dared return to Massachusetts, he would have faced the noose.[52]

THE "QUAKER INVASION"

As far as the magistrates and ministers of Massachusetts and Connecticut were concerned, the first major crime wave came with the "Quaker Invasion," from 1656 through 1669. On July 11, 1656, the *Swallow* sailed into Boston Harbor from the West Indies with Mary Fisher and Ann Austin aboard, marking the beginning of what Massachusetts Bay authorities considered a direct assault upon their government, religion, and society. Many who belonged to this religious sect, founded by George Fox in England, and also known as the Society of Friends, had been driven out of that country for their religious convictions and practices. Many sailed to the New World filled with missionary zeal, convinced that God had dispatched them to Massachusetts to topple Puritanism. And they were prepared to surrender their lives for their faith.

"Repent! A day of howling and sad lamentation is coming upon you all from the Lord," Mary Fisher and Ann Austin shouted to the curious crowd as they were immediately hauled off to Boston Prison. Governor Bellingham had been forewarned, so the religious pamphlets and "corrupt" Quaker books the two carried were quickly confiscated and burned. The windows of the prison were boarded up to prevent them from proselytizing to passersby. After five weeks behind bars (during which their bodies were scrutinized for marks of witchcraft—that is, any mole or unnatural protuberance where a witch's *familiar*, or imp, might suckle), the women were shipped back to Barbados.

"On Trial" or "A Quaker Trial," illustration by Charles Stanley Reinhart, engraved by James S. King from William T. Harris, Edward Everett Hale, Nelson A. Miles, O. P. Austin, and George Cary Eggleston, *The United States of America: A Pictorial History of the American Nation from the Earliest Discoveries and Settlements to the Present Time, 1909.* COURTESY OF PAUL ROYSTER, COORDINATOR OF SCHOLARLY COMMUNICATION, UNIVERSITY OF NEBRASKA, LINCOLN LIBRARIES

Ann Austin, who bore five children, said she "had not suffered so much in birthing them all, as she suffered under those barbarous and cruel hands."[53]

This humiliating body search was customary for any woman, man, or child suspected of witchcraft, and shows that Puritans considered Quakers in the same league as witches.

Quakers established the first Friends Meeting in Massachusetts Bay at Sandwich in 1658. The following year, Plymouth Court attempted to prevent more Quakers from entering the colony by seizing any vessel transporting any of "that cursed sect of heretics lately risen up in the World." Quakers are generally referred to in Plymouth and Bristol county records as "vagrants," a term of reproach for idle persons with "no lawful calling to earn their own bread."

Reverend John Higginson, a Salem cleric, called the "Inner Light" experienced by devout Friends "a stinking Vapour from Hell," while his colleague, the Reverend John Wilson, said he "would carry fire in one hand and faggots in the other in order to burn all the Quakers in the world!"[54]

For Massachusetts and Connecticut, the coming of the Quakers represented a major crisis of law and order. Members of this religious sect refused to take the required oath to support the Crown or to bear arms to protect New England from its enemies, and they would not pay taxes. Because their faith directed them to resist all signs of hierarchy, they flatly refused to doff their hats as was customary in deference to all magistrates and ministers. Puritans were horrified by the Quaker conviction that God revealed himself directly to the human heart. The educated clergy who led Puritans in daily faith were reviled and despised by these "Agents of Disorder," who rudely disrupted worship services by yelling out verbal abuses such as *Devil's mouthpiece!* at the parson in his pulpit. Quakers simply did not believe in ordained clergy or traditional worship services, nor did they see the need for baptism or the point of any formal religious creed.

Particularly difficult for Puritans to stomach was the fact that this troublesome sect respected no human authority and considered women equal to men, even permitting them to take active roles in worship services. Quaker missionaries challenged the church and civil law that Puritans had worked so diligently to establish in the New World, and the social order that accompanied adherence to those laws. As Non-Conformists, Puritans themselves had suffered severe persecution back in England. Many of their own religious leaders had been driven from their pulpits and even imprisoned through the efforts of Archbishop Laud and the established Church of England. It was ironic that when the Quakers arrived in determined droves, colonial administrators were quick to respond with new laws enacted solely to address the threat of "Vagabond Ranters" and the "Damnable Heresies" they seemed hell-bent on spreading.[55]

Laws to Punish "the Quaker heretics"

At its first session in 1656, following the landing of the *Swallow,* the Massachusetts General Court announced new laws to combat "the cursed sect of heretics lately risen up in the world commonly called Quakers, who take upon them to be immediately sent of God ... and do speak and write blasphemous opinions." The laws included:

→ a fine of £100 for any shipmaster knowingly transporting Quakers into the colony, and imprisonment if he did not carry them back to the place from whence they had come;

→ a sentence to the house of correction for the Quakers, where they were to be severely whipped, and by the master there be kept constantly to work and none suffered to converse with them;

→ a fine for anyone importing, dispersing, or concealing Quaker books or writings concerning their devilish opinions;

→ a fine on anyone defending the opinions of the Quakers and banishment for persistence in such defense; and

→ a whipping or fine for anyone who shall revile the office or person of magistrates or ministers, as is usual with the Quakers.

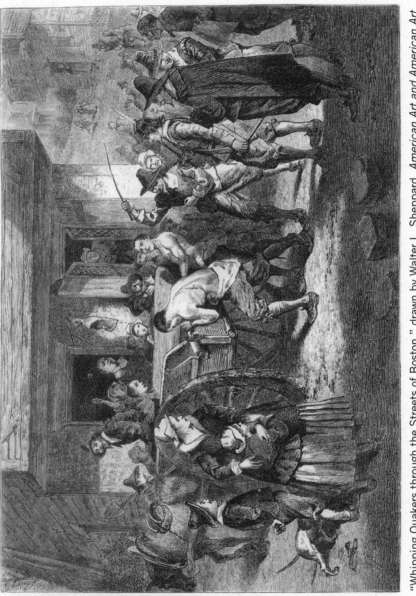

"Whipping Quakers through the Streets of Boston," drawn by Walter L. Sheppard, *American Art and American Art Collections, Volume I*, Walter Montgomery, editor, 1889. COURTESY OF PAUL ROYSTER, COORDINATOR OF SCHOLARLY COMMUNICATION, UNIVERSITY OF NEBRASKA, LINCOLN LIBRARIES

The colonies of Plymouth, New Haven, and Connecticut likewise enacted laws against "this malignant doctrine," so many Quakers were forced to find refuge in Rhode Island, where there were no such laws to prevent their settlement. Puritans were well aware of that colony's tolerance toward religious refugees fleeing persecution in other jurisdictions, and frequently referred to it as "Rogue's Island." Yet, Quakers kept returning to Massachusetts Bay, bound and determined to challenge the rules against them, causing one administrator to sigh in despair, "[F]or every one Quaker banished, ten rose in his or her place!" Thus, the laws against Quakers became tougher.

In 1657, the Massachusetts General Court ordered male Quakers to have an ear lopped off and "be kept at work in a House of Correction doing community service, until he can be sent out of court jurisdiction at his own expense." On the second conviction he risked losing his second ear and getting branded on the hand with an "H" for "Heretic." On the third offense, his tongue was to be bored through with a hot iron before he was banished again. Quaker women did not lose ears, but were generally stripped to the waist and whipped at the cart's tail or tied to the back of an ox-drawn cart and pulled through the streets.

"Take heed you break not our Ecclesiastical Laws," Governor John Endicott warned Quakers, "for then ye are sure to stretch by a halter!" A Massachusetts law passed in 1659 made death the penalty for any Quaker who returned to the colony to test the laws, after being twice banished.

In spite of the persecution, the sect found converts. Lawrence Southwick, his wife Cassandra, and their three adult children originally belonged to the Salem church, but in 1656 Cassandra was fined for skipping meeting. It turned out that the whole family had become Quaker converts, and the younger Southwicks landed in Ipswich jail for refusing to forfeit the 30 shillings levied upon each for missing six Sabbathday meetings. After the elder Southwicks fled to New York, their son Josiah, was cart-whipped, and his sisters ordered exiled to the West Indies to become indentured servants. However, no sea captain could be found who was willing to transport them.

In another case of conversion, Deborah, the wife of Robert Wilson, sauntered nude up and down the streets of Salem in June 1662, "in order to demonstrate the spiritual barrenness" of Massachusetts religion.[56] The Essex County Court considered her "distempered of mind," and thought the best action for her strange behavior was to

"Scourging a Quaker," engraving by Frank Thayer Merrill, from *A Book of New England Legends and Folklore in Prose and Poetry,* by Samuel Adams Drake, 1884. COURTESY OF PAUL ROYSTER, COORDINATOR OF SCHOLARLY COMMUNICATION, UNIVERSITY OF NEBRASKA, LINCOLN LIBRARIES

put her under her husband's custody. However, Goodman Wilson informed authorities that he thoroughly approved of his wife's public testimonial of faith, so the court quickly stepped in with appropriate punishment:

> *For her barbarous and unhuman going through the town is to be tied at a cart's taile with her body naked downward to her waist and whipped from Mr. Gidney's Gate till she come to her own house, not exceeding 30 stripes, and her mother Buffum and sister Smith, that were abetted to her, to be tyed on either side of her, at the cart's taile naked to their shifts to ye waist and accompany her.*

Evidently, Goody Wilson's demonstration was thought effective, for Lidia Wardell (or Wardwell) was also ordered to be "severely whipped and pay costs to the Marshal of Hampton upon her presentment for going naked into the Newbury Meetinghouse."

Guilt by association with Quakers also meant trouble. John Selado, the Wenham innkeeper (father of Sarah Good, hanged for witchcraft in 1692), broke the 1657 law against harboring "any of that cursed sect of Quakers," but agreed to pay the required 40 shillings, instead of going to jail, "to answer complaint for entertaining them" in his public house. On March 16, 1663, John Emery found himself before the *Court of Quarterly Sessions, Essex County,* "for entertaining Quakers, whom he bade welcome for a meeting at his house." He was to forfeit four shillings plus court fees, "for being kindly to bed and table and shaking the hands of two Quaker male vagrants." Several months later, Emery presented a petition, signed by selectmen and fifty Haverhill citizens, granting remission of the fine imposed on him.[57]

By 1676, the Massachusetts General Court had issued an order that allowed authorities to search out and arrest any and all Quakers.[58]

Judge Samuel Sewall recorded the general reaction in his diary when on June 21, 1677, "accompanied by five or so male companions, a female Quaker slipt" into the South Meetinghouse (Third Church of Boston) during the Sabbathday sermon. Margaret Brewster was "covered with a canvas Frock, her hair disheveled and loosened, straggling wildly down her neck and shoulders . . . [She was] smeared with soot, her face black as ink, led by two other Quakers and followed by two more. It occasioned the greatest and most amazing uproar I ever saw."

"God is displeased at you," Goody Brewster called out to the minister and his congregation during the solemn worship service. "God will show his displeasure soon!" Margaret Brewster's aim was to demonstrate humility. "I came into Priest Thatcher's House of Worship with my Hair about my shoulders, Ashes upon my head, my face colored black and sackcloth on—with nothing but Love in my heart." According to the Salem constable, she, like other Quakers, "was led by the spirit of the devil to ramble up and down the country like whores and rogues a caterwauling. There is but one God, and you do not worship that God which we worship."

The court sentenced Margaret Brewster to be stripped to the waist, tied to the cart's tail, and whipped out of Boston. "The will of the Lord be done," Margaret bravely told the judges. "I am contented."[59]

The New Haven Colony did not threaten Quakers with death, but presented them with choices: prison, whipping, or branding, followed by banishment. However, any male Quaker who came back after being dismissed from New Haven's jurisdiction, risked getting branded with the letter "H." Quaker women on the second offense "shall be severely whipt . . . and for every Quaker, he or she, that shall a fourth time again offend, they shall have their tongues bored through with a hot iron." In 1658, in New Haven, two Quakers received forty lashes for insisting there was no devil, and that "infants were not charged with Adam's sin until they themselves had sinned."

Connecticut records report the punishment dealt a Quaker named Humfry Norton before he was cast out of the New Haven Colony: "The drum was beat, the People gather'd. The offender was fetch'd and stripp'd to the Waist, and set with his Back to the Magistrates, and given in their View Thirty-Six cruel Stripes with a knotted cord, and his hand made fast in the Stocks where they had set his Body before, and burn'd very deep with a Red-hot Iron with H for Heresie."

Mary Dyer—Quaker Martyr[60]

Though Puritans preferred to rid the colonies altogether of these irksome religious practitioners rather than execute any one, many of those exiled kept coming back, well aware that they faced death in doing so. Indeed, they seemed determined to become martyrs. William Robinson, Marmaduke Stevenson, William Leddra, and Mary Dyer were eventually hanged at Boston Neck for their faith.

In his journal, Governor John Winthrop described "Vagabond Quaker" Mary Dyer as "a proper and fair woman of a very proud spirit . . . notoriously infected with error; one censorious and troublesome."

The Antinomian Controversy of 1636–38 had marked the first religious challenge to Puritanism in Massachusetts Bay Colony. When Anne Hutchinson was excommunicated and received her sentence of banishment, Mary Dyer and her husband walked out of the Boston church by her side. The Dyers were among some thirty-five families to join the Hutchinsons in exile in Rhode Island. Like Ann Hutchinson, Mary Dyer was convinced that one received God's grace through personal revelation without any aid from educated clergy and believed that women could preach every bit as well as men. The Dyers later returned to England and joined the Society of Friends there, returning to the New World some years later, afire with missionary zeal. Mary Dyer preached her way through Connecticut and Plymouth and finally landed in Boston, where she visited the Quakers in prison, before being banished to Rhode Island.

In 1657, Dyer returned to Boston determined "to look the bloody laws in the face!" She was immediately jailed, then sent out of the colony with the warning that if she came back, the penalty would be death. The next time she returned she was summoned before General Court with Marmaduke Stevenson and William Robinson. When Endicott ordered the Quaker men—on trial for their lives—to doff their hats out of respect to the Court, they refused.

"Neither I nor any magistrate wished to see them die," Governor Endicott explained, "but the law was the law and must be followed."

When the death sentence was announced to Mary Dyer in court, she replied, "The Lord's will be done."

"Robinson, Stevenson, and Mary Dyer Going to Execution," engraving by F. O. C. Darley, from *A Book of New England Legends and Folklore in Prose and Poetry*, by Samuel Adams Drake, 1884. COURTESY OF PAUL ROYSTER, COORDINATOR OF SCHOLARLY COMMUNICATION, UNIVERSITY OF NEBRASKA, LINCOLN LIBRARIES

"Friends or Quakers Going to Execution," engraving by F. O. C. Darley, from *Our Country: A Household History of the United States for All Readers, From the Discovery of America to the Present Time,* by Benson J. Lossing, 1895. PHOTOGRAPH COURTESY OF PAUL ROYSTER, COORDINATOR OF SCHOLARLY COMMUNICATION, UNIVERSITY OF NEBRASKA, LINCOLN LIBRARIES

On October 27, 1659, the day the Quakers were to hang, the authorities must have feared public demonstrations and loss of crowd control, since by court order, one hundred armed militiamen were on the scene.

Mary Dyer walked hand in hand between the two condemned men, toward the gallows at Boston Neck. William Robinson's final words upon the scaffold were silenced when a minister standing among the spectators called out, "Hold your tongue, Quaker! You are going to die with a lie in your mouth!"

Marmaduke Stephenson vowed that "New England's leaders would be cursed forevermore . . . Be it known unto all this day, that we suffer not as evildoers, but for conscience' sake." The remainder of his final statement was drowned out by drumbeats.

Mary was the last to ascend the ladder. The noose was around her neck and she was blindfolded when there came a sudden shout.

"Stop! She is reprieved!"

Mary Dyer's son was anxiously waiting in the jail cell when the sheriff brought his mother back. His horse was saddled, ready to take her back to Rhode Island, for he and his father had somehow managed to get her death sentence commuted to exile. Still, stubbornly determined to see the colony's laws against Quakers repealed, Mary Dyer returned to Boston seven months later.

"Are you the same Mary Dyer who was here before?" Governor Endicott asked her in court.

"I am the same."

"Then I must repeat the sentence once before pronounced upon you. And now it is to be executed."

Upon the scaffold, Mary Dyer was once more offered her life if only she would stay out of town. "I cannot," she replied, "for in obedience to the will of the Lord, I came, and in His will, I abide faithful unto death." On June 1, 1660, Mary Dyer became the first woman in New England to die for her religious convictions.

William Leddra—Last Quaker Executed

The last Quaker hanged was William Leddra on March 14, 1661, after he had also been banished several times. Leddra spent nearly a year in

Boston Prison chained to a log, and when dragged into court for trial, one leg was still attached to the log. The prisoner was offered liberty and passage to England or elsewhere out of Massachusetts, but declined the offer.

"Not having the Fear of God before his Eyes," . . . he returned into this Jurisdiction in a Rebellious and Seditious Manner contrary to the wholesome Laws of this Country, made for the Preservation of the Peace and welfare of the same." Leddra's reply was that "this governor was not his Judge and that he knew your Ministers are deluders and yourselves Murderers . . ." Banished from Essex County, Leddra spent nearly a year in Plymouth prison, where he was told he "might have his life and be at liberty if he would depart the colony."

The Quaker's brave reply was: "I am willing to die for it . . . for I speak the Truth." Three months before his execution, William Leddra wrote a letter to his fellow Quakers, that included the following excerpt: ". . . with a Pen of Trembling, that the Noise of the Whip on my Back, all the Imprisonments, and Banishing upon pain of Death, and after returning, the loud threatening sound of a Halter, did no more affright me . . . than if they had threatened to have bound a Spider's Web to my Finger . . ."[61]

Following the Restoration of King Charles II to the British throne in 1660, the numerous complaints from Quaker subjects about their treatment in His Majesty's colonies resulted in a decree prohibiting the use of corporal and/or capital punishment against Quakers. Colonial laws against members of the religious sect were thus briefly suspended. Yet on October 8, 1662, the Massachusetts General Court reinstated the *Cart and Whip Act Against Vagabond Quakers.*

Members of the controversial sect did hold political offices in Kittery and York County between 1648 and 1663, since Quaker entrepreneurs such as Nicholas Shapleigh and Richard Nason achieved considerable financial success through trade, lumber mills, and timber rights on the Maine frontier.

In 1662, however, York County Court launched its own attacks against Quakers. Ruling magistrate Richard Waldron, for example, had three Quaker women arrested, tied to carts, and whipped out of his jurisdiction. Quakers residing in the area were also fined for skipping Sabbath services.

There is no evidence that Rhode Island ever persecuted Quakers. This colony, in fact, even elected a Quaker, William Coddington, to serve as governor in the 1670s.

Not until the new Royal Charter of 1692 was enacted—promising Liberty of Conscience to all Protestants—were Quakers, like Anglicans and anti-Baptists, permitted to worship as they wished in their own churches and meetinghouses.

Part V

Sexual Deviants and Female Felons

If any man shall commit fornication with any single woman, they shall be punished either by enjoining to marriage, or fine, or corporal punishment, or all or any of these as the Judges in the Courts of Assistants shall appoint most agreeable to the Word of God.
—Massachusetts Bay Colony Law, 1642

The most common crime on the dockets during colonial days, after "disguised with drink," was fornication—or, as it was so indelicately known, "carnal copulation." Sixty-nine cases were prosecuted by the Plymouth Court between 1633 and 1691. From 1665 through 1689, it was fornication that brought approximately two-fifths of all female offenders before the bench, an increase of 20 percent over the previous thirty-five years.

Puritans and Pilgrims were convinced that due to Eve's rebellion against God and temptation of Adam in the Garden of Eden, women had less self-control over mind and body than men. Seventeenth-century society believed females more easily tempted by carnal desire and morally weaker in resisting sex than males. Howlong Harris of Providence, Rhode Island, was fined 5 shillings by the Newport Court of Trials in 1682 for fornication, then was acquitted when she testified to being "so surprised by drink that she was unable to resist the temptation to have sex with Thomas Deney."[62]

As early as the 1630s, both Massachusetts and Connecticut passed laws stating that a man could not court a maid without her parent's consent. Neither indentured servants nor licensed apprentices were permitted to marry until they completed their designated terms. The mean age for marriage between 1630 and 1675 in New England was twenty-six years for men and just over twenty years for women. Between 1676 and 1692, most men were twenty-seven years old when they wed, while women were generally twenty-two or twenty-three.

How could young people not be tempted by what clergy called "their carnal natures," particularly during regular harvest gatherings, corn-husking bees, and periodic militia drills? Single young adults frequently lived outside their family homes for lengthy spells of unchaperoned time, serving apprenticeships to learn a trade, or working as household servants and mother's helpers for relatives who might be ill or require assistance with a newborn.

Marriage was an honored institution and meant to last a lifetime. Since early New Englanders considered marriage a civil rather than a religious contract, couples were customarily joined by magistrates rather than by ministers in meetinghouses. A public announcement of the couple's intent to marry, known as *banns*, was posted prior to the event, usually by a paper notice nailed on the meetinghouse door. On the date set, the presence of witnesses was required and the marriage dutifully recorded. In March of 1680, the Ipswich Quarterly Court fined John Sandy not only for fornication, but also *"for marrying without being published."*

Historian Laurel Ulrich claims that between 1653 and 1727, the York County courts tried 274 fornication cases, 61 percent involving couples already married.[63] Suffolk County handled over 200 cases of illicit sex in the 1670s.[64] Offenders could be single men, single women, or couples recently married. Sex between a man and a single woman, if the man was married, was legally considered fornication rather than adultery. In 1654 the Essex County Court convened at Hampton and ordered John Ash "whipped ten stripes and bound to good behavior for filthy, lascivious carriages divers times with a wench." According to her Cambridge neighbors, Hannah Gray was a "lying little devil." Another young woman testified before the Middlesex County bench that her brother told her Hannah used to "entice the scollar boys from Harvard and use baudy language."

Couple making love, while the devil's imps spy on them. SEVENTEENTH-CENTURY WOODCUT, AUTHOR'S COLLECTION

Hannah's punishment was to stand in front of the meetinghouse with a paper sign on her head on which was written in capital letters: I STAND HERE FOR MY LASCIVIOUS AND WANTON CARRIAGE.

It was frequently a newly married couple who stood accused and were made to suffer punishment together. The *Boston Court Records* of 1638 reveals the tale of "John Bickerstaffe, censured to be severely whipped for committing fornication with Ales Burwoode . . . Ales Burwoode censured to be whipped for yielding to Bickerstaffe without crying out and concealing it 9 or 10 dayes."

On June 4, 1645, John Ellis was "whipped at the public post in Sandwich, for uncleanness with his wife before marriage, and his wife, to stand and witness his punishment."

John Baker and Susan Martin stood together before the Middlesex County Court in April of 1654, charged with fornication. He readily confessed to having "had the use of her body in a carnal way. Both were to be severely whipped twelve stripes apiece upon their naked bodies before the public concourse and also are enjoined to marry."[65]

Jacob Farrer and his then wife confessed to premarital sex in 1670. Farrer explained that the death of his father was one reason for their "great and crying sin . . . Had my father been yet alive," Goodman Farrer told judge and jury at the *Essex Quarterly Court of Sessions,* "he might have been a comfort to us in this hour of our temptation and trouble."

BRIDAL PREGNANCY AND BIRTHING BASTARDS

Bridal pregnancy was surprisingly common, and though a married couple might be embarrassed by a child who arrived too soon, historian Jack Larkin estimates that one-third of early-eighteenth-century New England brides were pregnant when wed. Although the couple would most likely have ended up as man and wife anyway, they were still usually fined and flogged. They could also expect to be chastised for "uncleanness" in front of the entire congregation at their local meetinghouse. From 1640 through 1685, over one hundred women were convicted of bearing children out of wedlock in Essex County. The standard fine for fornication was 40 shillings. When the woman only was required to pay this fine, it typically meant that her husband was not the child's father. If she refused to name the child's father, the fine levied on her would be higher.

Illegitimacy was a matter of great local concern because any child born out of wedlock might become the town's financial responsibility for many years to come. The usual period for "maintenance" was until a child was six, or until someone offered to take the child into his household as a servant or apprentice. Mothers, particularly those who were poor and indigent, had little or no say if local selectmen decided their fatherless child was best bound out to a foster family.

All the county court records describe couples in which the woman was either pregnant or a new mother was summoned to appear together with her husband before the authorities. Here are several examples from the *Essex County Court Records* of July 19, 1730,

> *John Baker of Ipswich & now wife Judith; child born within 5 months of marriage—40 shillings each.*

> *Patrick Bourne, laborer, & now wife Jane Britton, both of Wenham; child born April, 2 months after marriage; no proof against him, pleads not guilty; wife pleads guilty—40 shillings.*

> *Caleb Burbank of Rowley and now wife, Lidia, alias Garfield: 40 shillings each.*

If a couple refused to publicly confess to fornication before marriage and pay the fine levied, their child could be denied baptism, which in Puritan theology was to prevent a newborn soul his or her opportunity for everlasting life. Once a couple confessed to premarital sex, underwent the prescribed public humiliation, and forfeited the fine, there was seldom ostracism from the community. After all, marriage was supposed to be a lifetime commitment based on love between a man and a woman, and premarital pregnancy provided proof that God had already blessed the union with conception.

Women, particularly servants, were punished more severely than the males with whom they coupled, especially if they then bore an illegitimate child, and particularly if they dared to accuse their masters. Elizabeth Drew received twelve lashes in 1654 for naming her master as the father of her bastard. Because she stuck to her story, the Essex County Court judge ordered her whipped another twenty stripes, then she was forced to stand outside the meetinghouse wearing a placard that declared her A SLANDERER OF MR. ZEROBABELL ENDICOTT.

In 1639, Dorothy Temple was sentenced "for uncleanness and bringing forth a male bastard, is censured to be whipt twice; but she fainting in the execution of the first, the other was not executed."[66]

After 1668, a Massachusetts law allowed the mother's word to convict a man of fornication, thus punishing him with public whipping and a fine, as well as requiring his child support, "notwithstanding his denial." Confession was still preferable. Before the Essex County Court in June of 1696, "Moses Kimball admitted to having had carnal knowledge of Elizabeth Hodgkins" and was "ordered to pay maintenance and a fine of 40 shillings."

Clearly, it was a particular concern of local selectmen that the maintenance of illegitimate children not be put on town doles. On April 10, 1719, Maybell Evance stood before the Essex County justices for bearing an illegitimate child. She accused Gregory, a black slave belonging to Francis Norwood of Lynn. She was "whipt 15 stripes and costs" and was "to serve the selectmen of Beverly or their assigns five years toward the town's maintenance of her child."

The next day in court Gregory pleaded not guilty, "but she making oath and it appearing that it is a blackish negro child and that she dwelt at the same house and he offering to work hard and take the child and maintain it and she asked to be married to him. His punishment was to receive twenty whiplashes and to be sold out of the province "as the law directs" within six months, being imprisoned in the meantime."[67]

Rhode Island tended to be more lenient regarding crimes of a sexual nature. In 1682, for example, Ruth Bayly's punishment "for having sundry Bastards" was to pay the court £1, 6 shillings, 8d, or else receive fifteen lashes upon her naked back.

Elizabeth Dean of Salem, Singlewoman, accused John Gray of Salem, laborer, of fathering a male child born December 4. She paid 10 shillings, and at the next session, John Gray "freely offered to hold the town of Salem free of Elizabeth Dean's child's maintenance."[68]

William Dirkey was presented for fornication at Hampton Quarterly Court, where he was "ordered to be whipped not exceeding twenty stripes, and to put in security of £20, to save the town of Ipswich harmless from the charges of keeping the child, or else go to prison."

Elizabeth Dunwell of Topsfield was a repeat offender whose name appears in various court records of Essex County. She was "whipt 10 stripes for having a third bastard child." This time she named Thomas

Goodale as the father, "but since she had not accused him while in labor, he was dismissed."[69]

"Joseph Weed complained of by John Hoyt for fornication with his daughter, Rachel Hoyt. Weed confessed and the court fined him 40 shillings and maintenance of the child unless he marries Rachel."[70]

Single women accused of fornication occasionally begged the courts for mercy. In September 1682, Elizabeth Gould was sentenced to a whipping after accusing Ralph Farnum Jr. of Andover, then later admitted she did not know who fathered her child. After paying the fine, her corporal punishment was remitted and Elizabeth expressed penance by petitioning the court: "I confess I have sinned against God and my owne conscience and thereby have dishonored God and the country and have brought shame upon myself and Relations."[71]

Mary Redy was another sentenced to a flogging for fornication, who, after paying her fine, petitioned the court and was relieved of corporal punishment. In September of 1682, Mary declared before the bench at Essex County Court, that she was but "a poor destitute Creature . . . (and I) desire that your Honors would be pleased to show mercy to me, and desire your prayers for me that I might reform and leave all such wickedness through God's help." The *Middlesex County Court Records* note one single woman, already pregnant and incarcerated, caught in the act with her Boston gaoler. "I could not help it!" she cried before judge and jury. "The devil made me do it!"

Legal Role for Midwives

The testimony of midwives was crucial in cases of single women bearing bastards. The theory was that any woman at the peak of her labor, nagged to name the baby's father by the midwife in attendance, would inevitably speak the truth. Authorities then knew exactly who to go after for child support, absolving the town of economic responsibility. It was a surefire means of going after deadbeat dads. If the mother refused to name names, adultery or even prostitution might be assumed, and these were more serious crimes than giving birth to an illegitimate child.

Fifty-five-year-old Elizabeth Colby and her sister, Mary Challis, who was sixty-eight, were both practicing midwives. They testified in Essex

County Court that "being at the travail of Sarah Baisdell, Singlewoman, being near one week since, that in the extremity of the time of her travail, Mrs. Foss [another midwife] put it upon her to declare whose the child was, the said Sarah answered that it was Stephen Flanders, his child, and that she never knew any man else."

Ruth Eaton of Haverhill accused Ebenezer Kimball of Bradford, who was fined 50 shillings. Ebenezer Kimball was later "dismissed, as Ruth Eaton did not name him during her travail."[72]

WEARING THE SCARLET LETTER

The first case of adultery to come before New England courts appears in the *Plymouth Colony Records of 1639*, when Mary, wife of Robert Mendame (alias Mendlove) of Duxbury was accused on September 3, of "dallyance diverse tymes with Tinsin, an Indian, and committing the act of uncleanse with him . . . by his own confession by several interpreters . . . The Bench doth censure Mary to be whipt at cart's tail through the townes streets and to weare AD for Adultery upon her left sleeve for as long as she lives in this colony. If found without this badge of shame, then to be burned in the face with a hot iron." Tinsin's sentence was lighter. The Goodwife was the adulteress, so it was determined that "the Indian should be well-whipt with a halter about his neck at the post because the crime arose through the allurement and enticement of said Mary and he was drawn thereunto it."[73]

Adultery was legally defined by the marital status of the woman involved in the act. Whether she had relations with a married man or a single one, she had committed a grievous sin against her husband, and thus was seen as a threat to family harmony and community order.

In 1655, Mary Daly, a Maine resident, was charged with "daily frequenting a man's company in such a suspicious manner as caused neighbors to suspect her of incontinency."

The God of the Puritans was the God of the Old Testament, and this was the code they followed as lawmakers. According to the Book of Leviticus: "The man that committed adultery with another man's wife, even he that committeth adultery with his neighbor's wife, the adulterer and adulteress shall surely be put to death."

Book of General Laws of the Inhabitants of the Jurisdiction of New Plymouth:

> *It is ordered by the Court and Authority thereof that whosoever shall commit Adultery with a Married Woman, or one Betrothed to another Man, both of them shall be severely punished by Whipping two or several times . . . . . . once when the Court is in being, at which they were convicted of the Fact; and the second time as the Court shall Order; and likewise to wear two Capital Letters—A D cut out in cloth and sewed on their upper Garments on their Arm or Back; and if at any time they shall be found without the said Letters so worn while in this government, to be forthwith taken and publickly Whipt, and so from time to time as often as they are found not to wear the letters.*

James Britton and Mary Latham went to the gallows together in Boston on March 21, 1643/44, the only recorded execution for adultery in Massachusetts. Not only did Goodwife Latham betray her elderly husband, but she also bragged about it, making public jest of his inability to satisfy her wifely needs. After being rejected by the young man she adored, eighteen-year-old Mary had vowed to wed the very next fellow who came along. So, according to John Winthrop and *Boston Court Records,* she married "an ancient man who had neither honesty nor ability, and one for whom she had no affection." Disappointed in both love and marriage, Mary dallied with various men who plied her with wine and gifts in exchange for sexual favors. One was James Britton, whom Massachusetts Governor John Winthrop described in his Journal as "[i]ll-affected both to our church discipline and civil government." However, Britton's conscience eventually got the best of him, and he confessed to adultery before the court. At first, Mary Latham denied any liaison with Goodman Britton, but then confessed and proceeded to name twelve other lovers, including two married men, all who denied dalliance with the unhappy young woman. Britton's last-minute petition for a pardon was rejected.

Thomas Bird got in trouble with Plymouth authorities "for committing several adulterous practices and attempts, so far as his strength of nature would permit, with Hannah Bumpas, as he himself did acknowledge ... Sentenced by the court to be whipt two times, viz. the first time at the present Court and the second time betwixt this and the fifteenth day of July next. And the said Hannah Bumpas, for yielding to him, and not making resistance against him as she ought, is sentenced to be publickly whipt."

A couple of adulterers went to the New Haven gallows in 1650. Ruth Briggs was hanged in 1668 for double capital crimes of adultery and infanticide: "a defiant and disorderly woman whose dalliance and speech plagued New Haven for years."[74]

Unless there was a confession or witnesses came forward to testify, adultery was a difficult crime to prove. Thus, although the death penalty was on the books in Massachusetts Bay Colony, it was seldom carried out as a punishment for adultery. It was not a crime that warranted the death penalty in either Plymouth Colony or Rhode Island, nor was it a capital crime in Connecticut or New Haven after 1672. Punishment there was reduced to whipping and being branded on the forehead with the letter "A," or forced to wear a halter announcing your crime to all.

Between 1673 and 1774, there were thirty-eight indictments for adultery in New England. The most common punishment became a public whipping of twenty lashes, or up to the legal limit of thirty-nine stripes, at the judge's discretion, followed by the humiliation of being forced to sit at the foot of the gallows with a rope around the neck, the other end of it draped over the gallows. This was designed to encourage offenders to fully comprehend the deadly seriousness of their crime.

Ruth Read deserted her husband in Massachusetts and spent four years with another man in England, where she took his name and bore his child. In 1673, she returned "to these parts Imposing said child on her husband." The authorities gave her two months to depart the colony, or else suffer thirty stripes and stand in the marketplace upon a stool for one hour with a paper sign upon her breast that read: THUS I STAND FOR MY ADULTEROUS AND WHORISH CARRIAGE.[75]

Nathaniel Hawthorne, the beloved author of historical fiction, was surely aware of the law enacted in Massachusetts Bay Colony in 1694, requiring any woman convicted of adultery to wear the capital letter "A," "sewn conspicuously upon her garments." A Bowdoin College graduate with family connections in Maine, Hawthorne was surely familiar with the 1641 case of Mary Batcheller from Agamenticus (York, Maine) and that infamous minister, George Rogers, who represented Mary's own Arthur Dimmesdale.

We do present George Rogers and Mary Batcheller, wife of Mr. Steven Batcheller, minister, for adultery. It is ordered by ye Court [that] George Rogers, for his adultery with Mrs. Batcheller, shall forthwith have 40 stripes save one upon the bare skin, given him. It is ordered [that] Mrs. Batcheller, for her adultery, shall receive 40 stroakes save one at ye first town meeting held at Kittery six weeks after her delivery [of her child] and be branded with the Capital Letter A sewn conspicuously upon her.[76]

George Burdett, another York parson, was

indited by the whole bench for deflowering Ruth, contrary to the peace of our Sovereign Lord the King. Ruth, wife of John Gouch, found guilty by the Grand Inquest, of adultery with Mr. George Burdett, is therefore censured by this Court, that six weeks after she is delivered of Child she shall stand in a white sheete publiquely in the congregation at Agamenticus two Sabbath dayes and likewise one day at the Generall Courte, according to His Majesty's Laws.[77]

Mary Puddington was another paramour of the Reverend Burdett's who, at the same court session, was "indicted by the whole bench for often frequenting the house and company of Mr. George Burdett, minister, in his bed chamber, and elsewhere in a very suspicious manner, notwithstanding the said Mary was often forewarned by her said husband, and the constable to the great disturbance and scandal of the plantation."

Mary made a public confession before the court: "I do here acknowledge that I have dishonored God, the place where I live, and wronged my husband by my disobedience and light carriage, for which I am heartily sorry and desire forgiveness of this Court and of my husband and do promise amendment of life and manners henceforth." Having made this public confession the court then ordered her to kneel and beg her husband's pardon.

According to early *York Court Records*, the Reverend George Burdett, "turbulent breaker of the peace," was finally prosecuted as "a man of ill name and fame, infamous for incontinency, a publisher and broacher of divers dangerous speeches the better to seduce that weak sex of women to his incontinent practices." After paying his £40 fine, the minister was run out of town.

Another case of adultery involved Katheren Aines, a married woman of Plymouth, who was punished in 1656/7

> *for unclean and filthy behavior with . . . William Paule, Scotsman, and for the blasphemous words that she hath spoken, is sentenced by the Court to be forthwith publickly whipped at Plymouth and afterwards, at Taunton, on a publick training day, and to wear a Roman B for Bawd, cut out of red cloth and sewed to her upper garment on her right arm, and if she shall be ever found without it . . . to be forthwith publicly whipt.*

Alexander Aines, Katheren's husband, was ordered to witness her punishment. The court pronounced him "*guilty* for leaving his family, and exposing his wife to temptation of being a bawd." Alexander was sentenced to sit in the stocks while she and her lover, Goodman Paule, got flogged with the cat-o'-nine-tails. And Aines still had Katheren's prison fees to pay.[78]

Another wayward wife admitted to having taken a lover but justified her misbehavior by telling the court that her husband spent so much time hunting and fishing that he neglected to perform his conjugal duties. This woman and her lover were both locked in the stocks with the husband, since he was the one who led her to commit adultery.

According to the *Suffolk Country Court Records* of 1721, Jemima Colefix, the wife of a Boston laborer, "by the instigation of the Devil" committed adultery with a free black man. Her punishment was to "sit upon the gallows for one hour with a rope around her neck, the other end of it over the gallows." Then, on her way back to jail, she was "to be severely whipped 36 stripes, and forever hereafter wear a Capital A of two inches long and proportional bigness cut out in cloth of contrary color to her cloaths and sewed upon her upper Garment on her back in open view. Fifteen more lashes if she failed to do so."

Rhode Island tended to treat adultery more sympathetically than the other New England colonies, for it was not considered a capital offense there. The fine was just £10 in that colony, where adulterers received a mere fifteen lashes administered with enough time between that the wounds had a chance to heal between floggings.

The New Hampshire Statute of 1701 decreed that a couple guilty of having committed adultery was

> *to be sett upon the Gallows for one hour with ropes around their necks, its other end cast over the gallows. Afterwards both were to be severely whip't, and offenders forever after to wear a Capital Letter A of 2 inches long and proportionable in Bigness, cut out in Cloath of a contrary color to their Cloaths and Sewed upon their upper garments on the outside of their Arm or on their back in open View.*

"Pursuing Strange Flesh"

As far as we know, the term *homosexuality* was not used during the colonial period, and when the act does appear in court records, it is generally referred to as "pursuing strange flesh or unnatural lust." Ministers included it among the list of sins they believed drove God to destroy Sodom and Gomorrah. Sex with the same sex tended to get lumped together with disobeying one's parents, "nightwalking," drunkenness, "self-pollution" (or masturbation), fornication, and sleeping through Sunday sermons. To Puritans, all the descendants of Adam and Eve were ripe for any temptation that might cause them to turn away from the Will of God. What seemed to bother seventeenth-century people most was the idea of men spilling seed better spent on procreation, or "going forth to multiply."

Laws about homosexuality were unevenly applied. When two New Hampshire men were accused of sodomy in 1635, that colony's governor ignored the charge and refused to put them on trial. On September 5, 1641, one William Carsley was excommunicated from the Barnstable church for "carnall carriage" toward other men. Two men were executed for homosexual acts in seventeenth-century New England. William Plaine was hanged in New Haven in 1646 "for sodomising several men . . . and corrupting the youth of Guilford by masturbations . . . above a hundred times." Yet, it seems the real reason Goodman Plaine went to the gallows was that he had dared question God's existence. It was for this crime that authorities labeled him "a monster in human shape, exceeding all human rules for planting 'the seeds of atheism' into the young men he seduced." In 1655, John Knight was found guilty of a "sodomitical attempt" upon a young New Haven man and the court sent him to the scaffold.[79]

In 1655, the more conservative New Haven Colony added sex between females to its list of capital offenses, specifically mentioning lesbianism for the first time in any body of laws, and referring to the Bible (Romans 1:26) as "going after strange flesh, or other flesh than God alloweth by carnall knowledge of another vessel than God in nature has appointed."

These laws remained on the books when the New Haven and Connecticut colonies became one in 1665. As with any capital crime, two witnesses were required for conviction. Otherwise it was defined as "attempted sodomy," for which the usual punishment in Connecticut was a flogging, followed by several hours perched on a ladder next to the gallows with one end of the noose around the offender's neck and the other end of the rope draped over the scaffold. This simulated hanging was a punishment designed to force offenders to think long and hard about particular crimes they were guilty of committing.

Nicholas Sension of Windsor had a wife but preferred the company of young men. A respected member of the community and a representative on the Connecticut General Court, his advances toward men seem to have been common knowledge among neighbors and colleagues. What Sension termed his "fondest affections" focused on Nathaniel Pond, his servant, until Pond was killed fighting in King Philip's War. Sension managed to escape chastisement for more than three decades until finally charged with sodomy in 1677. One witness who testified against Sension's "sodomitical actings" claimed he once told the defendant "you will never leave this devilish sin till you are hanged." Sension was eventually fined, whipped, and forced to sit a spell beside the gallows with the rope around his neck. Then he was disenfranchised and cast out of his church congregation.[80]

According to historian Richard Godbeer, there are but two known cases in early New England courts of women committing "unclean behavior" together. Elizabeth Johnson faced the Essex County Court in 1642 for "unseemly practices between her and another maid." Her judges agreed that her most grievous crime was disobeying God, since "whenever the Word of God was read aloud, she had a habit of covering her ears with her hands."

Sara Norman, a married woman, and Mary Hammon of Yarmouth faced the Plymouth Colony Court in March of 1648/49 "for lewd behavior with each other upon a bed." Goodwife Norman, who was also accused of making "diverse lascivious speeches," was ordered to publicly apologize for her unchaste behavior. The judge was careful not to categorize the act as sodomy. Her partner, Maid Hammon, was remitted back into her master's service.

Early New England lawmakers considered sodomy solely a male crime and one requiring two eyewitnesses for conviction. John Alexander and Thomas Roberts were found guilty of "unclean carriage with one another" by the Plymouth Court in 1637, "often spending their seed one upon another," as proven by witnesses and their own confession. Alexander was whipped at the post and branded in the shoulder, then banished out of the colony.[81]

Although boys and girls both wore long skirts until boys were "breeched," or put into pants at about six years of age, our colonial ancestors strongly objected to any neighbors dressing in drag. In 1652, the Essex County Court charged Joseph Davis of Haverhill a 10-shilling fine for putting on female attire and "going from house to house in the middle of the night."

These same court records note that Dorothy Hoyt was to be whipped in 1677, unless her father paid her £2 fine for putting on men's clothing, considered "an abomination in the eyes of the Lord." Papa apparently refused to pay, so Dorothy fled Massachusetts Bay rather then suffer a whipping or give up her preference for male outfits.

In 1695, Massachusetts enacted a law against wearing clothing of the opposite sex, the punishment being a fine of £5, or a public whipping.

"A Horrible Case of Bestiality"

Buggery, or sexual relations with animals, was against Mosaic Law, since Leviticus 20:15 decreed: "If a man lie with a beast, he shall surely be put to death; and ye shall slay the beast." Four men were hanged for bestiality in New Haven and Massachusetts, the first being Thomas Granger of Plymouth Colony. Someone saw this seventeen-year-old indentured servant and herdsman belonging to Goodman Love Brewster in a Duxbury pasture, having sex with a mare, and reported it to the authorities. One can imagine Plymouth Colony gossips having a field day, cackling over this abhorrent crime. What people most feared at the time was that unnatural livestock might be born with human characteristics. Of Thomas Granger's crime, Governor William Bradford wrote in his journal: ". . . horrible it is to mention, but the truth of history requires it."

At first, Granger flatly denied the accusation. Then, trapped by the words of several eyewitnesses, he confessed in livid detail, even volunteering to identify which animals he favored. Besides the guilty mare he got caught with, he named one cow, two calves, a couple of goats, five sheep, and a turkey.

"No, not that one," young Granger told the court as the animals were rounded up to appear before judge and jury. "The ewe." Then, "Nay, 'twas the black one! 'Twas she I did tup." When asked how the practice of "such wickedness came about," the lad replied that he had learned to copulate with ewes and other livestock from a fellow servant who heard about the practice back in England.[82]

On September 8, 1642, Thomas Granger was forced to watch the animals slaughtered one by one before he himself was hanged. "A very sad spectacle it was," wrote Governor Bradford. "For first the mare and the cow and the rest of the lesser cattle were killed before his face, according to the Law, and then he himself was executed. The cattle were all cast into a great and large pit digged of purpose for them, and no use was made of any part of them. Since the perpetuator could not be positive which sheep was which, eight rather than a dozen animals were put to death."

Benjamin Goad of Roxbury, also seventeen, was executed for the same crime. Since there had been just one witness, the jury found him guilty by "confession upon apprehension." He regretted his behavior, which he told Judge Sewall was "the result of idleness and disobeying my parents." The court then informed Goad that: "The mare you abused before your execution in your sight shall be knock't on the head."[83]

In New Haven, three men went to the gallows for bestiality: Walter Robinson in 1635, George Spencer in 1642, and William Porter in 1662.[84] In October 28, 1681, one Thomas Saddeler, a laborer from Portsmouth, Rhode Island, in the jurisdiction of Providence Plantation, was arraigned for buggery with a mare and

> *for having not the fear of God before, nor carrying with thee the dignity of human nature, but being seduced by the instigation of the devil, on the third of September in this present year . . . at Mount Hope, in the jurisdiction of New Plymouth, a certain mare of a blackish color then and there being in a certain obscure and woody place on Mount Hope, near the ferry, didst tie her head onto a bush, and then and there, wickedly and most abominably . . . felloniously and carnally didst attempt, the detestable sin of buggery . . . thou didst commit and do, to the great dishonor and contempt of Almighty God and of all mankind, and against the peace of our Sovereign Lord the King, his crown, and dignity, and against the laws of God and this jurisdiction.*

Saddeler pleaded "not guilty" and requested a "trial by a jury of twelve men." Their final verdict was "Guilty of vile, abominable, and presumptuous attempts to buggery with a mare." The court judge then sentenced Thomas Saddeler to be "severely whipt at the post, and to sit on the gallows with a rope about his neck during the pleasure of the Court, and to be branded in the forehead with a Roman P to signify his abominable Pollution, and so to depart this government; all which was performed in the particulars."[85]

PEDOPHILIA—THE SPECTACULAR HUMFRY CASE

Some crimes were so heinous that it did not even occur to colonial authorities to declare a law until after the offense was committed. A stringent law against rape of a minor was passed in November of 1641 as part of the *Massachusetts Body of Liberties,* following the conviction of three men for sexual misconduct with nine-year-old Dorcas Humfry of Lynn in Massachusetts Bay Colony and her seven-year-old sister, Sarah, who "were found to have been often abused by diverse lewd persons and filthiness" over a period of two years. The same day that sentences were handed down on the three perpetrators, the Massachusetts General Court proclaimed the mandatory sentence of death for sexual intercourse with a child under ten years.

The case aroused even more shock and scandal throughout the colonies because the father of the victims, John Humfry, Esquire, was one of the most highly respected gentlemen in New England. A graduate of Trinity College, Cambridge, he was married to Lady Susan, a sister of the Earl of Lincoln, the powerful Puritan nobleman who helped to finance the Puritan migration to the New World in 1630. Humfry was among the original Dorchester Adventurers and another prime mover and chief financier for establishing Massachusetts Bay Colony. When the Humfry family sailed to Massachusetts in 1634, they brought along all six of their children.

After settling in Lynn, Humfry hired a joiner by the name of Jenkin Davis, who had a wife and son. Sir John had such confidence in this employee that when he traveled to the West Indies and England on business, he left his younger daughters in the care of Goodman Davis and his wife, Sarah. The predator is described by one local historian as "too vicious person to be allowed a place in such honest company," though Davis consistently denied having

> *any entrance to the girl's body. Jenkin Davis, for his abusing the fore-named Dorcas, ordered to be severely whipped at Boston on a Lecture Day, and shall be returned to prison till he may be sent to Lynn, so if he shall at any time go forth out the bounds of the said town without license of this court, he shall be put to death. Also he shall wear a hempen rope about his neck during the pleasure of this Court, so as if he be found to have gone abroad at any time without it, he shall be again whipped, and further, if he shall be duly convicted to have attempted any such wickedness upon any child after this present day, he shall be put to death. And he is to pay 40 pounds to Mr. Humfry for abusing his daughter.*[86]

On October 17, 1643, the Court allowed Davis, upon his wife's petition, liberty to leave off his rope till they required him to resume it.

John Hudson, "another vicious person" employed by Mr. Humfry, received a severe punishment from the same court, for a similar offense. Governor John Winthrop recorded this case in his journal: "Hudson did abuse Dorcas many times, so as she was grown capable of the man's fellowship, and took pleasure in it."

According to Lynn historians, "the extreme youth of these misses, rendered the crime the more aggravated, certainly in a moral sense. Yet the court seems *not* to have deemed Dorcas entirely blameless . . ." The child was ordered to be privately corrected by several magistrates of the court.[87]

The punishment meted out for the same crime was most severe on Daniel Fairfield, since he confessed to instigating this child abuse. Formerly an indentured servant, Fairfield was a married man with children, as well as a church member, and was considered a "man in good esteem for piety and sobriety." Winthrop reported that "both girls visited the house of Daniel Fairfield and were by him abused very often, especially upon the Lord's days and lecture days, by agitation and effusion of seed, and after by entering the body of the elder, as it seemed; for upon search she was found to have been forced . . ." Governor Winthrop argued for the death penalty, "for it is against nature as well as sodomy."

On June 14, 1642, Fairfield was ordered "whipped and to have his nostrils slit and seared, then to be confined to Boston Neck, so as if he be found at any time during his life to go out of Boston Neck . . . or beyond the low water mark, he shall be put to death . . . and he is also to wear a hempen rope about his neck, the end of it hanging out two foote at least and so often as he shall be found abroad without it, he shall be whipped; and he is to pay Mr. Humfry 40 pounds."

A year or so later, Fairfield was permitted to seek work within Boston limits and the islands, as long as he did not go farther than five miles from the Boston meetinghouse. On petition from his wife, Elizabeth Fairfield, on May 27, 1652, permission was granted him "to lay the rope aside," and finally, on October 14, 1656, Daniel Fairfield was "given liberty to go in one of the Colony's ships to England, as he desires."

After 1692, "carnal knowledge of any woman child under the age of 10 years" became a capital crime demanding the death penalty.

Although "to Ravish & Carnally Know," or rape, was on the books as a capital crime punishable by death, Massachusetts seems to have left punishment for rape up to the discretion of judge and jury. The most common penalty in the Bay Colony for rape was a severe whipping and a humiliating hour or so beside the gallows, with one end of the noose around the offender's neck and the other over the scaffold, the length of time "according to the Court's Pleasure."

However, in 1681, William Cheney, according to *Suffolk County Court Records*, a rapist from Dorchester, Massachusetts, was hanged "for Carnall Copulation with a maid by force against her will, she crying out." The court approved a reprieve for Cheney, then withheld it because the obstinate malefactor flatly refused to hear Cotton Mather preach an execution sermon. Thus, Cheney went to the gallows.

The first Connecticut law code in 1642 made rape punishable by death if the woman was married. The rape of a maid or single woman above the age of ten was punishable by death, or "at the discretion of the Court, by some other grievous punishment," a law renewed in 1648,

1660, and 1672. Connecticut and New Haven males convicted of rape after 1656 could expect to get the capital letter "R" branded on their cheeks.

The *Connecticut Acts & Resolves*, 1:296, stated that "Carnall copulation with a female child is a more heinous Sin than with one of more years . . . more inhumane and unnatural in itself and more perilous to the life and well-being of the child." New Hampshire law made rape a capital offense in 1679.

Incest carried the death penalty in the Connecticut and New Haven colonies, although Thomas Rood is the only person known to have been executed for it. He committed incest with his twenty-three-year-old daughter, Sarah. The Connecticut Court sought advice from clerics before announcing their verdict. The ministers all voted "Yea" to Rood's execution. After 1702, anyone guilty of the crime of incest was forced to suffer a severe whipping, stand upon the gallows for an hour or so, and wear the capital letter "I" whenever they ventured out in public.[88]

MOST TRAGIC OF FEMALE FELONIES—INFANTICIDE

Because premature deliveries and stillbirths were so common during the colonial period, infanticide was difficult to prove. For Puritans, any infant killed prior to baptism meant more than the tragedy of a dead child. It was truly a lost soul, since they believed there was no place in heaven for the unbaptized.

"Butcher of her own Bowels," was how the Reverend Cotton Mather put it to Elizabeth Emerson and "Grace, a Negro," so harshly in *Warnings from the Dead*, the sermon he preached just before the two were hanged for infanticide. Grandparents could also be held responsible, for in 1686, John and Ester Andrew of Lakenham went to the gallows for concealing their daughter Susanna's murder and secret burial of twins.[89]

The only woman believed to have ever been executed in Plymouth Colony was Alice Bishop in 1648, "for felonious murther by her, committed upon Martha Clark, her own child, the fruit of her own body."[90]

"Calling in the women," or summoning midwives at the hour of pending delivery, was imperative, for should a baby be stillborn, the midwife who attended the birth could testify in court that the mother had not committed infanticide, but that the death of the newborn was "by God's Hand," and thus, no case of murder.

In 1673, a woman living on the Isles of Shoals was accused "of being with child prior to marriage and neglecting to send for help at the time of Travell" and of later denying that she had given birth when midwives were sent to examine her. This new mother was whipped on two separate occasions while wearing a halter about her neck, and the suspected father also received a flogging, paid a fine, and was ordered to post a bond for good behavior.[91]

Dorothy Talbye and Her Daughter, Difficult

In the autumn of 1638, Dorothy Talbye, a farmer's wife, became the first woman executed in Massachusetts Bay Colony. According to Governor John Winthrop, Goodwife Talbye "was so possessed with Satan that he persuaded her by his delusions which she listened to as revelation from God, to break the neck of her own child." Dorothy Talbye threw her three-year-old daughter, Difficult, into a deep gully. She later told the authorities that had she been stronger, she would have killed her husband instead.

The Talbyes were members of the Salem church who attended meeting regularly and were "in good esteem for godliness." Yet neighbors reported hearing Goodwife Talbye "railing" against her husband. She refused to sew and cook for John and their four children and no longer kept the house clean, saying she was following God's orders. Dorothy Talbye claimed having experienced a divine revelation telling her she "was John Talbye's equal and that she should kill him and starve herself and their children. [B]y what right is my husband the master of my life?" she asked herself. After much patience and diverse admonitions for her melancholy and spiritual delusions, she was excommunicated by the church elders. When she failed to appear before the Court of Common Pleas, after having been indicted "for frequent laying hands on her husband to the danger of his life and for neglect of her duties as a wife and mother and for railing against the Court," she was publicly whipped. After this, according to John Winthrop, writing in his journal, "She reformed for a time and carried herself more dutifully to her husband."

At her arraignment, Goodwife Talbye stood mute until the magistrate warned that unless she put in some plea, either "guilty" or "not guilty," she would have to endure the dreaded *peine forte et dure* (or strong and hard) punishment. According to English law, every defendant accused of a felony was required to enter a plea. Anyone who refused after the third request was subject to *peine forte et dure,* by which the accused was made to lie prone upon the ground beneath a plank as heavy stones were placed upon it, their weight becoming heavier one by one, until the accused either entered a plea or expired.

Dorothy Talbye eventually confessed to infanticide but refused to repent. According to Goody Talbye, "only through death could her child escape the torment she herself had endured and be free from future misery and a life of poverty." Once condemned to die, she requested to be beheaded, considering it a more honorable and less painful death than the gallows, but this was denied. At her execution on December 6, 1639, in Boston, Dorothy Talbye denounced her executioner, refused to climb the ladder to the gallows, and pulled the cloth off her face to wrap it between her neck and the noose to ease the pain. The laws of this time made no distinction between an act of murder and insanity. Besides infanticide, Dorothy Talbye's crime was that she had rebelled against the traditional status of wives assigned by church and state.

Elizabeth Emerson's Tragic Tale

Michael Emerson had a large family and apparently found it difficult to manage his wayward daughters. Tim Swan was the handsome fellow next door whom Elizabeth Emerson identified as the father of her first illegitimate child.

Timothy's father, Robert Swan, sold some of his Haverhill lands to Michael Emerson in 1663, but the Swans were anything but neighborly. A cordwainer or worker in quality leather, Michael Emerson served the town of Haverhill at various times as town constable, tax collector, fence viewer, and grand juryman. When his twenty-four-year-old daughter, Elizabeth, gave birth to a baby girl on April 10, 1686, she dutifully informed her midwives that Timothy Swan was the newborn's father. However, Robert Swan refused to allow his son to be charged with fornication, and told the court he had "forbidden Timothy to go into that wicked house," and that his son had obeyed. Furthermore, Tim's father exclaimed, his son "could not abide the jade!" The senior Swan threatened to take the case to court in Boston if Timothy was formally accused of fathering Elizabeth Emerson's child, now named Dorothy.[92]

Three years before, the Essex County Court had sentenced Elizabeth's younger sister, Mary, to forfeit a fine or be *"severely whipped"* for fornication. Hugh Matthews of Newbury owned up to fatherhood and wed Mary Emerson.[93]

Goodman Swan, however, quickly dispatched his son, Timothy, to Andover to assist his brothers in operating the ferry across Merrimack River to avoid his responsibility.

Dorothy was being raised by her unwed mother in her grandparents' Haverhill home and was five when her mother, Elizabeth Emerson, was carted off to Boston and confined in prison nearly two years, then put on trial and executed for infanticide.

It was Sunday morning, May 11, 1691, when Haverhill's chief magistrate, Nathaniel Saltonstall, knocked upon the door of Michael Emerson's house. He was accompanied by several local midwives, one of whom was Hannah Swan, Timothy's mother. The other was Mary Neff (later taken captive by Indians with Elizabeth's elder sister, Hannah Dustin). Both midwives would later testify at Elizabeth Emerson's murder trial.

Goodman Emerson and his wife were at church while Elizabeth, feeling unwell, had remained at home. She was washing dishes when the suspicious visitors arrived. A neighbor, most likely Goodwife Swan, had reported her suspicion of Elizabeth's pregnancy to local authorities. The midwives led Elizabeth into an adjoining room to examine her and informed Magistrate Saltonstall that the young woman had recently given birth. A shallow grave in the backyard soon revealed two dead babies, yet with no marks of violence upon either tiny body. The umbilical cord of one infant was twisted around her neck. The midwives thought the other likely "never drew breath" and that "both died at time of travile for want or care."[94]

When asked where her babies had been born, Elizabeth Emerson replied, "On the bed at my Father's bed-foot."

"And did you call out for help?"

"No. There was nobody to call but my father and mother and I was afraid to call my mother for fear of killing her."

"Did you acquaint your father or mother afterward?"

"No, not a word. I was afraid."

"Did they not know before of your being with child?"

"Not as I know of. They were not told by me."

Later, when Michael and Hannah Emerson were questioned, Elizabeth's mother said, "This daughter was big," so she guessed she might be pregnant, but when asked, Elizabeth had denied it. They claimed they knew nothing of Elizabeth's secret backyard burial of the newborn twins.

This time, Elizabeth did not name Timothy Swan as the father, but identified forty-two-year-old Samuel Ladd, who had already sired eight offspring by his lawful wife. The son of one of Haverhill's original founders, Ladd was a respected citizen and reasonably wealthy. Thus, the adulterer was never brought to justice, nor even questioned. (Samuel Ladd was later killed by Indians in the February 22, 1697/98, raid upon Haverhill.)

Elizabeth must have feared her father's rage, for when Elizabeth was eleven years of age, Michael Emerson had been summoned before the Quarterly Court of Essex County to answer charges of child abuse brought against him: "for the cruel and excessive beating of his daughter with a flail swingle and for kicking her, was fined and bound to good behaviour."[95]

A wooden flail *swingle* is a farm implement used to thrash seeds from dried flax plants. Although corporal punishment was pretty much the norm in most New England families at this time, being disciplined and fined by any county court for physical abuse of one's own child was highly unusual. Goodman Emerson was "freed from bonds for good behavior," and records do not reveal which one of his daughters suffered this harsh treatment or what misbehavior might have brought about the punishment. Yet if Elizabeth was "haughty and stubborn," as she later admitted, having experienced such physical abuse within her own family may have led to her later reputation as a "jade."

On September 22 and September 25, 1691, the magistrates continued to question Elizabeth Emerson as she stood on trial for her life in Boston.

"Did you take the infants and hide them and sew them up in a cloth or bag?"

"Yes, I did."

"Did anyone help you do this?"

No one had helped her. She then went on to describe how she had first put the bodies in a drawer and later, when her father went away and her mother was "out milking," buried them in the yard.

Elizabeth Emerson was convicted and sentenced to hang

> for not having the fear of God before her eyes . . . but being led by the Instigation of the Devil after Malice of Forethought, the said two infants did Feloniously kill and Murther, and then in a small Bagg or clothe sewed them up, and conceal and hide in a Chest in the said Emerson House till afterwards, that is to say on Sabbathday, May the Tenth, 1691, she laid two Infants in the yard of the said Emerson's in Haverhill . . . and did secretly bury contrary to the peace of our Sovereign Lord and Lady the King and Queen their Crowne and dignity, the Laws of God and the Laws and Statutes.[96]

On June 11, 1693, Boston minister Cotton Mather preached his execution sermon entitled *Warnings From the Dead: An Holy Rebuke to the Unclean Spirit,* preached "on a Day when Two Persons were Executed for Murdering of their Bastard Children . . . and heard by one of the greatest Assemblies, ever known in these parts of the World . . . in the Boston Second Church on the morning that Elizabeth Emerson and a black indentured servant, named Grace, were hanged."

Though Elizabeth repeatedly insisted, "I did never murther those babes," Mather read a confession that he claimed she had written herself, although he complained in his diary of having "spent many and many a weary Hour . . . in Prison to save the Souls of those miserable Creatures."

Here is an excerpt from the alleged confession contained within that sermon by the famous Boston minister:

I am a miserable Sinner; and I have Justly Provoked the Holy God to leave me unto that Folly of my own Heart, for which I am now condemned to die . . . I believe, the chief thing that hath brought me into my present Condition, is my Disobedience to my Parents; I despised all their Godly Councils and Reproofs; and I was always of a Haughty and Stubborn Spirit. So that now I am become a dreadful Instance of the Curse of God belonging to Disobedient Children.

Cotton Mather considered it one of his finest sermons and quickly ushered it into print so it might be made available for everyone's edification.

Even as she climbed the ladder and the noose was placed around her neck, Elizabeth Emerson continued to deny responsibility for the death of her babies, repeating, "I never committed murther that I know of."

Worse than bearing an illegitimate child, to Puritans, was to keep any such birth secret. Each child represented a new soul that belonged to God, and thus might be counted among the predestined Elect. This is why a pregnant woman condemned to be executed for any capital offense inevitably received a reprieve until after the birth.

The unfortunate Elizabeth Emerson was caught by new legislation, for in 1692, the Massachusetts General Court sought approval of the King's Privy Council to make "concealing the death of a bastard child a capital crime."

Whereas many lewd Women that have been Delivered of Bastard Children, to avoid their Shame, and to escape Punishment, do secretly Bury or Conceal the Death of their Children: and after, if the Child be found Dead, the said Women do allege that the said Child was born dead; where it falleth out sometimes (although hardly it is to be proved) that the Child or Children were Murdered by the said Women their Lewd Mothers . . . Be it therefore Enacted . . . that if any Woman be Delivered of any Issue of her Body, Male or Female, which if it were born Alive, should by Law be a Bastard; and that they endeavor

privately, either by Drowning or secret Burying thereof . . . so to con-
ceal the Death thereof, that it may not come to light, whether it were
Born Alive or not, but be concealed: In every such case, the Mother so
offending, shall suffer Death, as in Murder, Except such Mother can
make proof by One Witness at the least, that the Child whose Death
was by her so intended to be concealed, was born Dead.[97]

Justice was usually swift in seventeenth-century Massachusetts Bay, but not so for Elizabeth Emerson. Her lengthy incarceration occurred because dockets at that time were jammed with prisoners accused of witchcraft, all waiting for the new Royal Charter to take effect and for the Supreme Count of Judicature to be established. Other than Reverend Cotton Mather's relentless visits to bring about her redemption, there is no record of anyone else coming to see her in prison. It is doubtful that Elizabeth Emerson ever saw her little girl again. Dorothy's mother seems to have been deserted by every member of her large family. Indeed, when Charles Henry Pope published his genealogy, *The Haverhill Emersons,* in 1913, beside Elizabeth's name, he wrote: "Let the mantle of charity cover her history."

Judge Sewall recorded the sad day in his diary: "Elizabeth Emerson of Haverhill and a Negro woman were executed after Lecture, for murdering their Infant children. Mr. Cotton Mather preached from Job 36:14, 'They die in youth and their life is among the unclean,' and made a very good sermon to a very great Auditory."

A violent footnote to Elizabeth's Emerson's fornication, "birthing bastards," and execution for infanticide, is her older sister's revenge against Native Americans six years later. When the Abenaki attacked Haverhill in 1697, Hannah Emerson Dustin was in bed, being tended by her nurse, Mary Neff, since she had given birth to her twelfth child less than a week before. Both women were taken captive to be marched to Canada and sold to the French. When the cries of Hannah's infant persisted, one Indian grabbed her from her mother's arms and smashed the tiny body against a tree. Later, camped on an island in the Merrimack River, near Concord, New Hampshire, Hannah, with the assistance of Mary Neff and a teenage male hostage, killed ten sleeping Indians and escaped by canoe. A few miles downstream, Goodwife Dustin suddenly remembered that the Massachusetts Bay authorities paid bounties for Native American scalps. The three immediately turned the canoe around and returned to the island to relieve the dead Indians of their scalps. For her deed, Hannah Dustin was not only awarded the bounties, but she was also heralded as a heroine for generations to come. The first statue erected to any female in New England was to commemorate Hannah Dustin's deed.

Part VI

The Second Colonial Crime Wave: Witches

Witchcraft is forbidden to be used in this colony and the penalty imposed by the authority we are subject to, is death.
—Rhode Island Colonial Laws, 1647

If any Man or Woman be a Witch, that is, Hath or Consulteth with a familiar Spirit, they shall be put to death.
—Exodus 22:18

Witchcraft represented a clear and present danger to seventeenth-century New Englanders. Belief in the malefic power of witches, who regularly perform evil deeds in the service of Satan, was part of the cultural heritage and traditional folklore brought from the Old World to the New, following centuries of witch persecutions in Europe. Prior to the Enlightenment and Age of Reason, with its new scientific discoveries, most people lived in a "World of Wonders." Tough times and tragic losses lacking logical explanations were often believed to be caused by witches who possessed the ability to injure humans and property through supernatural means.[98]

The loss of ships at sea in a sudden storm might be the cruel prank of a witch. The failure of seasonal crops, an unexplained accident, a healthy child suddenly dead, a cow no longer producing milk, a prize pig that drops dead, cream that will not churn to butter, sexual fantasies and nightmares—all these things could be blamed on a witch's malice. Perhaps one's present misfortune is the fault of that vindictive scold who shouted a curse at you last week.

The ancient conviction that women were more prone to witchcraft than men, so familiar in our own folklore and fairy tales, is rooted in the *Book of Genesis*, with Eve tempting Adam to defy God in the Garden of Eden, thus bringing about Original Sin. Misogyny was reinforced by books like *Malleus Maleficarum*, or *The Hammer of Witches*, written by two Dominican priests, Jakob Sprenger and Heinrich Kramer. Sanctioned by a Papal Bull in 1486, this text officially made witchcraft heresy and went through twenty-eight editions before 1600. It was the standard guidebook in Europe regarding the persecution and prosecution of anyone suspected of witchcraft. It describes in devastating detail the processes of identifying, apprehending, torturing, convicting, and executing witches.

Between 1630 and 1692, some 103 witchcraft cases were on New England court dockets, with some 40 accused of this capital crime prior to the Salem Trials of 1692. Twelve people were executed prior to 1692, although New England was gentler in its treatment of convicted witches. Here, they were hanged instead of being burned at the stake.

The *Records of the Quarterly Courts of Essex County* reveal that in 1652 John Bradstreet of Rowley confessed to familiarity with Satan. He was the youngest of the eight offspring of Anne Bradstreet, the country's first poet published in the English language, and her husband, Simon, a Massachusetts Bay founder and eventual governor. Young Goodman Bradstreet admitted having read a book of magic and told the court about hearing a voice and asking what work he had for him to do. "Go make a bridge of sand over the sea," the voice said. "Go make a ladder of sand up to heaven and go to God and come down no more." Although Bradstreet was acquitted of witchcraft, he was whipped and fined, "it being his second lie."[99] In 1692, a pet belonging to John Bradstreet became one of several dogs hanged for allegedly having served as "witches' familiars." The first person executed for witchcraft in Massachusetts Bay Colony was Margaret Jones of Charlestown in 1648, "for having a malignant touch." She was one of the few medical practitioners and midwives put to death for witchcraft in New England. Goody Jones, however, enjoyed little success at her chosen vocation since, according to Governor John Winthrop's detailed journal account: "Many persons she stroked or touched with any affection or displeasure were taken with deafness or vomiting or other violent pains or sickness; she practicing physic and her medicines being such things as (by her own confession) were harmless, as aniseed, liquors, etc., yet had extraordinary violent effects." Jones warned anyone who refused her medical advice and potions that their physical ailments would never be healed. "So their diseases and hurts continued, with relapse against the ordinary course and beyond the apprehension of all physicians and surgeons." Other evidence against her was the fact that "some things she foretold came to pass and [she] could tell of secret speeches which she had no ordinary means to come to the knowledge of."

Margaret Jones "had an apparent teat in her secret parts as fresh as if it had been newly sucked [by the witch's familiar] and after it had been scanned, upon a forced search, that was withered, and another began on the opposite side."

Nearly every woman and man accused of witchcraft was forced to undergo this humiliating and thorough body search. One surviving document from the Salem Trials of 1692 describes the results of such examinations endured by George Jacobs and the Reverend George Burroughs. Midwives had significant political roles here, too, because they were generally the persons summoned to strip and search the accused for "witch's teats." These were moles, warts, or any such protuberance any place upon their bodies where their imps suckled. Should any suspicious mark be discovered, a pin was then pushed through it. If this growth proved insensitive to pain, it was believed to be the spot favored by this witch's *familiar*, to gain nourishment.

Governor Winthrop noted in his journal that when Margaret Jones was "in prison, there was seen in her arms, in clear daylight, she sitting on the floor, and her clothes up, a little child which ran from her into another room, and the officer following it, it was vanished. The like child was seen in two other places . . . and one maid that saw it, fell sick upon it and was cured by said Margaret . . ."

According to Winthrop, this woman's "behavior at her trial was very intemperate, lying notoriously and railing upon jury and witnesses ... and in the like distemper she died." The governor also noted in his journal that at the very hour Margaret Jones was executed on June 15, 1648, "there was a very great tempest at Connecticut, which blew down many trees."

Ironically, Richard Bellingham and William Hibbens were both members of the General Court that convicted Margaret Jones at her trial. These two men were, respectively, brother and husband to Ann Hibbens, who would go to the gallows for the same crime in 1656.

Ann Hibbens—Hanged "for having more wit than her neighbors"[100]

Ann Hibbens sailed to Boston with her third husband, William Hibbens, and her brother Richard Bellingham and his wife. Both men quickly prospered in Massachusetts Bay Colony—Mr. Hibbens as a merchant, magistrate, and government assistant, and Bellingham as an administrator and, later, governor. Mistress Hibbens proudly showed off her husband's success by dressing in satin and wearing taffeta cloaks.

When the couple desired renovations on their house, it was Ann who took charge and hired carpenters. And when Mistress Hibbens was dissatisfied with the work the joiners did, she accused them of overcharging. They demanded £13 for the job they'd agreed to finish for £2. When ten men were summoned to settle the matter, Mistress Hibbens called it a conspiracy. She made more enemies by inviting other Salem joiners and neighbors to evaluate their work. These folks agreed the finished job was not worth half the amount the men were asking.

The situation grew so argumentative that the church elders were forced to arbitrate after John Davis, another joiner and church member, brought the controversy to their attention on September 13, 1640. Ann Hibbens had also requested her bed "be designed and carved like the chimney piece," but she also found fault with that job, dubbing the carpentry "toys and gewgaws." Goodman Davis accused her of "lying and bad behavior," and threatened to provide witnesses to testify against her. Several hearings were held in Boston's First Church, where Mistress Hibbens accused

Goodman Crabtree of deceitfulness and "slight doing of" his carpentry as well as breach of contract and "neglecting his work after he began it." She claimed Crabtree originally bargained for 40 shillings and ended up taking £13. The congregation warned Ann Hibbens "to mend her obstinate ways or face more serious charges." Five months later she had still not apologized to John Davis nor admitted being wrong. When charged with lying, her reply was, "My husband did give me leave."

"Execution of Mrs. Hibbens at Boston," by Frank Thayer Merrill, from *A Book of New England Legends and Folklore in Prose and Poetry,* by Samuel Adams Drake, 1884.
COURTESY OF PAUL ROYSTER, COORDINATOR OF SCHOLARLY COMMUNICATION, UNIVERSITY OF NEBRASKA, LINCOLN LIBRARIES

The church fathers decided that Ann Hibbens had been "proud and contemptuous to the carpentry crew, using speech unbecoming her gender." Since "nothing that comes from her tends to satisfaction, and all Mistress Hibbens's speeches tend to excuse herself and to lay all blame upon others . . . she refusing to lay down her pride and veil her pomp," "this bold and outspoken woman, in spite of her husband's plea for "patience and leniency for my dear wife," was excommunicated from church membership for "many and gross sins and offenses, proved against you by many witnesses and for your contempt and pride of spirit and for exalting yourself against your guide and head—your husband, I mean—when you should have submitted yourself, and because you have rejected the advice of Brethren and Sisters and the Council of your Elders, when they persuaded, advised, and earnestly exhorted you to be quiet and sit down satisfied . . . ." Ann Hibbens was dubbed "a leprous person to be cast out from amongst us . . . [for fear] of infecting others . . . "

This impertinent woman simply refused to do and act as the male authorities ordered, and "because the Lord hath not yet broken her spirit," she was evicted from the congregation.

Due to William Hibbens's high position, they did not dare go after this uppity woman while her husband was alive. Prior to his death in July of 1654, Mister Hibbens had served as a government official, court representative, even an agent for Massachusetts Bay Colony in England. Two years after his death, Ann, no longer wealthy woman, due to her husband's unwise investments, was arrested on charges of witchcraft. Since two witnesses were required by law to convict, the jury's first verdict was rejected and the case turned over to Massachusetts General Court in May of 1656, where Mistress Hibbens continued to enter a plea of "not guilty."

Part of the testimony for her witchcraft conviction was that when seeing several neighbors talking some distance away, she had accused them of gossiping about her and was able to reconstruct details of their conversation. This was proof that Ann Hibbens had preternatural knowledge, a skill that only witches possessed.

Sometime before her execution on June 19, 1656, Ann Hibbens, "being in health of Body and perfect memory," left a will naming three adult sons by her first husband who had remained in England. John Moore, the eldest, received a double portion of her whole estate, in part, two chests and one desk, with all things therein. Astute businesswoman that she was, Mrs. Hibbens named five overseers with power to sell her land and houses, "for the best advantage," and to administer her property "until my eldest son shall come over and be whole executor . . ."

At the time of her execution, Mrs. Hibbens's former minister agreed with the church elders that she was a "quarrelsome and obnoxious scold," but added that she was "hanged for having more wit than her neighbors." Ann Hibbens's worst offense and what got her cast out of church and put the noose around her neck was her refusal to play the role of dutiful and submissive wife. The church elders denounced her "pride of spirit" and complained that she did not "hearken to her husband," and even "made a wisp" of him.

Some two hundred years later, Ann Hibbens would become a rather unsavory character in Nathaniel Hawthorne's novel, *The Scarlet Letter.*

THE CONNECTICUT WITCH HUNTS

New England's first witch trial and execution took place in Connecticut when Alse Young of Windsor was hanged at Hartford May 26, 1647. Connecticut also hosted the last witch trial in New England, in 1768, when a Bristol teenager accused her aunt Norton of putting a bridle on her and riding her through the air to attend a gathering of witches two hundred miles away. Between 1647 and 1768, thirty-seven persons were indicted in Connecticut, of whom ten were executed and several banished. In the 1660s, this colony also endured the first witchcraft panic, or chain of accusations, with fourteen indictments against eleven different men and women. At that time, four persons were executed while five escaped.[101]

Mary Johnson, a Wethersfield servant girl, was a witch by her own confession. In 1648, she said it was her discontent with too many duties that made her call the Devil for help. She had a habit of muttering "The Devil take this" and "The Devil do that," when one day Satan showed up, offering to assist with her chores. Maid Mary's master blamed her "for not carrying out the ashes, so afterwards, the Devil came to clear the hearth" for her. Then her master ordered her to "drive out some hogs that broke into the field and the Devil fetched those hogs" and amused Mary by making them run around. This young woman already had a record, having been flogged for theft two years before. Now, before the bar on charges of witchcraft, she confessed to murdering a child, and admitted "committing uncleanness with both men and devils." Mary Johnson, in fact, gave birth to a child in prison. Her minister, the Reverend Samuel Stone, "was at great pains to promote her conversion from the devil to God," but when she was hanged, he "judged her very penitent, dying in a frame extremely to the satisfaction of them that were spectators of it."[102]

Connecticut had several witch couples. John Carrington, a Wethersfield carpenter, and his wife, Mary, came to New England in 1635. He got in trouble with the law for selling guns to Indians and was fined £10. Neighbors were suspicious of his incredible strength that enabled him to "[perform] works above the course of nature." He and Mary were executed together March 19, 1653, "for having entertained familiarity with Satan, the great enemy of God and mankind and by Satan's help, having done works above the course of human Powers."[103]

Nathaniel and Rebecca Greensmith were both indicted for committing witchcraft at Hartford in 1662. Nathaniel was a successful farmer but had previous convictions for theft, assault, and lying. They were not a popular pair. Greensmith was Rebecca's third husband, and she was even described by her minister as "a lewd, ignorant and considerably aged woman." Rebecca claimed the Devil appeared to her in the form of a stag and spoke with her frequently, and "to her horror and delight had use of her body."

Goody Greensmith confessed attending "a meeting of witches under a tree in the green and there we danced and had a bottle of sack." She willingly provided the magistrates with the names of others at the party, and added "the Devil promised us another merry meeting at Christmas," surely aware that the mere mention of celebrating Christmas horrified Puritans.

At her trial, Rebecca Greensmith implicated numerous Hartford-area residents against whom she'd long held grudges. She even joined in the prosecution of her own husband, testifying that "he met with strange red creatures and black dog-like creatures in the woods," which he said were "only foxes . . . I have seen logs that my husband brought home in his cart and wondered that he could get them into it, being a man of little body and ye logs such that I thought two men could not have done so."

Like John Carrington, Nathaniel Greensmith received the death sentence for possessing supernatural strength, and "for not having the fear of God before his eyes . . . and by Satan's help has acted things in a preternatural way beyond human abilities . . ." The couple went to the gallows together on January 25, 1663, and "at the precise moment they were turned off, a pure white stag ran out of the woods, dashed beneath the gallows, then disappeared back into the woods."[104]

Goody Knapp of Fairfield faced the court in 1653, "a victim of gossip and a jealous wife," according to Connecticut historian, George Clark. She deposed that Goodwife Mary Staples once told her of "an Indian appearing from the woods and offering two gods that shone brighter than day, but that she was fearful and refused."

A group of townspeople visited Goody Knapp's cell and urged her to "[d]o as the witch at that other place did and name all you know to be witches, so they are discovered." The convicted witch told them she must not say anything that was not true. Furthermore, she did not know any witches and "must not wrong anybody . . . I will not add to my condemnation by accusing other innocents . . ." But she promised that she would reveal names "just before going out of this world."

One friend who visited Goody Knapp in prison on the day she was to die, later reported that she "burst forth into tears, saying she 'knew not how she was tempted by the Devil . . . Never, never a poor creature was tempted as I am tempted; pray, pray for me.'"[105]

At the gallows and upon the ladder, Goody Knapp did give authorities several names, including one witch in town who "would be hanged within a twelve month."

Katharan Harrison Told Fortunes[106]

Katharan Harrison emigrated from England in 1651, and soon found a position as one of the servants in the Hartford household of wealthy merchant John Cullick. Katharan liked "to tell of Things to Come" and to read from the forbidden book on astrology she'd brought with her from

England. She enjoyed predicting the futures of the other servants, but when she got caught telling the fortune of Captain Cullick's daughter, he fired her for "evil conversation in word and deed."

There was illness and unexplained death in all three households where Goody Harrison worked. Townspeople were gossiping that this servant must be a witch because she could perform amazing tasks. For example, she "often spun such a quantity of fine linen yarn as was never seen, nor could any natural woman spin so much, so well."

Her husband, John Harrison, was a successful Wethersfield merchant, and though neighbors were impressed by her skills at spinning and tending the sick, Goody Harrison also had a reputation for being a "notorious Liar" and a shameless Sabbath-breaker. Her husband's death in 1666 left her a wealthy woman, and she proceeded to sue various neighbors in more than a dozen court cases. For most of these litigations, she did later apologize for "slandering with hasty, unadvised, and passionate expressions."

This Widow of Wethersfield was indicted for witchcraft in the spring of 1669. It was said she caused children to suffer fits and animals to sicken and die, and was even known to send bees to sting folks. Thomas Bracey recalled the misfortunes that befell him after he dared to quarrel with Goody Harrison. Her spirit had come to his bedside, where she attempted "to strangle him, pinching him as if flesh were pulled from bones." Joan Francis testified that four years ago, on the night her child was taken ill, Katharan Harrison, or her shape, appeared. "The Lord bless me and my child, why here is Goody Harrison!" she'd said, and then "laid the child between me and my husband, and the child continued strangely ill three weeks and then, did die."

Mary Hale told the court that "while lying in bed she saw an ugly dog with the head of Katharan Harrison in place of its own, and it walked over her and crushed her; then came a sharp blow on the fingers." On another night, this same witness heard the voice of a woman who said she had a commission to kill her, and she knew it to be the voice of Katharan Harrison."

Goodwife Gilbert had a black cap which she let Katharan Harrison borrow. Goody Harrison wanted to keep it but Gilbert refused to sell it to her. Later, "whenever I put it on, my head and shoulders became much afflicted."

Katharan Harrison pleaded *"not guilty,"* but ended up having three different trials, two of which ended in hung juries and the third, on May 20, 1670, resulting in conviction and the death sentence. She spent a year in prison, during which time she submitted a petition to the court explaining how she had been "made to suffer in person and estate." The magistrates eventually reversed their verdict and acquitted her, on the condition that following payment of fees due for her trials and imprisonment, she depart the colony "for thine own safety and for the contentment of neighbors."[107]

Swimming a Witch—The Cases of Elizabeth Clawson and Mercy Disborough[108]

Elizabeth Clawson and Mercy Disborough were two victims of "taunts and threats," who refused to confess to witchcraft in 1692. Goody Clawson of Stamford "was examined by the honorable Court but doth absolutely and peremptorily deny herself to be any such person."

John Finch accused both women at their trial of killing his daughter. "My child in an evening was taken very violently with screaming and crying insomuch that with all haste I opened her clothing and examined her body, but could find nothing that might expose it to that pain and misery." Daniel Westcott of Fairfield had "several discourses with the accused witch Clawson, "concerning her being angry with me." He told her "she never laid down to sleep in anger and how could that be when she continued angry with me?" Another witness defended Elizabeth Clawson, claiming they had been "near neighbors many years," and she "knew Goody Clawson to be a woman for peace ... [who] when she had provocations from neighbors, would say, 'We must live in peace, for we are neighbors.'"

When a woman named Katherine Branch came face-to-face with Mercy Disborough's "two fiery eyes" in court, she immediately "fell down in a fit." In spite of being forced to endure the humiliating body search for witch's teats, Mercy Disborough requested that she be given the water test to prove her innocence. Bound hand and foot, she and Goody Clawson both "swam like corks, even though some in the crowd tried to push one of them under."

Henry Gray, another witness against Mercy Disborough, had "a cow strangely taken." He "sent for his cart-whip and beat the cow . . . [T]hat same afternoon, Mercy Disborough appeared with a painful and mysterious injury. She lay on the bed and stretched out her arms, telling Goodman Gray, 'I am almost killed!'"

Elizabeth Clawson was exonerated, while Mercy Disborough was convicted. Disborough managed to cheat the hangman apparently, because so many neighbors and relatives petitioned for her pardon.

The ordeal known as *swimming a witch*, or dunking, endured by accused witches Clawson and Disborough, was not used again in Connecticut, nor was this legendary water test known to have ever been used on any witchcraft suspects in Massachusetts.

Following a meeting held in Hartford on October 17, 1692, the Reverends Joseph Eliot and Timothy Woodridge published *Ministers' Advice about Witches*, where it was announced that witchcraft convictions by swimming were "unlawful and sinful and cannot afford any evidence." This document further stated that "unusual marks upon bodies ought not be allowed as evidence." These clerics also rejected any "hysteria of specters upon the afflicted . . . As to other strange accidents [such] as dying of cattle, we apprehend the applying of them . . . as matters of witchcraft to be upon very slender and uncertain grounds."[109] This publication became available about the same time that Massachusetts Bay's general populace was rejecting the wisdom and validity of the Salem Trials.

THE SALEM TRIALS

I believe there never was a poor plantation more pursued than our New England . . . First, the Indian powwows . . . Then seducing spirits . . . After this a continual blast upon some of our principal grains . . . Herewithal, wasting sicknesses . . . Next, many adversaries of our own language , . . . Desolating fires also . . . And losses by sea. Besides all which . . . the devils are come down upon us with such a wrath as is the astonishment of the world.
—REVEREND COTTON MATHER, *THE WONDERS OF THE INVISIBLE WORLD*, 1693

The 1692 witch hunt and the infamous Salem Trials that resulted in the executions of twenty persons were caused by different circumstances than previous New England witchcraft cases. By 1692, many ministers and magistrates had become convinced that the Prince of Darkness was leading a conspiracy with the aim of destroying the Cities of God in the wilderness they had settled through their sacred Christian Covenant. Controversies within churches were increasing, and this seemed to indicate a breakdown of their theocracy with its former religious, social, and political stability.

From all indications, Satan seemed hell-bent on ruling New England, recruiting as many witches as he possibly could to help him in the effort. Many Puritan leaders and colonists believed in the Devil's Plot to take over New England, employing "a dreadful knot of witches." This pervading idea is basic to understanding why the Salem Trials took place in 1692, and the reason why so many persons from different towns and counties were arrested, convicted, and executed for the capital crime of witchcraft within a relatively brief eight-month period.

Determined to consolidate England's territories from Maine to New Jersey into the Dominion of New England, King James II revoked Massachusetts Bay's original charter in 1684. For the English settlers, this meant losing the autonomy they had enjoyed since 1629. When Sir Edmund Andros, the king's governor-appointee, arrived in Boston on December 20, 1686, accompanied by sixty soldiers, he was not welcome, and it was not long before he was sent packing. Massachusetts existed in legal limbo until 1693, awaiting a new royal charter. The new charter would eventually be negotiated by the Reverend Increase Mather and other colonial emissaries, with representatives of King William and Queen Mary, who occupied the English throne after James II was overthrown in 1689. Sir William Phips, born and raised on the Maine frontier and knighted for capturing Spanish ships and bringing gold and other treasure to the Crown, was appointed Royal Governor of Massachusetts.

Property became the basis for franchise under the new charter allowing the vote to "all freemen of honest and good deportment." The Elect (or covenanted male church members) were no longer the only group permitted the privilege and responsibility of voting. Franchise was now open to men of any Christian sect, including Anglicans, Baptists, and even Quakers. Any man, in fact, except a Catholic, could vote so long as they owned land. Thus, property rather than sainthood was what now provided political clout. This was a devastating blow to the established Puritan theocracy and a direct threat to clerical power. As the population of Massachusetts Bay Colony grew, land became less available, and this led to constant hassles among neighbors regarding boundaries and rights of ownership.[110]

The original English settlers had done their best to organize themselves into cohesive communities, but by the third generation, this former interdependence had often evolved into intense economic rivalry.[111]

A smallpox epidemic broke out in Boston in February of 1690 and spread rapidly, "raging much at Piscataqua" (Portsmouth, New Hampshire), according to one minister.[112]

It seemed to many that God had turned His back on them. If they were God's chosen people, trying so hard to live by His sacred covenant, why were times so terrible? How was it that so many Englishmen were being killed in Indian wars to the Eastward and English settlements burned to the ground in cruel, sporadic raids? Between 1688 and 1761, France and England were at nearly constant war with each other, as each European nation struggled for the domination of North America, drafting Native Americans as pawns. Terrified, destitute, and homeless refugees and orphans from frontier attacks streamed into Boston and Salem and other towns, and taxes levied upon citizens to support military forces just kept rising.

As the end of the seventeenth century approached, Massachusetts Bay colonists were living in a climate of fear. It was this insecurity that helped foster and feed the extremism that sparked the Salem Witch Hunt, a time when religious fanaticism, intolerance, and the abuse of human rights were permitted to take over the minds and hearts of ordinary people, as well as many of their religious and political leaders. The Puritans wondered how they might appease the Wrath of God whose hand had come down so heavily against them. Perhaps going after those *Devil's Agents* known as witches, might pacify Him.

The troubles started in Salem Village (now Danvers), when Betty Parris, the nine-year-old daughter of the local minister, Samuel Parris, began throwing fits and experiencing terrifying visions. Her eleven-year-old orphaned cousin, Abigail Williams, who resided in the parsonage with the Parris family, quickly demonstrated the same inexplicable behavior. According to eyewitnesses, she barked like a dog, suffered scratches and bites upon her body, and even attempted to throw herself into the blazing hearth. Prayers were said over the afflicted girls, a village fast was held, and Dr. Griggs made a house call, only to shake his head with the helpless diagnosis that in his opinion, the poor children were victims of some "evil hand."

The doctor's own niece, Elizabeth Hubbard, soon joined the growing number of stricken girls, who were badgered to name the persons responsible for their miseries. First targeted was Tituba, the Carib Indian, whom Samuel Parris had brought back from Barbados with her husband, Indian John, when he returned to Massachusetts after failing at business in the West Indies. The girls next pointed fingers at elderly Sarah Osborne and Sarah Good, that despised derelict who went from house to house, begging food and clothing. These three were likely targets, but before long, men, women, and children who lived in nearby towns, including some known to be devout church members and well-respected in their communities, were also being issued arrest warrants.

Surviving sermons and letters indicate the Salem Trials were not supported by all ministers and magistrates, but that there was dissension from the first. The Court of Oyer et Terminer ("to hear and determine") did not aim to execute all the accused. Plaintiffs were required to demonstrate evidence of harm done to them, as well as provide some indication that the person on trial had "trafficked with the devil." Judges and jury were generally convinced they were doing the right thing, and were careful to follow English legal precedents regarding witchcraft cases. Besides *Malleus Maleficarum,* or *The Hammer of Witches,* they also consulted *A Discourse of the Damned Art of Witchcraft* by William Perkins, published in London in 1608, and John Gaule's *Select Cases of Conscience Touching Witches and Witch Crafts* (1646).[113]

Colonial magistrates were also familiar with *Demonology,* the book written by James IV of Scotland and published in Edinburgh in 1597.

King James the First of England was a passionate and dedicated witch finder. He personally blamed malefic witches for stirring up the storm at sea that nearly drowned the Queen and His Majesty.

Some magistrates even consulted the colony's most influential ministers regarding criminal law, and then became overzealous in their determination to save New England from the Devil's clutches. This abuse of power by a few, through their leading on of witnesses and browbeating of defendants, is evident in surviving documents. John Proctor's *Letter from Boston Prison* tells of three teenage boys, including his own son, forced to endure physical torture by being "tied neck to heels until the blood ran from their noses."

Throughout the Trials, ministers continually called for days of fasting and constant prayers to seek God's guidance. On August 1, 1692, a group of leading clergymen, led by the Reverend Increase Mather, gathered in Cambridge to discuss "whether the devil could represent an innocent person in tormenting someone." Although they agreed he could, the elders thought "such things rare and extraordinary, especially when such matters come before Civil Judicatures."[114]

This spectral evidence remained controversial and troubling throughout the Trials. Many clergy, including Cotton Mather and his father, Increase Mather, spoke out against applying this as sole grounds for conviction. There was no possible defense when someone swore they'd seen your specter or shape, inflicting harm on another person. This is why those accused of witchcraft were kept in shackles and chains in prison— to prevent their specters from getting out to harm others.

Whatever was the matter with those afflicted persons? Their fits, screams, and visible torments, particularly when one of the accused was brought into the courtroom or glanced their way, were described by numerous eyewitnesses. Ordered by a judge to touch the afflicted, the alleged witch was supposedly able to draw the evil force back into his or her own body, immediately calming the afflicted.

Their sufferings have long been debated by scholars, novelists, and playwrights. Their fits were definitely not the result of eating rye bread contaminated by ergot, as one science buff theorized. The victims came from different towns, and the bread they ate was baked from rye grown in many different fields. Nor were the afflicted a bunch of bored teenage girls playacting for power, since some were males, while others, women in their thirties. The sufferings of some surely stemmed from religious anxiety. Others were haunted survivors of Indian warfare. Several of the afflicted Salem Village girls were refugees and orphans whose families had been slaughtered in frontier raids. Now reduced to working as servant girls in the homes of relatives or strangers, they suffered from what we now recognize as post-traumatic stress disorder.

It is also obvious from the documents that some of the afflicted were influenced by their peers, and that their alarmingly dramatic hysteria was supported, even encouraged, by some adults within the various communities. It is important to realize that most people living in Massachusetts Bay Colony in 1692 believed the afflicted to be "gifted persons" who were endowed with special spiritual insight. God had given them the power to spot witches and they alone had the ability to see specters. This is why their convulsions in court were viewed by so many contemporaries as mystical. It must have seemed to many spectators that they were witnessing Satan wrestling God for the very souls of these tortured persons, whose bodies had become battlegrounds for good versus evil. In the seventeenth century, "possession" was generally viewed as a mystical religious experience. It was as old as the Bible and a basic tenet of Christianity, as familiar to the faithful as the teenaged Saint Teresa of Avila, one good example from church history.

When the *Nonesuch* sailed into Boston Harbor on May 14, 1692, carrying the Reverend Increase Mather and the new Royal Governor, Sir William Phips, the jails were already jammed with persons arrested on grounds of witchcraft, all awaiting trials. The new Provincial Court could not be established until the following October when the Royal Charter took effect, so on June 2, Governor Phips set up the ad hoc Court of Oyer and Terminer to deal solely with witchcraft cases. William Stoughton, educated for both the church and the law, was appointed chief magistrate. A firm believer that the colony was presently under attack by what Cotton Mather first called an *Army of Devils*, Judge Stoughton was ruthless in his determination to rid New England of every single witch.

Crimes and conflicts from long-ago riffs with neighbors and earlier run-ins with the law now came back to haunt the accused. Village gossips wielded amazing power in a society where community surveillance had long been the norm—and those with prison records or who had been formerly convicted of crimes and misdemeanors were at greatest risk.

Goody Bishop Goes to the Gallows[115]

Bridget Oliver Bishop was the first to go to trial, and the first of the nineteen hanged at Salem in 1692. Although she was not the first to be arrested and imprisoned, hers was likely the easiest case for the judges to try, for Goody Bishop had been before the courts on numerous occasions. Now nearly sixty, this woman had a long-standing reputation as a troublemaker. Like many others arrested during the 1692 Salem Witch Hunt, Goody Bishop had previously been accused of witchcraft. She was still Thomas Oliver's wife in that tumultuous relationship when she'd faced the Court of Assistants in 1678/9. According to popular gossip, Goodman Oliver later died under suspicious circumstances, just as this woman's first husband (named Samuel Wasselbee) had, back in England many years before. Goody Bishop was well aware of her reputation around Salem as a bad neighbor. She once asked young William Stacey if his father would grind her meal at his mill which was located in a nearby town. When he wanted to know why, Bridget had replied, "Because folks around here count me a witch."

Two women testified at Goody Bishop's examination that her own husband had suspected her of witchcraft years ago. She'd even told him that she "was familiar with the devil as he came to her bodily and she sat up all night long chatting with the devil himself." The confessed witch Deliverance Hobbs claimed Goody Bishop had helped to distribute the sacrament at one witches' gathering she attended.

Samuel Gray deposed that Bridget Bishop "stared long" at his sleeping infant daughter and she died two weeks later. When Goodman Gray was himself dying several years later, he admitted that his accusation against Goody Bishop had been caused by the heartbreak he'd suffered over the death of his baby girl. Gray's retraction of his testimony against the accused witch was never noted during her trial, nor did she live to hear it.

The most damning evidence against Bridget Bishop turned out to be those *"poppets"* found inside the walls of her former house by a carpenter and his son. These homemade rag dolls, they testified, were stuck with pins—sure evidence of malefic witchcraft with intent to put a hex on others.

When Judge Hathorn urged Goody Bishop to confess, she remained as defiant as always. "I have done no witchcraft!" she insisted. "I know not what a witch is." Bridget Bishop was carted to the gallows only eight days after her verdict was handed down.

Writing up Bridget Bishop's case in *The Wonders of the Invisible World* (1693), the Reverend Cotton Mather said, "[T]here was so little doubt in the minds of the magistrates as to her guilt that there was little occasion to prove the witchcraft, it being evident and notorious to all beholders."

"Very much dissatisfied with the proceedings," Judge Nathaniel Saltonstall quit the bench. In doing so he made it clear that he did not condone the use of "spectral evidence" as sole grounds for conviction. Returning home to Haverhill, this magistrate soon found himself accused of witchcraft.[116]

On June 10, Chief Magistrate Stoughton asked Boston's leading clergymen to advise the court on the matter of spectral evidence. In *Return of the Ministers Consulted,* they approved its application in court, but strongly advised caution in its use.

The Ordeal of Captain Nathaniel Cary[117]

Captain Nathaniel Cary was a shipmaster and merchant from Charlestown who later became a judge himself. His wife, Elizabeth was arrested on grounds of witchcraft in 1692. Convinced that the magistrates, ministers, and the afflicted were all in the wrong, Captain Cary attempted to get his wife's trial moved from Essex to Middlesex County, which he considered less biased. On July 30, 1692, he managed his wife's escape from Cambridge Prison, likely by bribing the keeper or sheriff with hard cash. This rare personal account by the loving husband of an accused witch expresses in lively detail what it was like to stand before the Court of Oyer et Terminer charged with this capital crime. It was first published in *More Wonders of the Invisible World* by Robert Calef, a cloth merchant, who was vehemently opposed to the Salem Trials.

I having heard some days, that my Wife was accused of Witchcraft, being much disturbed at it, by advice, we went to Salem Village, to see if the afflicted did know her; we arrived there, 24 May, it happened to be the day appointed for Examination; accordingly soon after our arrival, Mr. Hathorn and Mr. Corwin, etc., went to the Meeting-house, which was the place appointed for that Work, the Minister began with Prayer, and were two Girls of about Ten Years old, and about two or three other, of about eighteen, one of the Girls talked most, and could discern more than the rest. The Prisoners were called in one by one, and as they came in were cried out of, etc. The Prisoner was placed about 7 or 8 foot from the Justices, and the Accusers between the Justices and them; the Prisoner was ordered to stand right before the Justices, with an Officer appointed to hold each hand, least they should therewith afflict them, and the Prisoners Eyes must be constantly on the Justices; for if they look'd on the afflicted, they would either fall into their Fits, or cry out of being hurt by them; after Examination of the Prisoners, who it was afflicted these Girls, etc., they were put upon saying the Lord's Prayer, as a tryal of their guilt; after the afflicted seem'd to be out of their Fits, they would look steadfastly on some one person, and frequently not speak; and then the Justices said they were struck dumb, and after a little time would speak again; then the Justices said to the Accusers, "Which of you will go and touch the Prisoner at the Bar?" then the most courageous would adventure, but before they had made three steps would ordinarily fall down as in a Fit; the Justices ordered that they should be taken up and carried to the Prisoner, that she might touch them; and as soon as they were touched by the accused, the Justices would say, "They are well," before I could discern any alteration; by which I observed that the Justices understood the manner of it. Thus far I was only as a Spectator, my Wife also was there part of the time, but no notice taken of her by the afflicted, except once or twice they came to her and asked her name.

But I having an opportunity to Discourse with Mr. Hale, minister at Beverly (with whom I had former acquaintance), I took his advice, what I had best to do, and desired of him that I might have an opportunity to speak with her that accused my Wife; which he promised should be, I acquainting him that I reposed my trust in him. Accordingly he came to me after the Examination was over and told me I had now an opportunity to speak with the said Accuser, Abigail Williams, a Girl of 11 or 12 Years old; but that we could not be in private at Mr. Parris's House, as he had promised me; we went therefore into the Alehouse, where an Indian Man attended us, who it seems was one of the afflicted: to him we gave some Cyder, he shewed several Scars that seemed as if they had been long there, and shewed them as done by Witchcraft, and acquainted us that his Wife, who also was a Slave, was imprison'd for Witchcraft. And now instead of one Accuser, they all came in, who began to tumble down like Swine, and then three Women were called in to attend them.

We in the Room were all at a stand, to see who they would cry out of; but in a short time they cried out, "Cary" and immediately after a Warrant was sent from the Justices to bring my Wife before them, who were sitting in a Chamber nearby, waiting for this. Being brought before the Justices, her chief accusers were two Girls; my Wife declared to the Justices, that she never had any knowledge of them before that day; she was forced to stand with her Arms stretched out. I did request that I might hold one of her hands, but it was denied me; then she desired me to wipe the Tears from her Eyes, and the Sweat from her Face, which I did; then she desired she might lean herself on me, saying, she should faint.

Justice Hathorn replied, she had strength enough to torment those persons, she should have strength enough to stand. I speaking something should be turned out of the Room. The Indian before mentioned, was also brought in, to be one of her Accusers: being come in, he now fell down [before the Justices] and tumbled about like a Hog, but said nothing. The magistrate asked the Girls, "Who afflicted [John] Indian?" They answered she [meaning my Wife] and now lay upon him; the Justices ordered her to touch him, in order to his cure, but her head must be turned another way, least instead of curing, she should make him worse, by her looking on him, her hand being guided to take hold of his; but the Indian took hold on her hand, and pulled her down on the Floor, in a barbarous manner; then his hand was taken off, and her hand put on his, and the cure was quickly wrought.

I being extreamly troubled at their Inhumane dealings, uttered a hasty Speech [That God would take vengeance on them, and desired that God would deliver us out of the hands of unmerciful men]. Then her Mittimus (or a warrant directing the sheriff or constable to bring the accused to prison) was writ. I did with difficulty and charge obtain the liberty of a Room, but no Beds in it; if there had [been], I could have taken but little rest that Night. She was committed to Boston Prison; but I obtained a Habeas Corpus to remove her to Cambridge Prison, which is in our County of Middlesex. Having been there one Night, next Morning the Jailer put Irons on her legs [having received such a command]. The weight of them was about eight pounds; these Irons and her other Afflictions, soon brought her into Convulsion Fits, so that I thought she would have died that Night. I sent to entreat that the Irons might be taken off, but all entreaties were in vain, if it would have saved her Life, so that in this condition she must continue

The Tryals at Salem coming on, I went thither, to see how things were there managed; and finding that the Spectre-Evidence was there received, together with Idle, if not malicious Stories, against People's Lives, I did easily perceive which way the rest would go; for the same Evidence that served for one, would serve for all the rest. I acquainted her with her danger; and that if she were carried to Salem to be tried, I feared she would never return. I did my utmost that she might have her Tryal in our own County, I with several others Petitioning the Judge for it, and were put in hopes of it; but I soon saw so much, that I understood thereby it was not intended, which put me upon consulting the means of her escape; which through the goodness of God was effected, and she got to Road Island, but soon found herself not safe when there, by reason of the pursuit after her; from thence she went to New-York, along with some others that had escaped their cruel hands; where we found his Excellency Benjamin Fletcher, Esq, Governour, who was very courteous to us.

After this some of my Goods were seized in a Friend's hands, with whom I had left them, and my self imprisoned by the Sheriff, and kept in Custody half a day, and then dismist; but to speak of their usage of the Prisoners, and their Inhumanity shewn to them, at the time of their

*Execution, no sober Christian could bear; they had also tryals of cruel
mockings; which is the more, considering what a People for Religion, I
mean the profession of it, we have been; those that suffered being many of
them Church Members, and most of them unspotted in their Conversation, till their Adversary the Devil took up this Method for accusing them.*

John Alden Jr., Mariner and Indian Trader[118]

One of the wealthiest and most highly respected men in New England,
John Alden Jr. was affectionately known as the "Tall Man from Bos-
ton," and was the eldest son of John Alden, the cooper who arrived on
the *Mayflower*, married Priscilla Mullins, and became immortalized in
Longfellow's poem. Now, seventy years old, John Alden Jr. had been a
Boston resident and church member for some thirty years when he was
arrested May 28, 1692, "for cruelly torturing and afflicting several Salem
Village Children."

A former soldier and mariner, Captain Alden had commanded vessels and recently been appointed to negotiate with the Abenaki to redeem
hostages captured during York's Candlemas Day Massacre. His own son,
taken captive earlier, was being held for ransom in Quebec. As a sea captain, Alden had long worked the Maine coast, trading for furs in Native
American villages. He spoke several Indian languages and in 1689/90,
helped finance and lead Massachusetts' failed expedition against French
forces in Quebec.

The Salem Village maids who were Captain Alden's accusers likely
never met the man, but his "trafficking with Indians" made him suspect.
Many young men had died in battles to the East, and Massachusetts Bay
Colony seemed to be losing the Indian wars. If the Devil was plotting to
conquer their Christian colony, as many believed, then Satan would surely
call upon heathen natives as well as witches for assistance.

"There stands Alden, a bold fellow with his hat on before the Judges,"
cried one accuser. "He sells powder and shot to the Indians and French,
and lies with Indian Squaws and has Indian papooses." When John Alden
glanced at the afflicted, they began to suffer fits, and when he put his hand
upon them, as ordered by the magistrate, they became quiet.

"I have known you many years and have been at sea with you," Judge Bartholomew Gedney told Captain Alden in court, "and I always accounted you an honest man. But now I do see cause to alter my judgment, for when you touched that poor child, the poor child came out of her fit."

"How is it that when I look upon you, Mr. Gedney, you do not fall down as well?" asked Captain Alden.

Mr. Gedney urged Alden to confess to witchcraft. "By doing so, give glory to God."

"I hope I should give glory to God, and never gratify the Devil," the Captain replied, "and that God will clear up my innocency."

It was said that when John Alden was taken to his cell, "The prison keeper seeing such a man committed, of whom he had a good esteem, was after this the more compassionate to those that were in prison . . ."

A fast was held at Alden's home a few weeks after his incarceration. Judge Samuel Sewall read a sermon, and the Reverend Cotton Mather and other ministers offered prayers. After fifteen weeks, Captain Alden broke out of jail and fled to Duxbury, where he hid out with Plymouth relatives. When the witch hunt was over and the Court of Oyer et Terminer dissolved, he turned himself in to the authorities, and on April 25, 1693, was acquitted by the First Superior Court.

On June 12, Judge Samuel Sewall noted in his diary: "I visited Captain Alden and his wife and told them I was sorry for their sorrow by reason of his imprisonment and that I was glad of his Restoration."

Writing in the third person, John Alden later told the tale of his ordeal, which was published by Robert Calef in *More Wonders of the Invisible World*. "An account of how John Alden was dealt with at Salem Village" follows, in the victim's own words:

I cannot but condemn this method of the Justices because of making this touch of the hand a rule to discover witchcraft because I am fully persuaded that it is a superstitious method . . . upon the Accusation of a company of poor distracted, or possessed Creatures or Witches; and being sent by Mr. Stoughton, arrived there the 31st of May and appeared at Salem Village, before Mr. Gedney, Mr. Hathorn, and Mr. Corwin

Those Wenches being present, who played their juggling tricks, falling . . . Then all were ordered to go down into the Street, where a Ring was made around Alden and more accusations made. Then was Alden committed to the Marshal's Custody, and his Sword taken from him; for they said he afflicted them with his Sword. After some hours Alden was sent to the Meeting House in the Village before the Magistrates, who required Alden to stand upon a Chair, to the open view of all the People.

The Accusers cried out that Alden did pinch them, then, when he stood upon the Chair, in the sight of all the People, a good way distant from them, one of the Magistrates bid the Marshal to hold open Alden's hands that he might not pinch those creatures. John Alden asked them why they should think that he should come to that Village to afflict those persons that he never knew or saw before?

Captain Alden appealed to all that ever knew him, if they ever suspected him to be such a person and challenged anyone that could bring in anything upon their own knowledge that might give suspicion of his being such a one. Alden spoke of the Providence of God in suffering these Creatures to accuse Innocent persons, and the Reverend Nicholas Noyes said that God by his Providence governs the World, and Keeps it in peace; and so went on with Discourse, and stop't Alden's mouth.

"There is not a word of Truth in all these say of me," Captain Alden protested, as the Marshal led him off to the Boston prison.

Goody Toothaker's Ironic Tale

Mary Allen Toothaker was terrified of Indians. A Billerica goodwife, she admitted to making a deal with the Devil because he had promised to protect her from those *Savages*. This fear was partly based upon the near loss of her eldest son, Allen, who was fighting Native Americans on the Maine frontier. When Allen finally returned home, he still had a four-inch open wound, "so deep that a knitting needle could be thrust into it."[119] Even his aunt, Martha Allen Carrier, claimed it would never heal, though after she was imprisoned for witchcraft, the former soldier's wound miraculously healed. Mary herself was safe in prison when another band of Native Americans attacked Billerica, killing six neighbors and torching the Toothaker homestead.

Mary's husband, Dr. Roger Toothaker, was a *"cunning person,"* that is, someone who practiced astrology and magic. Indeed, at her examination, Goody Toothaker explained how she and Roger "used to read many histories, especially one book that treated of the twelve signs, from which they could tell a great deal."[120]

According to the *Middlesex County Court Records of 1680,* Thomas Wilkinson, a Billerica swineherd, filed a suit against Mary Allen Toothaker, accusing her of adultery. Goodman Wilkinson had previously been chastised by the court for neglecting his land and "much mispence of precious time." Goody Toothaker pleaded not guilty to Wilkinson's charge, explaining how in February of 1669, Goodman Wilkinson had spent the night with the Toothakers on a return journey "from the bay." When Mary's husband stepped outside, Wilkinson proceeded to demonstrate "lascivious carriages."

He told Goody Toothaker he would get a shirt for her husband, and she'd replied she "knew not how to pay him for it." Wilkinson then boldly announced he would "take his pay for it if she were willing to lay her child out of her arms." Mary told the swineherd she "would see him hanged first." He then attempted to bribe her with cheese, "for he had great need." She told him again that she would see him hang first, for he had a wife of his own. Was he not ashamed to offer abuse to another man's wife?

"If you have such need, make haste home to your own wife!" Goodwife Toothaker told Thomas Wilkinson.

"You be hanged," Tom Wilkinson replied. "Look you here!" And with that he "walked to her with his nakedness uncovered in a most brutish manner."

"Are you not ashamed?" she asked him.

"If you will neither take anything, nor give anything, then adieu to you," he said, and to Mary Toothaker's great relief, Goodman Wilkinson left her house.

After doing his best to seduce Goody Toothaker by her own fireside, Wilkinson then threatened her husband, saying that "if he spake a word of it, it would cost him [Dr. Toothaker] all his estate in damages for defamation."[121]

Dr. Toothaker spent so much time at Beverly and Salem that he neglected duties of family and farm. This was a matter of grave concern on the part of Billerica selectmen, for, according to their records of March 12, 1682/3, "Roger Toothaker being sent for and spoken unto concerning many things amiss in his family; he desired they would exercise a little more patience toward him . . . and promised to make amends."[122]

Apparently Dr. Toothaker still failed to assume family responsibilities, for on December 15, 1684, local selectmen dispatched another letter to him at Salem, telling him "to come for his wife ye middle of next week, and they would help away with his family, in case of need and help fit them out."

If Roger did return home, he did not stay long, for his wife received charitable aid from the Town of Billerica, and two of the Toothaker children were placed in the households of other families.

On May 18, 1692, Dr. Toothaker was arrested on charges of witchcraft. A few years earlier, at a tavern in Beverly, he had boasted how his daughter killed a witch by the name of Mathias Button at Haverhill. The doctor claimed he'd taught Martha Toothaker Emerson a trick to deal with witches: When a person complained of being bewitched, all one needed to do was to put the afflicted person's urine into an earthenware pot, cap it tightly, and place the pot in a hot oven, leaving it to bake overnight. The very next morning the suspected witch would be dead. Recently, when Dr. Toothaker had been called to examine two sick children on the North Shore, he'd diagnosed their miseries as "caused by an evil hand."

Mary Allen Toothaker and her nine-year-old daughter, Margaret, were taken into custody May 28, the same day that Mary's sister, Martha Carrier, was arrested in Andover. Mary told the court she was "under great discontent and troubled with fear about Indians and used to often dream of fighting with them." She'd tried praying, "but was the worse for it and knows not but that the devil tempted her not to pray." The devil appeared to Mary in the shape of "a tawny man," who "promised to keep her from the Indians," and told her she "should have happy days with her son." So she'd made her mark with a finger on a piece of birch bark.

Summoned by the beating of a drum and the sound of a trumpet, Goody Toothaker traveled twice to witch meetings at Salem Village with her sister, Martha Carrier, Ann Foster, and the two Mary Laceys. The minister who "preached at the meeting of witches was a little man whose name is Burroughs ... they talked of 305 witches in the country and spoke of pulling down the Kingdom of Christ and setting up the Kingdom of Satan."

Mary Toothaker was convicted of being a "Detestable Witch," who did "wickedly, feloniously and maliciously, a Covenant with the Devil make, promising to Serve and praise him with her whole heart." On June 16, her husband, Roger Toothaker, was found dead in Boston Prison. Circumstances were suspicious enough that the coroner summoned a jury to determine cause of death.

"Twenty-four able and sufficient men appeared before me at the prison," said the foreman, Benjamin Walker. "We have viewed the body and obtained the best information we can from persons near and present at his death and do find he came to his end by a natural death.[123]

Widow Mary Toothaker and her daughter were released from Cambridge Prison the first week of February in 1693. It was the middle of winter and they had no home to return to, since it had been burned to the ground during the Indian raid of August 1. Once again, the family became charges of the town. Goody Toothaker's earlier fears proved well founded, for three years after her exoneration and release, Billerica suffered yet another Indian massacre. This time, Mary Toothaker was slaughtered, while twelve-year-old Margaret was taken captive and never heard from again.

Timothy Swan—Witchcraft Victim

Mary Toothaker was among the eighteen angry women who supposedly tortured Timothy Swan to an early death by means of malefic witchcraft. On trial for her life on August 5, Goody Toothaker told the magistrates that she hurt Swan by "clinching her hands or gripping a dishclout" while thinking of him. She also claimed she "went in spirit to Timothy Swan's," where she "squeezed his arms and throat." When asked if there was not someone who stirred them all up to hurt Swan, Mary Toothaker replied,

"Aye, a pretty elderly woman who was most busy about him and encouraged the rest to afflict."[124]

Young Goodman Swan was apparently quite the irresponsible rake. He is believed by most historians to have fathered Elizabeth Emerson's first illegitimate child, Dorothy. The only known grave marker of an alleged witchcraft victim is the crude stone belonging to Timothy Swan in the Old Burying Ground of North Andover, Massachusetts. He died February 2, 1692/3, at the age of thirty, "tortured, afflicted, consumed, and wasted," as "three or four at a time, their specters attacked him at his bedside with spindles, pins, spears and tobacco pipes."[125]

Timothy Swan was definitely one of those afflicted who accused others of causing him intolerable suffering by means of witchcraft. In spite of being seriously ill for more than a year, his name shows up in eighteen different cases. On July 15, 1692, Tim Swan struggled out of his sickbed to make a court appearance as one of the afflicted at Ann Foster's examination. Seventy-two-year-old Goody Foster admitted she had "hurt Swan by making a poppet out of rags, then sticking pins in these or tying knots in the rags and burning them." On July 22, Goody Foster's eighteen-year-old granddaughter, Mary Lacey Jr., testified to seeing Richard Carrier's specter burn Timothy Swan with a tobacco pipe in Swan's chamber.

"Sometimes we were in shapes and sometimes in body, but he did not see us. We rode upon hand poles and the devil was also there in the shape of a black man and high crowned hat and bid us to kill Swan by stabbing him to death and we also stuck pins into his likeness."

"And what else had you?" Judge Hathorn inquired. "Any hot irons or knitting needles?"

"Oh yes," replied Mary. "We had an iron spindle and Richard Carrier ran it through Swan's knee."

When Judge John Hathorn asked eighteen-year-old Richard Carrier (also "in the devil's snare") if he had helped to hurt Timothy Swan, the young man confessed he'd "helped Mary Perkins Bradbury (of Salisbury), to hurt Swan because they argued over a scythe."

"Had you any quarrel with Goodman Swan?" the magistrate asked.

Mary Lacey Jr. replied that they all came in upon Mrs. Bradbury's quarrel with him.

Her mother, also on trial for witchcraft, first denied afflicting Swan.

"Mother! Do not deny it!" exclaimed Mary Lacey Jr.

So Mary Lacey Sr. then explained, "The devil made his imps do it and there were hot irons held by the devil."

"Your daughter said it was an iron spindle," one magistrate noted.

"Yes, yes. 'Twas a spindle," replied Mary Lacey Sr.

And the younger Mary added, "Something of the quarrel between Goody Bradbury and Swan about thatching a house."

Mary Tyler Post Bridges of Boxford was arrested on July 28, "for committing sundry Acts of Witchcraft lately on the Body of Timothy Swan."

On August 2, her daughter, Mary Post of Andover and Rowley, was taken into custody on a formal complaint that Swan had filed with Ann Putnam and Mary Walcott of Salem Village.

At the end of July, Robert and John Swan appeared before Andover magistrate Dudley Bradstreet, to accuse Mary Johnson Clarke, of Haverhill, of "High Suspition [sic] of sundry acts of witchcraft" against their brother's body, for which they did "crave Justice."

Twelve-year-old Ann Putnam claimed she witnessed "Goody Clark stab Timothy Swan with a square ragged speare as long as her hand." When asked why she called it a ragged spear, she replied that it was "ragged like a file."

Defending himself against this army of enemies, Timothy Swan joined Mary Warren in taking out a warrant against Rebecca Eames in early August, and several weeks later, filed another complaint with two other Salem Village girls, against Francis Hutchins of Haverhill.

On August 19, the same day that Richard Carrier's mother, Martha, went to the gallows with four males convicted of committing witchcraft, Rebecca Eames of Boxford confessed to afflicting Timothy Swan with her son, Daniel Eames. Widow Mary Parker of Andover (hanged September 22) was accused by Mercy Wardwell and William Barker of joining them to afflict Timothy Swan. Timothy Swan was apparently back in court on September 4 to testify against Mary Bradbury.

"The Sheriff Brought in the Witch," from *The Witch of Salem, or Credulity Run Mad* by John R. Musick, illustration by Freeland A. Carter, 1893. COURTESY OF PAUL ROYSTER, COORDINATOR OF SCHOLARLY COMMUNICATION, UNIVERSITY OF NEBRASKA, LINCOLN LIBRARIES

Was it because six years before, young Timothy Swan had been accused of fathering a bastard, and, with the help of his father, refused to own up to his responsibility? Did he sexually abuse young women from four different towns, who later joined up to take their revenge? Or was it the father of the three Swans these citizens were actually after? This litigious malcontent, Robert Swan Sr., had been before Essex County Court several times, hassling over what he considered his personal boundary rights in Haverhill. Considered malicious by his neighbors, the senior Swan was accused of "making mischief" against their livestock and grabbing adjacent lands through intimidation.[126]

Goodman Swan even instructed his sons to knock down fences and destroy apple trees bordering his land, threatening abutters until they moved away. Robert Swan continually expressed disdain for authority, and the county court took note of the senior Swan's "seditious manner," in his assertion that "men were led about by ye laws like a Company of Puppy Dogs."[127]

Timothy Swan was already dead of his strange malady (one cannot help but wonder if it might have been "French pox," as syphilis was then known) by the time Elizabeth Emerson was executed for infanticide on June 8, 1693, leaving six-year-old Dorothy an orphan.

The Reverend George Burroughs—"Ruler of Hell"[128]

"Oh, dreadful, dreadful! Here is a minister come!" When twelve-year-old Ann Putnam Jr. envisioned the specter of a clergyman, she was "grievously affrighted," and wondered, "What, are ministers witches too?"

The girl told magistrates seated high above the bench and presiding at the Oyer et Terminer Court, that she had threatened "to complain of him, even though he was a minister, should he be a wizard." She claimed she was "immediately tortured by him, racked and almost choked . . . he tempted me to write in his book, which I refused with loud outcries, and said I would not write in his book though he tore me all to pieces . . ." Ann Putnam said he told her his name was George Burroughs, and he admitted to bewitching his first two wives to death.

In her damning testimony, Maid Ann then told Mr. Burroughs it was "a dreadful thing that he, a minister who should teach children to fear God, should come to persuade poor creatures to give their souls to the devil."

George Burroughs was born in Virginia to a successful merchant and his wife.[129] Following his father's return to England, his mother brought him to Massachusetts, "so she might enjoy God in his ordinance in New England," and in 1657, she joined the church congregation at Roxbury. George graduated from Harvard in 1670, and a few years later, married the first of three wives. He served as minister in frontier settlements at Falmouth and Casco (now Portland, Maine), until King Philip's War devastated those English villages. He escaped to a nearby island with some members of his congregation and sent dispatches back to Boston describing Indian attacks and requesting military reinforcement.

In 1680 Burroughs was offered the pulpit at Salem Village Meeting House, which he hoped would prove a permanent post, since Puritan ministers generally served one church for a lifetime. George Burroughs, his pregnant wife, and two small children moved into John Putnam's household while waiting for the parsonage to be made ready for occupancy. The £93, 6 shilling annual salary promised Burroughs—one-third in money and two-thirds in the usual *minister's rates* provided by parishioners in rye, barley, malt, corn, beef, pork, and butter—was never paid him. Burroughs refused to preach until receiving his due, while John Putnam and others tried to get the court to force him to preach as agreed. His salary in arrears, Burroughs was forced to borrow money from Putnam in September of 1681, to cover funeral expenses following his wife's death in childbirth.

Although his salary needs were still not being adequately met, the minister did his best to serve the contentious Salem Village church, during which time he remarried. Burroughs' second wife was Sarah Ruck Hathorn, a war widow whose husband was killed fighting Native Americans in Maine. Sarah's former brother-in-law was Magistrate John Hathorn, the judge who would later condemn George Burroughs to death for witchcraft. In June of 1683, the growing family moved to Casco,

"The Reverend George Burroughs at His Witchcraft Trial," originally published in Frank Leslie's *Illustrated Newspaper,* February 4, 1871. COURTESY OF PAUL ROYSTER, COORDINATOR OF SCHOLARLY COMMUNICATION, UNIVERSITY OF NEBRASKA, LINCOLN LIBRARIES

Maine, where Burroughs had been offered one hundred acres to help encourage resettlement of the former English village destroyed by Indians. Major Benjamin Church, leader of this endeavor, soon had high praises for George Burroughs: "As for the minister of this place, I am well satisfied with him, he being present with us in the fight." At this time, Burroughs was one of only two clergymen in all of Maine.

Hoping still to collect salary due him, Burroughs returned to Salem Village, only to find that John Putnam and several other church members had filed a suit against him: "Action of Debt for two gallons of Canary Wine, and cloth, etc., bought of Mr. Gedney on Lieutenant Putnam's account for the funeral of Mrs. Burroughs." The minister was arrested for debt yet managed to stay out of jail because friends paid bail and convinced authorities that these debts were "due to the poor minister's bereavement over his first wife's death." Although the case was dismissed, Goodman Putnam fostered a grudge against the minister that he would carry into court when Burroughs later stood trial for witchcraft.

Driven away once again when the French and Indians attacked Casco on May 20, 1690, George Burroughs moved his family to the better-fortified settlement at Wells. It was the Reverend George Burroughs who penned the vivid descriptions of the January 25, 1691/2 Candlemas Massacre against York, where some fifty English settlers were slaughtered and about one hundred taken captive and marched through the snow to Canada.

Simply surviving such devastating attacks was enough to make ordinary folks suspect Satan himself might be shielding Mr. Burroughs while so many others died. Why, even York's minister, the Reverend Shubael Dummer, was killed as he attempted to mount his horse and escape. That Puritan cleric was then stripped naked as Abenaki warriors jeered and danced around his corpse.

Jonathan Walcott and Thomas Putnam, fathers of two of Salem Village's afflicted girls, swore a complaint against George Burroughs. The warrant for the minister's arrest was delivered to the chief magistrate at Piscataqua April 30, 1692, "to apprehend the body of Mister George Burroughs, at present preacher at Wells in the Province of Maine and convey him with all speed to Salem . . . he being suspected of a confederacy with the Devil . . ." He was also being accused of "Baptizing converts to the Devil and leading Satanic masses in the woods," and of "causing the deaths of many English soldiers to the Eastward." The Maine minister, widowed again, was taken into custody by the field marshal of the Province of New Hampshire and Maine on May 2, while eating dinner with his third wife and eight children and stepchildren.

Burroughs was already in prison when his dead wives supposedly paid a visit to the bedchamber of Ann Putnam Jr. Wearing winding sheets, their "pale, dead faces" told the girl they had both been murdered by their husband, George Burroughs. Supposedly, he stabbed the first "beneath her arm, then covered the wound with sealing wax," and the specter removed her shroud to show Ann the exact spot.

These ghosts of the minister's former wives claimed he was "a cruel man" to them, and that "their blood did cry out for vengeance . . ." The dead wives told Ann Putnam Jr. they "would ascend to heaven and wear white robes, while Burroughs would be cast into hell."

Ann's uncle John Putnam deposed that George Burroughs "was a very harsh and sharp man to his wife," and that "there were differences between them." He claimed that the minister, then living in his household, had forced his first wife to "write, sign, and seal, and swear a covenant never to reveal his secrets." Other Salem villagers testified Burroughs kept both former wives "in a strange kind of slavery." According to Susannah Sheldon, another afflicted accuser and war refugee, "The first wife, he smothered and the second, he choked."

Described as a puny man, George Burroughs's phenomenal physical prowess was legendary among his contemporaries. He was rumored to have accomplished feats "beyond the strength of a giant," and the man's seemingly supernatural powers would be used as evidence against him in court. He could supposedly hold a gun with a seven-foot barrel with just one finger. The gun was so heavy that two strong men could not keep it steady without using both hands. The minister made nothing of taking it up behind the lock with but one hand and holding it out at arm's end, like a pistol.

The Little Wizard could lift a full barrel of molasses and tote it with just the two fingers of one hand. Someone reported seeing him carry a barrel filled with cider from a canoe to the shore. Such feats of strength simply could not be accomplished "without diabolical assistance," according to the Reverend Cotton Mather.

When Burroughs told the Court of Oyer et Terminer that an Indian in Maine could do the same thing, his accusers replied that was simply Satan assuming the shape of an Indian.

The most damning evidence against George Burroughs however, stemmed from his unorthodox religious beliefs and practices, which is why the Reverend Cotton Mather and other conservative clerics considered him the "Ruler of Hell." Like later confessions of William Barker Sr., George Burroughs's case contained implications that threatened Puritanism at its very core. Burroughs's theology, gleaned from the original documents, sounds not unlike Baptist religious practices. Salem Trial records frequently allude to those accused as being unable to pray or frequently absent from the meetinghouse, but now authorities had a Harvard-educated minister in custody who could not even recall when he last took Holy Communion. When the magistrate asked him to say when his last sacrament occurred, Mr. Burroughs replied, "It was so long since, I could not tell." The man on trial for his life was a gospel minister, yet he neglected to celebrate the Lord's Supper regularly. Furthermore, he confessed that only one of his children had been baptized. Puritans believed wholeheartedly in infant baptism. Baptists did not, so according to Puritan practioners, this put George Burroughs in league with the Devil. Back in 1644, Massachusetts even made the refusal to present a new baby for holy baptism a crime punishable by banishment.

In a paper Burroughs read to the jury in his own defense, he denied any possibility of demonic obsession by witches. "Witches have no power to torment other people at a distance," the minister wrote. When asked what he thought of the afflicted persons, he replied, "It was an amazing and humbling providence," but he "understood nothing of it."

Chief among George Burroughs's eight accusers of his heading a "Hellish Rendezvous" of witches was Mercy Lewis, a victim of the 1684 Indian raid on Falmouth. After her parents were slaughtered in that massacre, the Burroughs family kindly took the orphan into their home. Now, at age seventeen, Mercy Lewis was a servant working in the household of Thomas and Ann Putnam. The Putnam men led the faction refusing to pay Burroughs's back wages from serving the Salem Village Meetinghouse. Mercy joined Ann Putnam Jr. in accusing the minister of murdering two wives. She deposed that George Burroughs "did grievously torture me and urged me to write in his black book, which was filled with spells and names written in blood." She testified that Burroughs told her "the Devil was his servant," and he "could raise the Devil anytime." Mercy Lewis claimed that this minister, in whose home she had once lived, "carried me up to an exceedingly high mountain and showed me all the Kingdoms of the earth and told me that he would give them all to me if I would write in his book, and if I would not, he would throw me down and break my neck." Mercy Lewis said she told him she "would not sign even if he threw me down upon one hundred pitchforks!"

One confessed witch, Deliverance Hobbs, testified at Burroughs's trial that she had attended a meeting of witches where the minister preached and had "pressed them to bewitch all in the Village." He also "administered a sacrament there of red bread and red wine like blood."

Seventeen-year-old Elizabeth Hubbard was another afflicted person who testified against him. "There appeared a little black-beard man to me, in blackish apparel. I asked him his name and he told me his name was Burroughs. Then he took a book out of his pocket and opened it and bid me to set my hand to it. I told him I would not. The lines in this book were red as blood. Then he pinched me twice and went away. The next morning he appeared to me again and told me he was above a wizard, he was a conjurer . . . I believe in my heart Mister George Burroughs is a dreadful wizard."

Another confessed witch, William Barker Sr. of Andover, identified this minister as the ring leader who summoned all the other witches to meetings with his trumpet. Mary Warren also claimed seeing George Burroughs "sound a trumpet to call witch gatherings, and the wine they drank there was real blood." Mary Lacey Jr. swore this cleric headed the entire Satanic Congregation.

Judge Samuel Sewall, who had been Burroughs's friend since their student days at Harvard, attended Burroughs's execution August 19. "By his speech, prayer, presentation of his Innocence," Sewall said, "Mr. Burroughs did much move unthinking persons . . ."

At the gallows the minister delivered his own sermon, during which he expressed forgiveness toward all who had accused him and urged the magistrates to reevaluate the Trials which he considered altogether wrong.

According to Robert Calef, a critic of the Trials, "Burroughs' speech for the clearing of his innocency, uttered with such solemn and serious expression, and such composedness, and fervency of spirit, was very affecting and was met with the admiration of all present."

Yet as the minister spoke, several afflicted girls pointed at the ladder, claiming they saw the Devil dictate words into Mr. Burroughs's ear. The doomed cleric then amazed spectators by reciting the Lord's Prayer from beginning to end without stumbling, a feat believed impossible for any witch to manage. This drew tears from many and raised fears that the spectators would hinder the execution, until thirty year old minister Cotton Mather calmed the crowd, with words of warning from astride his horse: "The Devil has often been transformed into an Angel of Light." Quoting the Bible, Mather informed spectators that "the Devil and his agents have the power to become saints and angels in order to deceive." Mather further reminded everyone that George Burroughs, "like all the other witches, had received a fair trial in the court of law by honest and worthy men."

In his August 19 diary entry, Judge Sewall wrote, "George Burroughs, John Willard, John Proctor, Martha Carrier, and George Jacobs were executed at Salem, a very great number of Spectators being present. Mr. Cotton Mather was there . . . says they all died by a Righteous sentence. All of them said they were innocent . . . Mr. Burroughs by his speech, Prayer, protestation of his Innocence, did much move unthinking persons . . ." In the margin, Samuel Sewall scribbled, *Dolefull Witchcaft!*

In 1710, Massachusetts General Court received a moving petition from Charles Burroughs, the minister's "elder son in ye name with the rest, praying that our dear and honored father's Attainer be taken off and they be allowed fifty pounds restitution…We have all the reason in the World to believe he was innocent by his careful Catechizing of his Children and upholding religion in his family and by his Solemn and Savory written Instructions from prison. We were left a parcel of small children helpless and a mother-in-law with one small child of her own to take care of, whereby she was not capable to take care of us by which our father's small estate was most of it lost and expended and we scattered."[130]

"The Reverend George Burroughs at His Execution, Salem, Massachusetts, August 19, 1692," illustration by Kendrick in William T. Harris, Edward Everett Hale, Nelson A. Miles, O. P. Austin, and George Cary Eggleston, *The United States of America: A Pictorial History of the American Nation from the Earliest Discoveries and Settlements to the Present Time, 1909.* COURTESY OF PAUL ROYSTER, COORDINATOR OF SCHOLARLY COMMUNICATION, UNIVERSITY OF NEBRASKA, LINCOLN LIBRARIES

CONFESSION—CHIEF GOAL OF MINISTERS AND MAGISTRATES

Whatever hath a tendency to put witches into confusion is likely to bring them unto confession too. Here cross and swift questions have their use.

—COTTON MATHER. *THE WONDERS OF THE INVISIBLE WORLD*,
BOSTON, 1693

Over fifty persons confessed to witchcraft in 1692, the highest number being residents of Andover, which then bordered Salem Village. The majority of confessing witches offered elaborate and imaginative details on exactly why, where, and how they signed the Devil's Book, pledging to serve Satan, and where and how they had been baptized by him.

For Puritans, a witch's confession held hope of salvation rather than damnation, helping to ensure the whole community further protection from the Devil and his agents. In Christian theology, confession leads to God's forgiveness. Witches who confessed could repent of their sins and be redeemed through God's grace. Thus, magistrates and ministers urged the accused to "Confess for the sake of your eternal soul." Confessions in court were what the judges most ardently sought. Confessions also reassured magistrates they were doing the right thing: serving God by saving New England from Satanic Rule. To gain these confessions, children, one even as young as four years of age, were coerced by the court to testify against their parents, on trial for witchcraft.

The ones most feared were those accused witches who stubbornly refused to confess, since they still possessed the power to direct their specters to inflict harm upon innocent people. This is why accused witches were kept in shackles and chains inside prison walls. By midsummer, it must have been clear to most people that no one who had confessed in court had gone to the gallows, nor were they chained and locked in manacles in their cells. Those who got hanged were the ones who denied ever having served Satan, even as they were led up the ladder and the noose placed around their necks. All who confessed remained in prison. Some were brought to court to serve as powerful witnesses against others, and they were yet alive. Many lied in order to save themselves, while others chose death rather than confess to things that were not true, for they were convinced that telling such lies in the eyes of God was but a sure path to hell.

When Ann Foster was questioned on July 21, the judges urged her confession by telling her that "God will give you more favor than others, inasmuch as you relent . . . you cannot expect peace of conscience without a free confession." Like Mary Toothaker and William Barker Sr., the Widow Foster not only confessed to the capital crime of witchcraft, but she also told the magistrates the precise number of witches currently in their colony.

Ann Foster and the Two Laceys — Three Generations of Witches[131]

The Andover Witch Hunt reached a peak in the late summer and early fall with fifty residents arrested, a higher number than from any other New England town. Andover also had the most children accused of witchcraft and taken into custody. Andover had suffered several Indian raids, and like Salem Village, had experienced controversy within its church. Citizens here were being taxed for the support of two ministers: the elderly Francis Dane, who disapproved of the Salem Trials, and Thomas Barnard, a thirty-four-year-old Harvard graduate who originally supported the Trials with its use of spectral evidence for conviction, but later changed his mind.

Elizabeth Phelps Ballard had a lingering illness. When the usual medicinal herbs did not ease her suffering and the local doctor was unable to identify cause or cure, her husband suspected she might be a victim of witchcraft. Like everyone else, Joseph Ballard had heard about the strange goings-on at Salem Village. So in mid-July, he went there to fetch a couple of those girls reported to have the ability to spot witches. Before long, two of them were standing at Elizabeth Ballard's bedside, claiming the poor woman was definitely bewitched. Ten days later, Goody Ballard was dead.

Ann Foster was the likely suspect, and Joseph Ballard lost no time in taking a warrant out against her. The seventy-two-year-old woman was arrested July 15, and four days later, Goodman Ballard filed formal complaints against her daughter, Mary Lacey, and her eighteen-year-old granddaughter, Mary Lacey Jr. The prevalent belief was that witchcraft ran in families. Since parents are the teachers of their children, the art and practice of witchcraft must surely be passed from mothers to daughters and sons. Thus, if one family member was accused of witchcraft, then all the kinfolk in that suspect's immediate and extended family stood in danger of being charged with the same crime.

These days, the Foster-Laceys would be labeled a dysfunctional family. Like impoverished women beyond childbearing age and those with kinship ties to accused or convicted witches, families in conflict were at greater risk of being "cried out against." Persons with long-standing quarrels with neighbors, resulting in someone's misfortune, or anyone previously suspected or accused of witchcraft, were the ones most apt to be arrested. Ann Foster's case contained all of these elements. Hers was a family tainted by trouble and one certainly considered "out of God's favor" by the Andover community.

Born in England, she was the widow of Andrew Foster, a Scotsman who was one of the town's earliest settlers and lived to be over one hundred years of age. According to the *Andover Selectmen Records,* Mary Foster Lacey's husband, Lawrence, had been publicly chastised "for excessive drinking and for absenting meeting." In 1689, Ann Foster's other daughter, Hannah Stone, pregnant with her seventh child, was murdered by her drunken husband during an argument over a sale of land. Hugh Stone had committed Andover's first murder and went to the gallows at Boston for slashing his wife's throat.[132]

Was it any wonder that Ann Foster found it "difficult to pray"? As she told the Court of Oyer et Terminer at Salem, she "formerly frequented public meeting to worship God but the devil had such power over me that I could not profit there and that was my undoing."

Ann Foster was ordered before the bar four different times during the month of July. Her confession is surely one of the most imaginative and detailed: "The Devil appeared to me three times in the shape of a bird. Such a bird as I never saw the likes of before."

Asked why she thought this bird was the Devil, she replied, "Because he came white and vanished away black. He had two legs and great eyes and sat upon a table." The bird told her that if she promised to serve Satan two years, she would "have prosperity . . . Many things were promised by him, but were never performed."

Ann Foster accused the Reverend George Burroughs and said Martha Carrier forced her to sign the Devil's Book, and was the one who'd made her a witch. They "rode to Salem Village witch meetings together on a pole and Ann carried bread and cheese in her pocket." Once, when they were "in the air above the tree tops, the stick broke, causing she and Goody Carrier to fall to the ground." Martha was not hurt, but Ann's knee was still giving her trouble. Goody Foster told the magistrates there were "305 witches in the whole country and they would ruin this place and set up the Devil's kingdom." Ann Foster admitted to bewitching John Lovejoy's hog, "hurting Timothy Swan," and "causing the death of Andrew Allen's child, as well as making the other very sick." (This three-year-old and his father both died of smallpox in 1690, in Andover's first smallpox epidemic, believed to have been brought to town by Martha Carrier's family.)

Goody Foster's bewitchment method was to make poppets out of rags and tie knots in them, stick them with pins, or burn them. The persons her poppets represented suffered whenever she pinched, pricked, or burned them in the fire. She insisted that her daughter, Mary Lacey, had never been a witch. Ann Foster likely confessed to witchcraft in a desperate attempt to save her daughter and granddaughter, even though they both confessed. At one point all three generations were examined before the bench at the same time.

"Do you not acknowledge that you made your daughter a witch thirteen years ago?" Judge Hathorn asked Ann Foster again.

"I know no more of my daughter's being a witch than what day I shall die upon," the grandmother replied.

Yet Mary Lacey accused her mother in court. "Oh, the Devil hath got hold of us!" she cried. "How shall we get rid of the evil one?" When the judges demanded to know whom Goody Lacey had afflicted and how she did it, the accused told the court that she "took a rag, cloth or any such thing, and rolled it up together. Then whatsoever I do to that rag or cloth is done to the person it represents." She admitted to having tortured Joseph Ballard's wife, and said "the Devil helped her into Timothy Swan's chamber at the window so she could afflict him with an iron spindle and once, with a tobacco pipe." Furthermore, she'd ridden to Salem Village witch meetings with Martha Carrier and her mother on that very same pole. When Mary Lacey, Jr. was brought into the courtroom, she immediately accused her mother with these condemning words, "Where is my mother who made me a witch and I knew it not? Why did you give me to the Devil twice or thrice over?" To which Mary Lacey Sr. told her daughter she was "Sorry at the heart for it. It was through the Wicked One."

Mary Jr. told the magistrates she had only been a witch "not above a week . . ." then added, "Well, maybe for a year." At the time of the Laceys' arrest, the Andover constable and two other men and women made a search for poppets and discovered a "purse of rags and tape and another parcel of quills tied up though no one in the family seemed to know what it was all for."

The Devil had appeared to Mary Lacey Jr. in the shape of a horse, and "put thoughts in my mind not to obey my parents . . . He came in the night when I was in bed and said he would set up his Kingdom and we should have happy days and it would be better times for me if I would obey him. But the Devil has proved a liar from the beginning."

When asked how it was that persons of the town did not see her when she rode out upon poles at night to afflict others, the eighteen-year-old replied, "Sometimes we leave our bodies at home, but at other times we go in our bodies and the Devil puts a mist before people's eyes and will not let them see us." She'd also ridden to Salem Village on a stick, where she recognized the minister, George Burroughs, "a pretty little man who comes to us sometimes in the shape of a cat." She saw Satan as "a black man, with a high crowned hat," and he told them all to "make more witches if we can and says if we will not make other person set their hand to the book, he will tear us into pieces."

The plaintiff then went on to describe the Witches' Sabbat which she'd attended with her mother and grandmother. "The bread was brownish and the wine red. They had a table and earthen cups and there were so many that there was not bread enough for all."

When Ann Foster was brought back into the courtroom, Mary Jr. called out to her: "Oh, Grandmother! Why did you give me to the Devil? Do not deny it! You have been a very wicked woman in your time!"

"Here is a poor miserable child, a wretched mother and a grandmother," announced one magistrate. "Here is living evidence that witchcraft is an art conveyed from mother to daughter."

When Mary Lacey Jr. asked "the Lord to comfort her" and "bring out all that are witches," the magistrates were hopeful that "she may be snatched out of Satan's snare," for there seemed "to be something of repentance" in the younger woman. Indeed, eighteen-year-old Mary Lacey soon became an eager and useful witness. Released from her cell to attend court sessions, she was carted from one town to another to testify against others on trial for their lives in the courts of Essex, Middlesex, and Suffolk counties.

Ann Foster was convicted of witchcraft and sentenced to die but did not survive to hang. She died on the Third of December, after twenty-one weeks in prison during one of the coldest winters then on record. A document in the *Massachusetts Archives* (Volume 135, #159) reveals that Goody Foster's son, Abraham, had to pay the keeper of the jail £2 and 10 shillings in prison fees before carting her corpse back to Andover for burial.

The Guilt of Rebecca Eames[133]

Rebecca Blake Eames was burdened by a heavy conscience. Not only had she committed adultery, but she'd even contemplated suicide. Furthermore, her adult children were a constant worry. Why, she even suspected her son, Daniel, now twenty-eight and married with children of his own, might have given himself to the Devil. Rebecca's daughter, Hannah, was the wife of Andover constable Ephraim Foster, whose job it was to arrest anyone from Andover and Boxford formally accused of witchcraft. And

Rose Foster, their twelve-year-old daughter, was among Andover's own group of afflicted accusers.

Born in Gloucester, Rebecca was fifty-one in 1692, and a resident of Boxford. In 1661, she married Robert Eames, a local selectman. On August 9, Rebecca's son-in-law took her into custody on Timothy Swan's formal complaint. Goody Eames refused to confess at first, vehemently denying having ever been baptized by the Devil, although she did confide that Satan had appeared to her. Goody Eames was examined on August 19, the same day that five convicted witches were hanged, including George Burroughs and Martha Allen Carrier, the King and Queen of Hell.

"Were you at Gallows Hill in Salem to see the other witches hang?" the inquisitor asked Rebecca Eames. He was referring to the five women who had been executed on July 19.

"I was at a house below," Goody Eames replied. "The woman there had a pin stuck in her foot but I did not cause it."

"Have you been a witch twenty-six years?" Judge Hathorn asked.

"No. I can remember but seven years."

Later, Goody Eames said, the Devil promised to give her powers to avenge herself upon those who had offended her. Rebecca Eames complained of being taunted by young girls, Mary Lacey Jr. in particular.

Goody Eames confessed on the last day of August, 1692, explaining how she "got baptized by the devil in Five Mile Pond, three years ago it was, as was her son, Daniel." Thus, she implicated her own son, who soon joined his mother in prison. Rebecca thought "Daniel might have been Satan's servant about thirteen years," since "he used dreadful bad words when he was angry and had bad wishes."

Mary Lacey Jr. testified that Goody Eames "gave Daniel to the devil when he was but two years old." Rebecca Eames could not recall this, but "perhaps it happened during an angry fit." In court, Goody Eames said she had "been discontented since being in league with the devil."

The magistrates wanted to know what happened twenty-six years before that had made her "give herself to the devil, soul and body." She was then in "such horror of conscience," she admitted, that she'd "taken a rope to hang herself and a razor to slit her own throat. And this was by reason of her crime of adultery and the devil won her allegiance by promising her that she would never be brought out, nor would her sin ever be discovered, so she would not suffer damnation."

Rebecca Eames had been carrying a terrible burden of guilt since 1665, when she had slept with her brother-in-law, Moses Tyler, the Boxford resident who was then married to Rebecca's sister, Prudence Blake. Prudence died in 1689 and Moses remarried Widow Sarah Sprague, a mother of eight. The eldest of these, now Moses Tyler's stepdaughter, was Martha Sprague, the *afflicted* sixteen-year-old who was Andover's chief accuser in 1692.

The Devil came to Rebecca Eames in the shape of a horse, "a very ugly colt, and a ragged girl came with him and they both persuaded me to afflict." She confessed to hurting Mary Warren and "another fair face." Her specter, not her body, "rode upon this devil-horse." When asked where she kept the spear she used to afflict others, Goodwife Eames replied she had only an awl.

"And did you afflict Timothy Swan?"

"Yes, I did torture, afflict, consume, waste, and torment Goodman Swan, but I am sorry for it," she said, vowing to "fall down on my knees to ask forgiveness" of all those she had hurt.

Though condemned to death on September 17, along with eight others called before the magistrates the same day, Rebecca Eames managed to escape the gallows. On December 5, she prepared a petition to send Governor Phips from prison. The document demonstrates a desperate woman fighting for her life:

> . . . *your poor and humble petitioner having been here closely confined in Salem prison near four months and likewise condemned to die for the crime of witchcraft which the Lord above he knows I am altogether innocent and ignorant of as will appear at the great day of judgment* . . .

In her personal document, Goody Eames reasoned she should not be executed, because the only evidence against her was spectral and her own confession, "which the Lord above knows was altogether false and untrue." She claimed she only confessed because she was

> *hurried out of her senses by the afflicted persons, Abigail Hobbs and Mary Lacey, who both of them cried out against me . . . mocking me and spitting in my face, saying they knew me to be an old witch and if I would not confess it I should speedily be hanged . . . The petitioner does beg and implore of your Excellency to take it into your pious and judicious consideration to grant me a pardon of my life, not deserving death by man for witchcraft or any other sin that my innocent blood may not be shed . . .*

In spite of this bold request, Rebecca Eames remained in Salem Prison for seven months. She was exonerated on the General Gaol Delivery of early February and returned to Boxford. Though Goody Eames lived to be eighty-one, the witch troubles within her family apparently broke her husband's health, for according to the *Boxford Vital Records*, Robert Eames died July 22, 1693, at the age of fifty-three.

Goodman Barker's Colorful Confessions[134]

William Barker told the magistrates exactly what they wanted to hear, and then baffled them with his prediction of universal religious freedom, with no particular guarantee of an afterlife. The forty-six-year-old Andover farmer was arrested by Constable Ephraim Foster on August 29, while working his fields in the north end of town. Two Boxford men who regularly attended the Andover Meeting House had taken out formal complaints against him, claiming he "woefully afflicted and abused Abigail Martin Jr., Rose Foster, and Martha Sprague by witchcraft, contrary to the peace of our sovereign Lord & Lady, William & Mary, King and Queen of England."

Goodman Barker hardly had a chance to say good-bye to his wife and children before climbing into the oxcart to travel the fifteen bumpy miles to Salem. His thirteen-year-old niece, Mary Barker, and another local woman named Mary Marston, rode with him, all accused of afflicting the same three girls.

The world had gone hard for Goodman Barker. His father, Richard, was one of Andover's original proprietors. A surveyor by trade and the father of nine, the elder Barker had made large land investments but was now in poor health. The most arable land was already in the hands of William's elder brother, while as a younger son, his legacy amounted mostly to swampy acreage.

"Being a poor man and having a large family," William Barker could not manage his debts. The eldest of his seven children was just fourteen, and before the week was out, this son, William Barker, Jr., would also be taken into custody on grounds of witchcraft. Of course, everyone knew the poor were more easily tempted by the Devil, who, according to a sermon by Cotton Mather, "loves to fish in troubled waters."

Goodman Barker told the authorities at his examination that he'd "been in the Devil's snare for the past three years. Satan promised him a comfortable life and promised to pay all his debts, if he would sign his book in blood." This happened the day Barker had gone "into the woods to fetch a stray cow and came upon the shape of a black dog which looked very fiercely upon me . . ."

In court Goodman Barker then proceeded to accuse Elizabeth Dane Johnson and Abigail Dane Faulkner, both daughters of Andover's senior minister, of being the witches who had enticed him "to this great abomination."

Barker's confessions reveal a man gifted with a lively imagination. He obviously enjoyed performing before the judges and spectators, even incorporating elements of medieval folklore to further dramatize his unique confessions. The Devil "has a cloven foot," and he'd "attended one meeting at Salem Village where some blades had Rapiers by their sides." Goodman Barker claimed their ringleader was George Burroughs. The farmer claimed that "the devil carried his shape to Salem on a stick," since he himself had been too busy carting hay and English corn" that day. At the witch gathering, Barker's specter "heard the trumpet sounding and bread and wine [which the witches present there called "the Sacrament"] was served, though he had eaten none of it himself."

He told the authorities there were about a hundred and seven witches in the country and that "Satan's design is to abolish all the churches in the country and set up his own worship." When asked to describe the Kingdom the Devil was hoping to set up on Earth, William Barker told the horrified magistrates that it would be "a place where all persons should live bravely; all should be equal; [where] there would be no Day of Resurrection nor of Judgment, and neither punishment nor shame for sin . . ."

Surely this was blasphemy! Why, this poor husbandman who had become an Agent of Satan was now informing them that all their ministers were in error! What this accused man was saying was the very antithesis of the Calvinist doctrine upon which the Massachusetts Bay Colony had been established. This philosophy of religion described by William Barker before the Court of Oyer et Terminer that day was unimaginable in the 1690s. Politically, this promise of religious freedom was a prediction of something not to be realized until the adoption of the Bill of Rights and the United States Constitution in the eighteenth century. Goodman Barker also told the magistrates the precise number of witches now at work in Massachusetts Bay Colony, who some of them were, and how they practiced their arts. This was welcome news, since the authorities were determined to capture every single one of these Devil's Agents plotting to overthrow their colony.

"In the spring of the year, they came from Connecticut to afflict at Salem Village, but now they have left it off," said Barker, claiming that "the Grandees told him there are about 307 witches in the country" who are "much disturbed with the afflicted persons because they are discovered by them." When asked what the witches thought of the judges, Barker replied that they "curse the judges because their Society is brought under." Barker said he believed the afflicted persons to be innocent, and that they "[did] God good service . . . Nor did he know nor hear of one innocent person taken up and put in prison and everyone currently in custody is guilty." Barker's testimony was welcome news to the magistrates, for it

Gravestone of William Barker Sr., Old Burying Ground, Academy Road, North Andover, Massachusetts. It reads: HERE LYES BURIED THE BODY OF WILLIAM BARKER WHO DIED MARCH THE 4 1718 IN 73 YEAR OF HIS AGE. COURTESY OF THE NORTH ANDOVER HISTORICAL SOCIETY

was read by them as assurance that they were performing God's work through these witch trials. Goodman Barker also had provided them with further proof of the Devil's conspiracy.

On September 16, William Barker Sr. again appeared before the bench, where he owned up to his confessions. He told the judges he was "heartily sorry" for what he had done, and for "hurting the afflicted persons who were his accusers." He "prayed for their forgiveness and begged the pardon of God and the Honorable Magistrates and of all God's people." He vowed to "renounce the devil and all his works . . . and to set my heart and hand to do what lies in me to destroy such wicked worship . . ." Still, William Barker Sr. was a guilty man and a confessed witch, with prison fees to pay. It wasn't long before the wily farmer broke jail and found his way to freedom.

153

SALEM TRIALS BROUGHT TO AN END

. . . To take away the life of any one, merely because a Spectre or Devil, in a Bewitched or Possessed person does accuse them, will bring the Guilt of Innocent Blood on the Land . . .

It were better that ten suspected witches should escape, than that one innocent person should be condemned. I had rather judge a witch to be an honest woman, than judge an honest woman as a witch.

—INCREASE MATHER, *CASES OF CONSCIENCE CONCERNING EVIL SPIRITS PERSONATING MEN*, BOSTON, 1692

On October 3, fourteen ministers gathered to discuss the legal and moral basis of the Trials and the validity of spectral evidence upon which nineteen had gone to the gallows at Salem. The clerics prepared a written statement, including a plea to the court "to permit only provable evidence in future witchcraft trials." This significant document, *Cases of Conscience Concerning Evil Spirits Personating Men, Witchcrafts, Infallible Proofs of Guilt in such as Are Accused with that Crime*, was also presented as a sermon by the Reverend Increase Mather, still the most influential minister in Massachusetts and president of Harvard College. In it, the ministers noted "the Powers of imagination in the minds of the afflicted," and concluded that innocent people had been put to death. They clearly aimed to put a stop to the witchcraft trials.

The people had had enough. Crops had fallen fallow due to sheer neglect as curious citizens attended examinations and trials of the accused. Those with family members in prison failed to bring in the harvest or cut enough wood for the approaching winter because they so often journeyed to Salem, Boston, or Ipswich to deliver food, blankets, and prayers of hope to family members locked in prison.

The accusers had gone too far, even daring to target Lady Mary Phips, the governor's wife. When Andover's afflicted named a high-ranking Bostonian, the furious gentleman threatened a costly law suit against his accusers. The senior minister of that town called the entire proceedings *"Our Sin of Ignorance,"* and organized several citizens' petitions that were dispatched to Governor Phips and the court. Following

Portrait of Judge Samuel Sewall (1652–1730), merchant and magistrate. Engraving by O. Pelton, from a portrait painted by Nathaniel Emmons, 1728, at the Massachusetts Historical Society. LIBRARY OF CONGRESS, PRINTS & PHOTOGRAPHS DEPARTMENT, WASHINGTON, D.C.

the execution of eight more victims, whom the Reverend Nicholas Noyes nicknamed the "Firebrands of Hell," on September 22, the Salem Trials were brought to a sudden halt by Governor Phips, the Crown, and the power of public opinion.

The Court of Oyer et Terminer was dissolved by order of the governor on October 15, causing Chief Justice William Stoughton to quit the bench in disappointment and disgust, exclaiming, "[But] we were to have cleared this land of witches!"

Fifty-two cases were still pending and awaiting trial. Many persons, previously convicted and sentenced to die, also remained in prison, awaiting execution. The new Superior Court of Judicature, or *Court of Assize,* was convened under the new charter on January 3, 1692/3, with confession now the sole legal grounds for conviction. Forty-nine of those accused received immediate amnesty and were released upon payment of gaol fees. Three of the confessed witches were found guilty, but soon received the governor's pardon.

Unable to meet her own prison fees, Lydia Dustin, finally exonerated of witchcraft, the capital crime she had been accused of several times, was not permitted to return home to Reading with her two daughters and sixteen-year-old granddaughter, Elizabeth Colson. In March, the sixty-seven-year-old widow perished in Cambridge Prison, for want of 6 shillings.

AFTERMATH OF THE SALEM TRIALS

We have cause to be humbled for the mistakes and errors which have been in these Colonies, in their Proceedings against persons for this crime . . . but such was the darkness of that day . . . we walked in the clouds and could not see our way.
—THE REVEREND JOHN HALE, MINISTER OF BEVERLY,
A MODEST INQUIRY INTO THE NATURE OF WITCHCRAFT,
BOSTON, 1702

In the years that followed, some publicly expressed regret and begged forgiveness for their role in the Trials. In January of 1696, twelve jurors signed a formal apology, confessing that "we ourselves were not capable to understand, nor able to withstand, the mysterious delusions of the powers of darkness and Prince of the Air." To "surviving sufferers," they expressed their "deep sense of sorrow for our errors in acting on such evidence to the condemning of any person; and do hereby declare that we justly fear that we were sadly deluded and mistaken, for which we are much distressed, and do humbly beg forgiveness . . . and do declare, we would, none of us, do such things again, on such grounds, for the whole world." Judge Samuel Sewall who at first supported the Trials, changed his mind following the arrest and execution of his Harvard College friend, George Burroughs. Although Sewall served on the bench of the Court of Oyer et Terminer, he came to realize that innocent people had been put to death. When his daughter died in 1696, he took it as a sign that God was displeased with his behavior. Burdened by "the blame and shame of it," Sewall asked the minister of his Boston church to read his personal apology for "errors in judgment" aloud to the entire congregation.

On August 25, 1706, Ann Putnam Jr., among the most active of all the accusers, stood up in the Salem Meetinghouse as the minister read her apology: ". . . that I, then being in my childhood, should . . . be made an instrument for the accusing of several persons of a grievous crime, whereby their lives were taken away from them, whom now I have just grounds and good reason to believe they were innocent persons; and that it was a great delusion of Satan that deceived me in that sad time . . ."

Abigail Faulkner's Brave Petition[135]
Married to a mentally unstable but well-to-do farmer, Abigail was the youngest of four daughters of the Reverend Francis Dane, Andover's senior minister, whose family was hardest hit of all during the 1692 Witch Hunt. Twenty-six members of Mr. Dane's extended family were accused and arrested. Five of his grandchildren were imprisoned, while two of his daughters were convicted witches, and two nieces executed.

Abigail Faulkner was accused of witchcraft along with her sister, several nieces and nephews, and her own two daughters, ages eight and ten, who confessed to being witches and testified against their own mother. Goodwife Faulkner refused to confess since she was convinced this would be to tell a lie before God. Abigail Faulkner was convicted and condemned to die, but after four months in prison, was able to "plead her belly." She was released on bail and sent home, her trip to the gallows postponed until after the birth of her seventh child. Her death sentence was finally commuted by the new Superior Court of Judicature, and Goodwife Faulkner was released at the General Gaol Delivery.

Yes, the witches were free, but they all quickly discovered that they no longer had any legal status, nor could they reclaim their former property or respect within the community. In 1703, Abigail Dane Faulkner penned this moving petition to the General Court at Boston:

> I am as yet suffered to live but this only as a Malefactor convicted upon record of ye most heinous crimes that mankind can be supposed to be guilty of, which besides its utter ruining and defacing my reputation . . . will certainly expose myself to Imminent Danger by new accusations which will thereby be the more readily believed will remain a perpetual brand of infamy upon my family. I do humbly pray that the High and Honorable Court will please to take my case into serious consideration and order the Defacing of ye record against me so that I may be freed from ye evil consequences thereof.

Goodwife Faulkner was begging the court for a *Reversal of Attainers*. She formally requested to have her sentence legally revoked and her name cleared. Twenty-two survivors and the families of those who had been put to death soon followed, addressing their own petitions to the General Court, and asking for reparations for the loss of life and property suffered during the 1692 Witch Hunt. In 1711, the Attainers were reversed, the court declaring "their convictions, judgments, and Attainers repealed, reversed, and made null and void and that no corruption of blood or forfeitures of goods and chattels be incurred and they be reinstated in their just Credit and reputation."

Nearly £600 was paid out, in varying amounts, to the majority of the victims or to their survivors. It was not until 1957 that the Commonwealth of Massachusetts passed a resolution to clear the names of all the victims of the 1692 Witch Hunt. Only the names of those whose families signed the 1704 Petition appeared on the 1711 legal Attainer document, so the State Legislative Committee on Constitutional Law passed a bill 246 years later "to reverse the attainers, judgments, and convictions for witchcraft of all the condemned."

Part VII

Crimes against Property

Andrew Low Jr., for breaking into Mr. Ling's house, where he brake open a cupboard and took from there some strong water, and 6d in money, and rasac't the house from room to room, and left open the doors, for which fact being committed to prison, broke forth and escaped, and still remains horrible obstinate and rebellious against his parents, and incorrigible under all the means that have been used to reclaim him. Thereupon, it was ordered that he shall be as severely whip't as the rule will bear, and work with his father as a prisoner, with a lock upon his leg, so that he may not escape.

—New Haven Court Records, 1643

Throughout New England's first few generations the majority of robberies were committed by overworked and underfed or disgruntled servants. Horses and hogs were common targets but ownership of wandering livestock could be easily determined by a nick or clip in an animal's ear. Clothing was inevitably endangered property since, as seventeenth-century probate inventories reveal, textiles were second only to silver and real estate in estimated value. And cloth could be quickly exchanged for ready cash on the open market. If it could be ascertained that no one was home at the time a house was broken into, penalties were lighter.

Robbery, along with breaking and entering, became more frequent as population and urbanization increased. With the growth of trade and commerce a new merchant class developed and the gulf between rich and poor deepened. These wealthy gentlemen aimed to live like their counterparts in Old England, outfitting stylish Georgian mansions with carpets, drapery, furniture and objets d' art imported from Europe. After 1711, robbery "in the field or highway" was made a capital offense on the second conviction instead of the third as formerly had been the case. In January of 1715, Boston selectmen noted "the great perplexity" residents felt with the alarming increase of thievery in the city and decided to offer financial rewards for any who apprehended these criminals. That same year the Massachusetts General Court made these property crimes punishable upon first conviction since the 1692 Provincial Law, designating robbery a capital offense only on the third conviction had done nothing to reduce incidents of theft. In 1770, with more vagrants and "strolling poor" flooding into the larger towns, breaking and entering was deemed a capital offense whether or not the dwelling place was inhabited and "apt to be injurious to the goods and lives of others" at the time of this particular property crime. Furthermore, burglars would suffer punishment "without benefit of clergy," demonstrating how seriously authorities now viewed these crimes against property.

"TIEFIN'"

Tiefin' (or theft) was the most common crime committed by the poor and disenfranchised during the colonial period, and what they were most apt to steal was food, live chickens, and clothing. Sarah Booker, a York spinster, was prosecuted for stealing three skeins of linen yarn in 1769. In 1653, The *Maine Court Records* also note that Alice Berry, wife of Richard of Yarmouth, was sent to the stocks for stealing a neck cloth from William Pearce's wife. She was soon in court again, "for going into the house of Samuel Arnold, and taking bacon and eggs when there was nobody at home. Sentenced for this and other doings of like nature ... to sit in the stocks for an hour each at Yarmouth and Plymouth." Apparently, public humiliation did not deter hungry Alice, for the following year, she was found guilty in Plymouth Court of going into Benjamin Hammond's house, where she "feloniously tooke away a woman's shift, new made, but without sleeves, and a piece of pork." In 1655, she was required to either pay a fine or return to the stocks "for thievish milking [of] the cow of Thomas Phelps."

Simon Bradstreet, Andover's founding father and chief magistrate, and a future Massachusetts governor, repeatedly had problems with a servant named John. In the spring of 1661, Mr. Bradstreet took the matter to the town constable:

You are hereby required to attach the body of John to answer such charges brought against him for stealing pigges, capons, malt, bacon, butter, eggs and for breaking open a cellar door in the night several times.

Evidence presented at court revealed John to be "in the habit of stealing chickens from Mister Bradstreet, then building a fire behind the barn to roast them, enjoying some himself and sharing the rest with servants from neighboring households."[136]

The *Boston Court Records of 1679* reported a "Thomas Davis of Medfield convicted in Court by his own confession of Stealing a pair of blew drawers etc. from Hannah Manning, Widow, and having formerly been convicted of the like and other Crimes."

The Court of Assistants had previously declared Goodman Davis one of a pair of "Incorrigible Thieves." His sentence was fifteen stripes at the whipping post and payment of treble damages to the widow. Upon release from prison, he was ordered to immediately depart Boston.

Most convicted Massachusetts thieves got twenty lashes at the whipping post, and were ordered to serve a spell in stocks or pillory. In addition, any person convicted of stealing was required to make three-fold restitution of the stolen item, or else replace the estimated value of each stolen item. Since few impoverished persons or servants could manage this, these thieves were reduced to becoming another man's servant, or receiving an extension of their previous term of servitude.

After New Hampshire made branding for burglary its punishment, burning upon forehead or cheek became the penalty for burglary throughout the New England colonies, although the hot iron was generally reserved for repeat offenders in Massachusetts. New Hampshire law specified the "B" brand on the right hand for the first offense, the left hand for the second, and any evildoer who committed theft on the Lord's

Day received a "B" burned in the center of the forehead. According to *New Hampshire Court Records*, one of the offender's ear was then nailed to a board and lopped off, followed by ten stripes at the whipping post. The third offense meant a trip to the gallows.

In 1677 Ipswich, according to the *Essex County Court Records*, George Major was convicted of "burglary and stealing pork and beef from John Knight, was fined and ordered to be branded on the forehead with the letter B and bound to good behavior." In 1681, George Fairfax, a Boston servant already convicted of two previous burglaries, including one on the Sabbath, was found guilty of stealing silver clasps, buckles, and money from his master, Timothy Dwight. Fairfax was severely whipped and branded with a "B" on the forehead. Soon sold off to another master, the court still required him to make the threefold restitution to Mr. Dwight.

Connecticut established its own laws regarding burglary in 1735. The letter "B" was to be branded upon the forehead on the first offense, with the malefactor's right ear nailed to a board and cut off, followed by ten lashes at the whipping post. On the second offense, another "B" was to be burned into the thief's face and the other ear cropped, followed by twenty-five whiplashes, with hanging on the third offense. In 1736, Massachusetts law also made death the penalty on the third conviction, should the item stolen be valued at £3 or more.

Native Americans accused of theft generally received even harsher sentences. In 1659, Rhode Island decided that Indians convicted of theft involving more than 20 shillings who could not make restitution would be exiled "into slavery to any foreign country of the English subjects. And the plaintiff was to be reimbursed from the sale price of the Indian." This practice was fairly common. A "notorious thief who broke out of jail" and "was lurking dangerously about Plymouth Colony," was sold to Barbados, "to satisfy his debts and to free the colony from so ill a member."[137]

Punishments also included branding and mutilation, the same as white thieves. The *Essex County Court Records*, November 1672 reports "Thomas Robbin, an Indian, for excess in drink and for Breaking into the house of the Worshipfull Mr. Simon Bradstreet." He was sentenced to be branded on the forehead with a letter B, and to pay costs to the Andover constable."

Boston Judge Samuel Sewall noted in his diary on July 1, 1685: "An Indian was branded in Court and had a piece of his ear cut off for burglary."

Money crimes increased dramatically along with New England's population and rising economy, and in turn, penalties for crimes against property became increasingly stringent. By 1704 the laws of Massachusetts, New Hampshire, Connecticut, and Rhode Island included the death penalty for counterfeiters. The usual punishment was branding on the cheek or forehead, and double reimbursement was required to be paid any persons so defrauded.

Counterfeiting was not too difficult a crime to commit, given apprenticeship and experience with the printing press, but it was a crime that threatened government finance and so had to be dealt with severely.

In 1704, with the final choice of penalties left to the judge's discretion, a guilty counterfeiter could be branded on the right check with "F" for Forgery, flogged up to forty lashes, put in the pillory, get an ear cut off and be sent to gaol. The double damages the incarcerated money-maker was required to reimburse his victim, as well as all prison fees, were to be collected from the malefactor's estate, rather than covered by his or her questionable cash.[138]

Prior to 1805, Massachusetts counterfeiters still risked losing an ear and spending a year in jail. The convict's goods were seized to pay prison fees, or the debt could be worked off by becoming an indentured servant to another man for up to seven years. A forger might get an ear cropped or be branded with an "F" on the right cheek, after being locked in the town pillory for an hour or so. A "T" for Thief, "B" for Burglary, or any other brand resulted in lifelong, visible scars, warning fellow citizens not to risk doing business with this scoundrel in the future.

The *Boston Chronicle* published the following item on November 20, 1769: "We hear from Worcester that on the eighth instant one Lindsay stood in the Pillory there one hour after which he received 30 stripes at the public whipping-post, and was then branded in the hand. His crime was Forgery."

Highway robbery and breaking and entering were more serious crimes, "apt to be injurious to the Goods and Lives of others." These crimes also called for the capital letter "B" to be burned into the forehead, an hour beside the gallows with the rope around the neck, and a whipping up to the legal limit of thirty-nine stripes on the second offense, with death on the third conviction. As highway robbery increased in the early eighteenth century, lawmakers added a prison sentence of six months to branding, and death on the second conviction. Road travel was apparently becoming increasingly dangerous at this time, for during a session in 1761, the Massachusetts General Court made highway robbery a capital offense upon the first conviction.[139]

ARSON

It is not usual for Providence to permit the Devil to come from Hell to throw fire on the tops of Houses; this might cause a whole town to be burnt to Ashes.
—INCREASE MATHER, *CASES OF CONSCIENCE*, BOSTON, 1692

Though relatively rare, arson was always considered a felony, and it was a crime that terrorized all citizens, since most structures were made of wood and built close together. There were laws forbidding "tobacco taking," as smoking was then called, "within twenty Poles of any House, or so near as may endanger the same, or near the Barn, Corn, or Haycock, as may occasion the firing thereof ... nor in any Inn or common Victual House ..." One 1672 Massachusetts law specifically targeted "those who set fires in certain seasons in the woods or commons so as to endanger the corn fields."

Indeed, Native Americans understood the power of fire to terrorize the colonists. Indians frequently employed fire as a weapon of war. Barns, houses, and outbuildings were nearly always torched during attacks on English villages. The Abenaki, Wabanaki, Micmac, and other New England Algonquin tribes also regularly burned livestock in these raids. These warriors observed that unlike the Frenchmen who had come to Canada mostly as fur trappers and beaver traders, the English seemed determined to remain forever upon these lands. Unlike most Frenchmen, the English had brought along their families, chopped back the forests, dammed the rivers and streams to build mills, raised towns, and operated large farms. The Indians understood the dependence of these particular white immigrants upon their tame beasts. Surely without their precious live-stock, these troublesome English would simply board their ships and sail back across the sea from whence they had come.

Even when the perpetrator was a colonist, arson was difficult to prove since everyone cooked over open hearths—although cautious housekeep-ers did keep buckets of sand and water within easy reach to douse errant sparks. When arson was committed, it was a crime most apt to be carried out by disgruntled servants, Native Americans, or slaves, frequently as an act of revenge against masters.

Henry Stevens faced the Essex County Court of Assistants on Novem-ber 1, 1641, "for carelessly firing the barn of his master, Mr. John Humfry." His sentence was to serve Humfry another twenty-one years to compensate for the loss of his master's corn and hay.

Threats of arson were also taken seriously. The *Essex County Court Records* of November, 1647, note that Ann Haggett, wife of Henry Haggett, was fined "for wishing the curse of God on Rice Edwards: that fire might come down from heaven and consume his house, as it did Goodwife Ingersoll's barn."

In 1652, the Massachusetts General Court imposed the death pen-alty for arson on "anyone over the age of fifteen who willingly and mali-ciously burned a dwelling house or public building, barn, mill, malt house, storehouse, shop, or ship." This was later modified to make arson a capital offense only if a building happened to be occupied at the time.

Edith, the wife of Salem mariner Mordecai Craford, was indicted by the grand jury of Essex County's Court of Assistants "for not hav-ing the fear of God before your eyes and being Instigated by the devil, did wittingly, willingly & feloniously fire the dwelling house lately your husband's in Salem and more lately belonging to Captain Thomas Savage or Anthony Ashby at or upon the tenth day of September last." William Curtis testified to being at Mr. Ashby's the night the house burned and claimed Goody Craford "fired it sure enough." Several witnesses swore in court that they had heard Anthony Ashby say he "would have Goody Craford hanged . . . for she was a witch and if she were not a witch already she would be one and therefore it was as good to hang her at first as last."

Samuel Archard testified to being at Mordecai Craford's house the day following the fire and heard Ashby and Goody Craford talking. Ashby said he "wished her not to finish the house for he would provide a warmer house for her and that she had said enough to hang her." Goody Craford pleaded "not guilty," claiming she would "be tried by God and Country." The jury returned the verdict in her favor. Mordecai and Edith Craford subsequently sued Anthony Ashby for defamation, unjust molestation, and false imprisonment. Ashby lost the case and was also liable for court costs.[140]

"Black Jack" Hanged for Arson

In September 1681, a slave who went by the name of Black Jack was executed in Boston for torching a house. On the night of July 14, Jack, who belonged to Samuel Wolcott of Wethersfield, allegedly set Lieutenant William Clark's house on fire in Northampton, "feloniously, by taking a brand of fire from the hearth and swinging it up and down to find victuals." Black Jack admitted to being careless, but judge and jury had evidence that led them to believe he had set the fire on purpose. He was "sentenced to be hanged by the neck till dead, then to be taken down and burnt to ashes in the fire with [the body of] Maria, negro." Maria, another slave, had been previously convicted of setting fire to her master's dwelling place in Roxbury, along with a second house. She pleaded guilty before the Court of Assistants and went to the gallows at Boston the same day as Jack.[141]

In 1709, Sabina, a slave belonging to Haverhill magistrate Nathaniel Saltonstall, "feloniously blew up and destroyed her master's house to the danger of his family," after robbing it. Sabina was not executed but was required to pay the sum of £168 to the colony treasury, and to reimburse her master £12 for his losses, a sum she obviously did not have. Tom, her fellow slave in the Saltonstall household, offered to pay back the money. Instead the court ordered her to be "sold beyond the sea" as a means of paying her debt, as well as removing potential danger from the community.[142]

A sixteen-year-old Native American girl from Marblehead named Hittee failed at her first attempt at arson, but later, in 1712, managed to successfully burn down her master's house. According to the *Massachusetts Supreme Judicial Court Records*, March 25, 1712, she was sold out of New England.

PART VIII

The Third Colonial Crime Wave: Pirates

"Now then, me bullies: would you rather do the gallows dance and hang in chains until the crows pick your eyes from your rotten skulls? Or would you feel the roll of a stout ship beneath your feet again?"
—CHARLES LAUGHTON, IN THE TITLE ROLE OF THE 1945 FILM, *CAPTAIN KIDD*

DISNEY AND JOHNNY DEPP HAVE CARRIED THE MYTHS AND LEGENDS first dreamed up in books like Robert Louis Stevenson's *Treasure Island* and in countless illustrations by Howard Pyle and N. C. Wyeth into the twenty-first century. Yet these imaginative, romantic renditions seldom reflect the true state of affairs of piracy during the colonial era. During the late seventeenth and early eighteenth centuries, pirates plagued the Atlantic seaboard, as well as many other parts of the world, threatening commerce and lives. The Massachusetts General Court passed a law against piracy on October 15, 1673. Eleven years later, piracy on the high seas was made a capital offense, which included "to entertain, harbor, or trade with privateers, pyrates, or other offenders."

With the new Provincial Charter of 1692, the property crimes of arson and piracy were added to the list including murder, sodomy, bestiality, concealing bastards, incest, and rape, as capital crimes calling for the death penalty.

The majority of buccaneers who plundered and captured colonial ships along the New England coast hailed from Great Britain, and were intent upon confiscating any goods that could possibly be sold. As commercial trade with the West Indies and foreign nations increased, these "Brethren of the Coast" became such a menace and scourge to ship owners, merchant seamen, coasters, and local fishermen, that stricter laws were soon passed against any persons aiding and abetting these "sea-robbers" who sailed beneath various Jolly Roger flags.[143]

Newport, Rhode Island, sent out many legitimate privateers under the English flag with permission to plunder and prey upon French vessels or any ships belonging to the enemies of England. Yet there was a fine line between legal privateering with government permission and bold piracy, and it proved a line dangerously easy to cross. The "freebooters" plaguing the Atlantic Coast were a multicultural mix of homeless adventurers. Many were escaped slaves and disgruntled indentured servants who had suffered abuse from their masters. Others were former members of pirate crews captured off other vessels during bold sea attacks, or men kidnapped as beggar boys from the streets of London, Bristol and other ports. Some were prison escapees or men on the run from debts owed. For the most part, pirates lived short and violent lives, yet they prided themselves on being free men, and generously shared their stolen booty with shipmates.

Captains of pirate vessels were customarily elected by democratic vote, with every man aboard sworn to secrecy. Crew members abided by a list of articles that included specific rules regarding the allocation and maintenance of pistols, cutlasses, and daggers, the equitable distribution of profits, the amount of compensation paid for the loss of any limb, and the honorable treatment of all captured females. In the Articles of the *Revenge,* the penalties for ungentlemanly conduct were clearly spelled out by Captain John Phillips: "If at any Time we meet with a prudent Woman, that Man that offers to meddle with her, without her Consent, shall suffer present and immediate Death."[144]

Yet these scourges of the seas were villains and thieves whose oft-repeated slogan was, "No prey, no pay!"

New England's first trial and execution of pirates took place in 1673, when William Forrest, John Smith, and Alexander Wilson swung from the scaffold at Boston. This event took place just after the Massachusetts Court adopted the death penalty for piracy on October 15, 1673. Massachusetts executed five pirates in 1675, and thirteen more in 1689.

The grandest execution of "Raiders & Sea Robbers" was staged at Newport, Rhode Island, on July 19, 1723, when twenty-five pirates were hanged alongside their captain, Charles Harris. This well-advertised event "was attended by a vast multitude from every part of New England . . . Their Black Flag, with the Portraiture of Death having an Hour-Glass in one Hand, and a Dart in the other, at the end of which was the Form of a Heart with three Drops of Blood falling from it, was affix'd at one Corner of the Gallows. This Flag they call'd '*Old Roger*,' and often used to say they would live and die under it."[145]

"Never was there a more doleful sight in all this land, then while they were standing on the stage waiting for the stopping of their Breath and the Flying of their Souls into the Eternal World. And oh, how awful the sounds of their dying moans."[146]

Rhode Island, however, did not adhere to Boston and London's custom of chaining its executed pirates in metal cages and keeping them on public display to serve as dire warnings and lessons in morality for the living.

DIXEY BULL—PIRATE OFF PEMAQUID

There arose up against us one Bull, who went to the Eastward a trading, and turned Pirate and took a Vessel or two, and plundered some Planters thereabouts, and intended to return into the Bay, and do mischief to our Magistrates here in Dorchester and other places. But as they were weighing Anchor, one of Mr. Short's men shot from the shore and struck the principal Actor dead and the rest were filled with Fear and Horror . . . afraid of the very Rattling of the Ropes . . .

—ROGER CLAP, *MEMOIRS,* 1640

Dixey Bull was the first of many pirates to plague the Massachusetts coastal waters, and he was one of the few who got away. The son of a reputable London family who was described by Governor John Winthrop as being "of adventurous disposition" sailed to Boston in 1631. He was likely sent to New England by Sir Ferdinando Gorges, who, eager to see his Agamenticus lands settled by Englishmen, granted the young gentleman some land in what would become York County, Maine. In June of 1632, as Dixey was trading woolen coats and blankets for Indian beaver pelts around Penobscot Bay, some French sailors seized his shallop in shallow water, stealing all the wares from his small open sailboat. These same Frenchmen had previously rifled the Penobscot trading post maintained by the Plymouth Colony.

Incensed, Bull returned to Boston where he collected a crew of fifteen men and headed back Down East. Hard as they hunted, Dixey Bull and his crew failed to locate the French sea-robbers. With supplies and morale running low, Captain Bull decided to attack and plunder several trading vessels, even capturing new crew members to sail with him.[147]

Fur trader turned pirate captain, Dixey Bull launched a surprise attack upon peaceful Pemaquid Village, where they looted the warehouse filled with merchandise valued at more than £500, then set it and other buildings afire. As they sailed off, Captain Bull's second-in-command, manning the tiller, was killed by musket shots coming from the fort on shore. Apparently, seeing a comrade's blood spilled, Dixey Bull's crew of wannabe pirates panicked and decided to a man, upon an immediate career change

Meanwhile, back in Boston, as John Winthrop tells the tale in his journal, a search-and-seize mission was organized to go after Captain Dixey Bull. Massachusetts Bay sent out a ship with twenty armed men to join another expedition sailing out of Piscataqua. Maritime historians consider this the earliest organized naval fleet and the first hostile fleet outfitted in New England.

Winthrop went on to describe this mutual naval effort:

At a meeting of all the Massachusetts Bay Assistants on December 4, it was agreed, in regard that the extremity of the snow, frost had hindered the making ready of the bark . . . that those of Piscataqua had sent out two pinnaces and two shallops, above a fortnight before, to defer any further expedition against the pirates till they heard what was done by those . . . By letters from Captain Neal and Mr. Hilton, it was certified that they had sent out all the forces they could against the pirates viz. four pinnaces and shallops and forty men, who coming to Pemaquid, were there wind-bound about three weeks.

... Dixy Bull & fifteen more of the English, who kept about the east, were turned pirates, and had taken divers boats, and rifled Pemaquid. Here upon the governor called a council, and it was agreed to send his bark with twenty men, to join those of Piscataqua, for the taking of said pirates.[148]

With the weather working to Dixey Bull's advantage, the search was called off, and New England's first pirate was never captured or brought to justice. Though some claimed he "went over to the French," Captain Bull eventually made his way back to England, his pirate career over nearly as soon as it began.

CAPTAIN KIDD—THE PIRATE WHO WAS FRAMED

As the seventeenth century turned into the eighteenth, Boston Prison was crowded with captured buccaneers, including the notorious Captain Kidd, the most unfortunate pirate ever to sail the seas. Privateer turned pirate, he unwittingly became the hapless victim of political intrigue.

The son of a Puritan minister, William Kidd was born in Scotland about 1655 and went to sea as a young man. He soon became a highly respected mariner and sea merchant. In August of 1689, William Kidd arrived on the Caribbean island of Nevis, in command of a twenty-gun vessel that he had captured from the French and renamed *Blessed William*, after the King of England. Preferring piracy to privateering, most of Kidd's eighty-man crew mutinied, taking the ship with them, abandoning Kidd.

Richard Coote, Earl of Bellomont, then governor of Barbados, recommended Kidd, now a captain without a vessel, assume command of a new government ship and serve king and country once more as a privateer. William Kidd was soon summoned to England to negotiate this royal commission and obtain funds for outfitting a ship to engage in covert missions. In April of 1696, Captain Kidd sailed out of Plymouth, England, commander of *Adventure Galley*, a 287-ton vessel with thirty-four guns and a crew of one hundred men, committed to defending the English Crown against its French enemies and all sea-robbers and raiders. Kidd's mission was also to protect British commercial interests in the Indian Ocean and Eastern seas, where piracy had become rampant.

When Lord Bellomont became the governor of New York and Massachusetts, he joined other investors in helping to finance Captain Kidd's ventures. His orders were to return to Boston where he was to deliver "the whole of goods, Prizes, Merchandizes, Treasure, and other things that shall be taken from pirates."[149]

By December Kidd was in the South Atlantic and on the lookout for a new crew, since many on the *Adventure Galley* were ill or dead of scurvy. In desperate need of supplies as well as mariners, Captain Kidd sailed for Madagascar on the Arabian Coast, arriving there in January 1697. According to Captain Kidd's later testimony, it was here that his new crew also threatened mutiny, along with his very life, if he would not permit them to give up privateering for the more lucrative career of piracy.

It was on the deck of the *Adventure Galley* too, that William Kidd accidentally killed his gunner, William Moore, leader of the mutiny against him. The captain called Moore "a lousy dog," to which Moore replied, "[I]f he was a dog, it was Kidd who made him so." The captain then grabbed a wooden bucket bound with iron hoops and slammed it down on the gunner's head. Moore died of head wounds the following day.

It was at this point that privateer William Kidd unwittingly crossed over into the illegal territory of piracy, and with his crew was soon plundering ships, including several belonging to the East India Company. In January of 1698, they seized the *Quedah Merchant*, which was flying French colors. This handsome vessel was owned by Mukhlis Khan, the Great Moghul himself, with whom England wished to stay on the best of terms.

When Kidd attacked the Moghul's ship, he stole money, silk, calico, and other costly textiles, sugar, opium, and iron. Captain Kidd renamed his captured ship *Cara Merchant*. Representatives of the East India Company were incensed and demanded immediate restitution. They filed formal complaints with the Crown against Captain Kidd. (Kidd's later defense in court was that the two Indian ships he captured had been sailing under French passes issued by the French East Indies Company at the time, which made them enemy vessels of England, and thus, Kidd claimed, "lawful prizes for any privateer.")

By the spring of 1699, Kidd was back in the West Indies, where he sold off much of his confiscated cargo. He was spotted in a sloop, carrying sixty pound weight of gold, a hundred weight of silver, and a number of bales of valuable East India textiles, estimated to be worth more than £30,000.

A message was dispatched informing Captain Kidd that he would receive a King's Pardon if he brought ship and treasure back to Boston. Kidd would then receive safe passage since he claimed to have left another ship loaded with gold and other valuables anchored off the African coast.

On his way back to Boston, Captain Kidd stopped at Gardiner's Island at the tip of Long Island, home to a previous financial backer named John Gardiner. Here, the captain supposedly unloaded (and, perhaps, buried) most of what he had plundered, taking care to get a properly signed receipt from Gardiner. This treasure was believed to have later been confiscated by the Earl of Bellomont at the time of William Kidd's trial.

The captain insisted that every bit of treasure had been legally seized from ships sailing under French colors, and furthermore, he had written passes to prove it, passes that he had previously turned over to Lord Bellomont. These documents also certified that Kidd plundered the two Moorish ships against his will and had been coerced into acts of piracy by his crew. These documents mysteriously disappeared.

Kidd's influential supporters on both sides of the Atlantic totally deserted him, and back in London, the Lords of Trade issued a letter demanding "apprehension of the obnoxious pirate Kidd." No one was more surprised than Captain Kidd when, on orders of the Earl of Bellomont, he was arrested and thrown into Boston Prison. Accused of piracy, William Kidd was now an embarrassment to the Crown. The King—and the English merchants—were anxious to keep trade with the East India Company intact. For the rest of his miserable life, Kidd remained a victim of international intrigue and deceit.

William Kidd spent nearly a year in Boston Prison, incapacitated by sixteen-pound leg irons, before he was transported back to England. Prior to 1700, anyone accused of piracy faced trial and judgment before England's High Court of Admiralty. On February 3, 1700, Captain Kidd and several other pirates, shackled and dragging chains, were led aboard the British man-of-war *Advice*, and taken to London for trial.

The unfortunate captain spent another year in London's Newgate Prison, awaiting trial. Just before being taken into court, William Kidd wrote a letter to the authorities, testifying to his innocence.

> *I took no ships but such as had French passes, for my justification. In confidence they would and ought to be allowed for my defense. I surrendered myself to my Lord Bellomont . . . But my Lord Bellomont, having sold his share in my ship and in ye Adventure Prize, thought it his Interest to make me a pirate, whereby he could claim a share of my Cargo, and in order to it, strip't me of ye French passes, frightened and wheedled some of my men to misrepresent me, and by his letters to his friends, advised them to admit me a pyrate . . . whatsoever my fate must be, I shall not contribute to my own destruction by pleading to this Indictment, till my passes are restored to me . . . I am not afraid to die, but will not be my own Murderer* [150]

They first put William Kidd on trial for murder:

> *. . . being moved and seduced by the instigations of the Devil . . . did make an assault in and upon William Moore upon the high seas with a wooden Bucket, bound with iron hoops, giving said William Moore . . . one mortal bruise of which he did languish and die.*

The defendant pleaded "not guilty," claiming that Moore, who served as gunner aboard the *Adventure Galley*, was the same man who had led the mutiny against him. Yet other crew members from that ship testified against their former captain, likely in order to save their own lives.

Now that the authorities could have Kidd executed for the murder of William Moore, they proceeded to put him on trial for piracy. The beleaguered captain continued to demand that the French passes he gave Lord Bellomont in all good faith, be produced as proof of his innocence. He was well aware that his life depended upon those two documents.

When the sentence of death was pronounced, Captain Kidd addressed the court, "My Lords, it is a very hard judgment. For my part, I am innocentest of them all, only I have been sworn against by perjured persons."[151]

Captain Kidd was as unlucky in death as in life. Six members of his former crew were executed along with their captain, but as he was being hanged on May 23, 1701, the rope snapped, and he dropped onto the mud below. According to eyewitnesses, Captain Kidd had consumed so much rum and brandy prior to his march to the gallows that he felt no pain, nor was he aware of either his fall or cheers from the crowd of spectators. Hanged again, Captain Kidd's body was then dipped in tar, wrapped in chains, then placed in a steel cage, where exposed to sun, storms, and seagulls, his bones hung for many years, a dire warning to all who passed his way.

Two hundred years later, the documents that would have spared the captain's life turned up in the archives of the British Public Records Office. William Kidd had been telling the truth all along.

Re-created by such storytellers as Robert Louis Stevenson and artists Howard Pyle and N. C. Wyeth, Captain Kidd became a great deal more menacing after death than he had ever been in life. Some believe he may have buried his booty rather than squandering it, as did most pirates, and legends persist as to where Captain Kidd's treasure lies. Ballads have been written and sung about his life and death, and several movies made.

CAPTAIN JOHN QUELCH—A PRIVATEER HANGED FOR PIRACY

England and France were again at war, and five well-to-do Boston merchants had the 80-ton brigantine *Charles* outfitted for privateering. On July 13, 1703, Joseph Dudley, governor of the Massachusetts Bay Colony, commissioned the *Charles* to attack French shipping "in pursuit of the Queen's enemies" off Acadia, Newfoundland, and New England.

Daniel Plowman, captain of the *Charles*, became gravely ill before the ship sailed out of port. He quickly dispatched a letter to the ship's owners, warning them that his crew was likely dangerous, and suggesting that when the vessel went to sea, it carry a different captain and crew. With Plowman still confined to his sickbed, the crew mutinied, locking the captain in his cabin. They wanted John Quelch, the ship's lieutenant, to assume command. Captain Plowman was pulled out of his bunk, pleading his life be spared. This was not to be, and poor Plowman was tossed overboard, along with several other ship's officers, as *"Old Roger"* was hoisted up the flag pole.

During the next three months, Captain Quelch captured nine Portuguese vessels off Brazil, unaware that England and Portugal had recently become allies. The booty they confiscated consisted of "a considerable quantity of gold dust, some [gold] bars, silver and gold coins, ammunition, rum, Brazilian sugar, and fine textiles, which they are violently suspected to have gotten and obtained by felony and piracy from some of Her Majesties' Friends and Allies . . ."[152]

When the *Boston News-Letter* of May 15–22, 1704, carried the following announcement—"Arrived at Marblehead, Captain Quelch in the Brigantine that Captain Plowman went out in and said to come from New Spain and have made a good voyage"—the merchants who owned the *Charles* immediately became suspicious. They assumed their vessel to be sailing the Caribbean on a privateering commission against France. The men filed a formal complaint, accusing John Quelch of *"felonious piracy."* Governor Joseph Dudley sent his relative, Paul Dudley, then attorney general, in hot pursuit. Dudley's assignment was to locate the *Charles* at Marblehead and find the gold dust and other booty believed to have been confiscated from Portuguese vessels. Captain Quelch and his pirate crew were soon caught and brought into Boston Harbor.

Judge Samuel Sewall described the capture and execution of Quelch and his crew in his diary entry of June 7, 1704: "Colonel Nathan Byfield, Mr. Palmer and myself have rec'd an Order from the Governor to search for and seize Pirates and their Treasure, and to hold a Court of Enquiry for this end at Marblehead, because Captain Quelch in the Charles Galley arrived there . . . A chase for pirates that ended with the Trial and hanging of one John Quelch, Commander of the brigantine, Charles, and his crew for piracy and murder."

Twenty-five of the original forty-three crew members from the Charles were locked in Boston Prison, from which eighteen soon managed to escape. Those who remained were arraigned on June 13, 1704, before the Court of Admiralty, in what was the first admiralty trial ever held in New England. Three of the men agreed to "Stand within the Bar, as witnesses on Her Majesty's behalf"—that is, to testify against their shipmates.

Captain Quelch pleaded "not guilty" and asked the court if he "might not have Council allowed him upon any matter of law that might happen."

Though the judges considered "the articles under which Captain Quelch was arraigned [as] plain matters of fact," he was assigned a respected Scots lawyer then living in Boston.

On the last day of June in 1704, six pirates were marched through the streets of Boston to their execution at Scarlets Wharf. The convicts were ushered to the scaffold by forty armed guards, the provost marshal, several town constables, and two clergymen. The lead militiaman carried the Silver Oar, which was the traditional emblem of a pirate execution. Prior to being hanged, thirty-eight-year-old John Quelch told one minister that although he was not afraid of death nor of the gallows, he did fear what was to follow, saying, "I *am* afraid of a Great God, and a Judgment to come."

Upon the scaffold, the condemned captain removed his hat and gallantly bowed to the crowd. "Gentlemen, 'tis but little I have to speak. What I have to say is this: I desire to be informed for what I am here. I am condemned only upon Circumstances. I forgive all the World . . ."

When one member of the crew told the crowd to "beware of false company," Captain Quelch shouted, "They should also take care how they brought money into New England to be hanged for it."

" 'Tis very hard for so many men's lives to be taken away for so little gold!" another doomed former crew member lamented.

On June 30, 1704, Judge Sewall recorded the event in his diary:

> When I came to see how the River was cover'd with People, I was amazed. Some say there were 100 boats—150 boats and Canoes, said Cousin Moody of York. Mr. Cotton Mather came with Captain Quelch and six others for Execution from the Prison to Scarlett's Wharf, and from thence in the Boat to the place of Execution . . . Mr. Mather pray'd for them standing upon the Boat. Ropes were all fasten'd to the Gallows. When the Scaffold was let sink, there was such a screech of the women that my wife heard it sitting in our Entry next the Orchard . . . a full mile from the place.

Never one to miss an execution, the Reverend Cotton Mather preached the *Brief Discourse Occasioned by a Tragical Spectacle in a Number of Miserables*

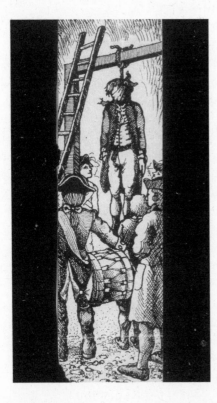

Eyewitnesses often sketched executions to be later sold as souvenirs or covers for printed gallows sermons. Although this pirate's name is unknown, his clothing tells us that the execution took place in the early 18th century. The condemned man climbed the ladder to the scaffold, where the sheriff or hangman draped a cloth over his face. Before being turned off the rope that broke his neck, the pirate heard the militia man's drum-roll. EARLY-EIGHTEENTH-CENTURY BROADSIDE, AUTHOR'S COLLECTION

Under Sentence of Death for Piracy. In this sermon, soon printed and widely circulated, Mather discussed the dangerous fine line between privateering and piracy. "Privateering so easily degenerates into the Piratical . . . the Privateering Trade is usually carried on with an un-Christian Temper and proves an Inlet unto much Debauchery and Iniquity."

THE PICKLED HEAD OF CAPTAIN JOHN PHILLIPS

John Phillips was a skilled and respectable carpenter living and working in England until, apparently struck by wanderlust, he decided on a career change. He signed on as a shipwright on a vessel bound for Newfoundland. Captured by pirates en route and taken aboard the *Good Fortune*, the young man willingly surrendered, preferring piracy over instant death. John Phillips embraced his new life with great enthusiasm, soon earning a reputation for cruelty that even included abusing female captives—something definitely counter to the traditional code that all pirates were expected to follow.

Beginning in the fall of 1718, in an attempt to protect British shipping interests and merchants, and to hopefully bring an end to international violence at sea, King George the First put forth an "Act of Grace," or a proclamation offering clemency to any pirates who pledged to reform and desist from further acts of piracy. Those who turned themselves in to British authorities were promised pardons, particularly if they proved willing to name other such sea scoundrels and help hunt them down. Some crew members of the *Good Fortune* wished to petition for King's Pardons, while others preferred to keep sailing beneath the *Skull and Crossbones*.

John Phillips decided to sign his name requesting a pardon, but once back in England, he learned that several men from his crew had already been arrested and imprisoned, presumably awaiting execution. So John Phillips boarded the next vessel bound for Newfoundland. He jumped ship in a New England port and with four other unworthy seamen, seized a Boston schooner at anchor, claiming it as their own. They renamed the stolen vessel *Revenge* and elected John Phillips captain.

In 1723, Phillips captured the sloop *Dolphin* off Cape Ann, and its crew was forced by Phillips to join his crew on the *Revenge*. One was a Wenham fisherman by the name of John Fillmore, who, along with Edward Chessman, the ship's carpenter, had also been forced into piracy by Phillips. These two would lead the mutiny against their pirate captain.

According to the *Boston News-Letter* of April 30–May 7, 1724, Captain John Phillips and his crew captured some thirty-four different vessels of various sizes and types from Newfoundland and New England to Barbados in little more than a year.

John Rose Archer, who served as Captain Phillips's quartermaster, learned the art of piracy while serving under Edward Teach, the most notorious pirate of them all, that evil, loathsome fellow known as Blackbeard. Archer had given up this perilous life in 1724, for the tranquil life of a fisherman, and was aboard the new sloop *Squirrel* out of Cape Ann, headed for the fishing grounds off Newfoundland, when he met up with

Phillips's ship, *Revenge*. The pirate captain coveted the *Squirrel* for speed, and so attacked Archer's sloop off the Isles of Shoals. A cannon shot, a puff of smoke and black flag unfurled, and Captain John Phillips, notorious for preying upon innocent fishing fleets, quickly made the *Squirrel* his own. Phillips not only confiscated John Archer's vessel, adding its crew members to his own, but he also appointed John Rose Archer as the *Revenge*'s new quartermaster.

During one particularly fierce fight against another pirate ship, John Phillips was hit in the head with a hand-spike, suffering a severe head injury. Though gravely wounded, the captain managed to draw his sword and mortally wound his assailant, but the *Revenge* could not escape another vessel out of Cape Ann that was in pursuit. The next day, Captain Phillips was dead of his wounds, and his captors cut off his head and pickled it in hard liquor, to verify his death.

When they arrested those of the crew still alive, authorities took Phillips's severed head back to Boston with them. The head of this late (but hardly lamented) pirate captain hung in the courtroom throughout the crew's Admiralty Trials for "Piracy, Robbery, and Felony," which began on May 12, 1724. Most of Captain Phillips's crew members had been kidnapped off other vessels and consequently had been looking for any possible chance to escape.

During the trials, crew member John Fillmore managed to convince members of the Admiralty Court that he was forced into piracy against his will. He then testified against another pirate on trial, one William White of Wenham, age twenty-two, as well as accusing John Rose Archer of malicious piracy. Fillmore received a verdict of "*not guilty*," while White was hanged on June 2, "before a multitude of spectators, where he died most penitent." The pirate flag flown by Captain Phillips and his pirate crew waved at the end of the gallows stage: death as a skeleton, its heart pierced by a dart and blood dripping from it, and on the other side, an hourglass, showing how quickly time—and the sands of life—run out.[153]

Twenty-seven-year-old quartermaster Archer also ended his days on the Boston scaffold on June 2, but unlike many of the pirates who were executed, he "dy'd very penitent, with the assistance of two grave Divines to attend him."

"I greatly bewail my Profanations of the Lord's Day and my Disobedience to my Parents," John Rose Archer informed the crowd of spectators.

And my cursing and swearing, and my blasphemy of the Name of the glorious God. Unto which I have added the Sins of Unchastity, and I have provoked the Holy One . . . to leave me unto the Crimes of Piracy and Robbery, wherein I have brought myself with the Guilt of Murder also. But one wickedness that has led me as much as any to all the rest, has been my brutish Drunkenness. By strong Drink I have been heated and hardened into the Crimes that are now more bitter than Death unto me.

Pausing, he then surveyed the crowd before adding, "I *could* wish that the Masters of Vessels would not use their men with so much severity, as many do, which exposes us to great temptations." Had Captain Phillips still been alive, he surely would have understood that the quartermaster's words were meant for him.

From the gallows, the pirate corpses were rowed to an island in Boston Harbor, where, picked at continually by seagulls and vultures, they hung in chains in a gibbet for years, "to be a Spectacle and so, [serve] as a warning to others."

CAPTAIN WILLIAM FLY—"A VERY HARDENED WRETCH"

Born in Bristol, England, William Fly went to sea early and was in Jamaica when invited to serve as boatswain on the *Elizabeth,* a slave ship bound for Guinea on the African Coast. Plotting with several other disgruntled crew members en route, young Fly soon became the leader of a murderous mutiny. He pulled the *Elizabeth's* captain out of bed, and as Captain Green begged and bargained for his life, William Fly whipped him senseless with his cutlass and threw the bleeding man into the sea. The black flag was hoisted, and the pirate crew proceeded to slaughter every officer aboard except for the ship's surgeon, carpenter, and gunner, whose skills they would need. When another British vessel sailed by, shouting a friendly greeting to the late Captain Green, Fly hollered back, "Oh, he is very well, Sir, and at your service!"

Now a pirate ship, the confiscated vessel was rechristened *Fame's Revenge*, and Captain Fly and his crew got busy plundering their prey. They captured ships off the coasts of New England and North Carolina. Near Newfoundland, they even went after a whaling ship, whose captain they cruelly wrapped in chains, before finally killing him.

On June 3, 1726, Captain Fly and his crew spotted a sloop at anchor off Cape Hatteras. It was the *John & Hannah*, bound for Boston. When the gracious captain invited Fly and a few mates into his cabin for a bowl of punch, Fly confessed that he and his comrades were "Gentlemen of Fortune," and that this particular sloop was a finer vessel than *Fame's Revenge*, and they must have her immediately. The captain refused to give up his ship without a fight, so Fly sank it and took the captain aboard *Fame's Revenge*. William Fly continued to pillage his way up the New England coast until finally captured off Brewster, Massachusetts.

It is a fearful thing to fall into the Hands of the Living GOD.

A

SERMON

Preached to some miserable

PIRATES

July 10. 1726.
On the *Lord's Day*, before their Execution.

By *Benjamin Colman*,
Pastor of a Church in *Boston*.

To which is added some Account of said Pirates.

Deut. XVII. 13. *And all the People shall bear and fear, and do no more so presumptuously.*

BOSTON, N. E. Printed for *John Phil. p* and *Thomas Hancock*, and Sold at their Shops. 1726.

"A Sermon Preached to Some Miserable Pirates, by the Reverend Benjamin Colman, On the Lord's Day, before their Execution," Boston, July 10, 1726. COURTESY OF MILNE SPECIAL COLLECTIONS, UNIVERSITY OF NEW HAMPSHIRE LIBRARY

The trials of twenty-seven-year-old William Fly and his crew members were held on July 4, 1726, before Lieutenant Governor Dummer and the judges of Admiralty Court, including Samuel Sewall. When accused of killing the captain of the *Elizabeth*, Fly replied, "I shan't own myself guilty of murder. I did not strike nor wound Master or Mate. 'Twas Mitchel done it! The Captain and his Mate used us barbarously. We poor Men can't have Justice done us . . . They used us like dogs."[154]

Since Captain Fly had coerced many members of his crew into committing acts of piracy, twelve were eventually acquitted. Boldly defiant on the day of his hanging, William Fly flatly refused to go to the Boston meetinghouses to listen to his own execution sermons. The Reverend Benjamin Colman preached to the condemned pirates on the Sunday before they were scheduled to be hanged, and the Reverend Cotton Mather held the congregation spellbound with his own sermon, *They Die Even Without Wisdom*. When published in 1726, it was entitled, *The Vial Poured Out Upon the Sea*.

Clutching a nosegay and decked out in colorful clothing and bright ribbons, Captain William Fly marched through the streets of Boston to the gallows, grinning, waving, and bowing to spectators all along the way. When the hangman fumbled with some knots in the rope, Fry chided him "for not knowing his trade," and, according to Cotton Mather, "rectified matters with his own hands."

The *Boston News-Letter* of July 7–14, 1726, reported on the event:

On Tuesday, the 12th Instant, about 3 p.m. were executed for Piracy, Murder, etc., three of the Condemned Persons mentioned in our Last viz. William Fly, Capt., Samuel Cole, Quarter-Master, and Henry Greenville . . . Fly behaved himself very unbecoming even to the last. Their Bodies were carried in a Boat to a small Island calle'd Nick's-Mate, about 2 Leagues from the town, where the above said Fly was hung up in Irons, as a spectacle for the warning of others, especially sea-faring men; the other Two were buried there.

William Fly enjoyed but a brief career as a bloodthirsty sea scoundrel, but the pirate's body and bones garnered public attention for many years to come, wrapped in chains and hanging from a gibbet on an island off Boston Harbor.

PART IX

Early Prisons

A prison is the grave of the living, where they are shut up from the world and their friends, and the worms that gnaw upon them are their own thoughts and the Jailer. 'Tis a house of meager looks and ill smells; for lice, drink, and tobacco, are the compound; or if you will, 'tis the Suburbs of Hell; and the Persons much the same as there.
—JOHN DUNTON, *LETTERS FROM NEW ENGLAND*, LONDON, 1686

PUNISHMENT IN SEVENTEENTH- AND EIGHTEENTH-CENTURY NEW ENGLAND was usually immediate. Most lawbreakers were quickly sentenced, served a spell in stocks or pillories, got flogged at the whipping post, or paid their fines, and returned home. Early prisons were chiefly holding places where the accused were detained while awaiting trials to be held at the next scheduled court session.

In 1632, two years after the first murderer in New England, John Billington, was executed at Plymouth, the Massachusetts General Court ordered its first prison constructed at Boston, although several years would pass before it was ready to hold any lawbreakers. Standing in the middle of town and surrounded by a stockade fence, Judge Samuel Sewall referred to it as the "Stone Prison." According to the *Essex County Court Records* of September 1663, the County "allowed £50 to build a prison at Salem out of lands already seized which were the Quaker's Lands."

HOUSES OF CORRECTION

After 1640, Massachusetts Bay Court decreed that each county should also have a house of correction. Instead of simply serving as a place to lock up lawbreakers until it was time for their trials, these less-common facilities were places where misbehavior would hopefully be "corrected" through manual labor and by learning a useful trade. Any offender so committed "shall first be whipped not exceeding ten stripes." A house of correction was considered the best place to send common drunkards, disobedient servants, vagrants or vagabonds, or "idle persons who will not worke to earn their own bread," and unmanageable young people, including "Youths, who in the time of worship in the meeting-house commit disorder and Rudeness."[155]

These correctional facilities actually marked the beginning of the notion of criminal reform in American penology.

In 1679, the General Court of Masschusetts Bay Colony ordered the construction of a house of correction in each county at county expense "for the keeping and setting to work of rogues, vagabonds, common beggars, and other lewd, idle and disorderly persons." This law was never fully implemented due to prohibitive costs, so gaols continued to serve this function in many places.

Specifications for houses of correction were sometimes spelled out. The *Connecticut Public Records of 1640* did not provide detailed plans but simply offered broad strokes:

> *Forasmuch, as many stubborn and refractory persons are often taken within these libertyes, and no meet place is yet prepared for the detyneing and keeping of such to their due and deserved punishment, it is ordered that there shall be a House of Correction built of 24 feet long and 16 or 18 broad, with a Cellar, either of wood or stone.*

In 1667, Connecticut ordered every county to have a jail, and in 1701, "voted four sufficient prison-houses be maintained in this Colony."[156] In these jails or prisons, inmates were usually thrown together without regard to gender or age or severity of crimes committed. The following

1726 description of a Connecticut quod or gaol, however, demonstrates a conscious attempt to separate prisoners according to gender.

It is ordered by the justices of Windham that a gaol be built with all possible expedition 31 feet long, 18 feet in breadth. The gaol to be 10 feet high, built of logs, all framed into posts, to be divided into two rooms by a board partition.

Prisons and workhouses were expensive to build and maintain, which is why some villages put lawbreakers inside crude wooden cages. When there was an actual prison building, it was seldom secure. According to one early report, "the keeper locked in two men, who came out without the door being unlocked." One inmate testified to seeing "a man pull up one of the boards overhead in the prison with his hand, going into the chamber of the prison, and others went out under the groundsill and some went out next to the worke-house [or house of correction]." As for Salem Prison in 1672, "any man having no instrument except his own hands could come out as he pleased."[157]

LIFE IN PRISON

The number of prisoners in one cell varied at any given time. During the Salem Trials of 1692, more than 150 persons were jammed into the prisons of Boston, Salem, Ipswich, and Cambridge. Seventeenth and early-eighteenth-century prison conditions were deplorable, aggravated by the stench of unwashed bodies, *nightjars* (or chamber pots), rotting food, and vomit. Inmates were inevitably covered with flea bites that caused constant itching and frequently resulted in infection. Manacles and chains chafed skin into open sores. Mice and rats scampered over bodies lying on vermin-infested straw, pausing to gnaw at anything that smelled tempting.

Inmates were required to pay their own room and board, even though they might be proven innocent at trial or would eventually be executed. George Burroughs, the minister hanged for witchcraft on August 19, 1692, still owed prison-keeper John Arnold 17 shillings and 6 pence when he died.

Bill presented by John Arnold, Keeper of the Boston Prison, March 1692. Itemized are the cost of blankets, chains, and shackles for ten prisoners, as well as transportation costs for several of those accused of witchcraft. The list also testifies to the continual need for prison repairs, including new locks and nails. COURTESY MASSACHUSETTS STATE ARCHIVES, BOSTON

Even if found innocent of a crime, prisoners were required to reimburse charges incurred for blankets and the rental of any fetters or chains. Prisoners or their families even received bills from blacksmiths for making manacles. Then, there were transportation charges due the constable or sheriff who delivered you to cell and court, plus an additional amount to pay the man who whipped you. Land and livestock belonging to prisoners were sometimes confiscated by authorities to cover these costs. According to the *York County Records* after Eunice March gave birth to a child in York Gaol in April, 1765, Robert Rose, the prison-keeper presented her with a bill for expenses, which likely included the services of a local midwife.

The job description of a *turnkey*—also known as gaoler, underkeeper, or deputy sheriff—included maintaining copious records for every person in his custody. In an era long before finger printing, mug shots, and DNA, his books contained a physical description of each prisoner, along with his or her age, place of residence, specific crime, and date of incarceration. "Sworn to the faithful discharge of his duties," the gaoler was also required to record every prisoner's release date, and by what authority he or she had been discharged. Should any prisoner escape, the gaoler was held responsible and fined for negligence.

In September of 1672, Edmond Bridges deposed before the Court of Quarterly Sessions that John Gould "demanding his prisoner at Salem court last November could get answer only that he had broken prison and run away. Also that the keeper of Salem Prison had often been known to take prisoners out of the prison to help him about his own occasions, and sometimes men have run away."

Anyone caught helping a prisoner to escape or providing him with a tool to make his way out of prison would be punished with thirty-nine lashes and a steep fine. "In June of 1670 the Salem Quarterly Court sentenced John Baker whipped ten lashes "for twitching the prison lock of Salem at noon day."

In 1699, Katherine Price, the indentured servant of one Boston prison-keeper, was caught aiding and abetting suspected pirate, Joseph Bradish. Because he was unsuccessful in his escape attempt, she was not formally charged.[158]

Help a debtor out of prison, and his debts became yours to pay. Should the debtor not be apprehended, the gaoler himself would be required to reimburse the creditor.

When a prisoner broke out of jail, it was up to the gaol keeper and the local constable to sound the "hue and cry," meaning, provide a description of the escapee, and give chase. This colonial version of an APB from the *Essex County Court Records* of June 19, 1675, sounds quaint to modern ears:

To the Constables of Wenham (& other towns), June 19, 1675. To make diligent search for James Booth, alias Garritt, who broke prison this last night at Salem and made an escape. He is of middle stature, brownish hair and complexion; a blemish in one of his eyes, of a drawning speech, a taylor by trade.

The gaoler received a stipend each time he turned the key and locked a lawbreaker in a cell, usually about 3 shillings, then the equivalent to a field laborer's daily wage.

The Court of Quarter Sessions in Salem, in March 1657, decreed "Theophilus Willson, keeper of the Ipswich prison, to have three pounds a year and five shillings for every person committed into the prison; the prisoners before being released to pay their charges for food and attendance; others to be allowed only bread and water." Gaoler Willson was originally paid 2 shillings for putting fetters on a prisoner and removing them later, but later got a raise, reflected in the *Ipswich Quarterly Court Records of May 1661*: "Mr. Willson, prison keeper, allowed 3li. 7s. for his salary and for 'hue & cryes.'" Willson apparently found success as a prison-keeper for a number of years:

Warrant, dated November 22, 1673, to the keeper of the prison at Ipswich for the arrest of Richard Craw: Due to Theophilus Willson for Richard Croye; for turning the key, 5s; for his diet, 2s. 6d; for being apprehended and bringing him to Salem, 3s.

The courts provided additional funds "for dieting ye prisoners." Food could be brought in by a prisoner's family and friends with the keeper's permission, while the gaoler's wife was expected to cook for those incarcerated.[159] The prison-keeper's family was generally required to reside on the premises in an attached or adjacent house that belonged to the court or county. Regular chores of a gaoler's children might be to deliver daily meals to the prisoners, passing food on wooden trenchers through the grate or bars of the cell.

When the weather grew cold, gaolers were also expected to supply prisoners with sufficient firewood, or even to remove them from the cell to the keeper's own home, as at York in 1674:

> *In regard of the coldness of the present season and the Inconveniency and unfitness of the Prison to entertyne prisoners this Winter Time, it is therefore ordered that until a more convenient prison be erected or season be more moderate, it shall be lawful for John Parker, Majesty's Gaolkeeper at York, to remove his prisoners to his house. Prisoners shall have their liberty to come to meeting on the Lord's Day with the Keeper of the Gaol.*[160]

During the winter of 1735, Joseph Young, Keeper of His Majesty's Gaol at York, submitted a "Humble Petition" to the Supreme Court of Judicature in Boston, for "an earnest request that I may have an order upon the county treasurer for the third quarter's pay for the prisoner's subsistence with allowance made to provide fuel without which the poor woman cannot subsist . . ."

The convict was Patience Boston, sentenced to death for murder. This pregnant Native American woman had received a stay of execution until after she had given birth. Concerned for his prisoner's health, Gaoler Young wrote:

> *Your Honors are very sensible that by reason of the further depreciating of our province bills the allowance for a prisoner's diet falls very short and if I must also provide firewood, and have nothing allowed for it, the burden will lie heavy.*

Although the position of a gaoler commanded respect, it was generally considered a stepping-stone to a more-lucrative future position. One York prison-keeper was issued a license to operate a nearby tavern, while

Robert Rose, keeper of the York Gaol in 1760, supplemented his income with a barbershop on the premises. The same Robert Rose is listed in the *York County Records of 1765* as *Innholder,* and "late Master and Keeper of the House of Correction."[161]

Keeping gaol was a busy and demanding job, for repairs on the building always seemed to be required. In 1735, Joseph Young earned an additional £5 for digging a cellar at York Gaol. The turnkey was frequently called upon to leave town in order to fetch prisoners and cart them to prison, or to make certain they got to court on time whenever they were scheduled to appear.

Circumstances beyond the deputy sheriff's control sometimes made his job more difficult. *The York County Records* of October 1695 reported that:

> *It being hazardous travelling with prisoners to the Common Gaol by Reason of the Indian Enemy, and the gaol being much out of repair . . . the Sheriff shall constitute any house which he thinks most convenient for a common county gaol for the present.*

Some jailers were also expected to administer the mandatory lashes at the whipping post before locking prisoners into their cells.

Connecticut implemented a workhouse act in 1727 that provided "a house of correction be erected in Hartford, New Haven or New London, according to the liveliness of these towns to secure the boon." The County Court was to appoint "an honest, fit person to be master, with powers to set at work, shackle, [and] whip . . . in the interest of discipline . . . Each person committed was to be put into a humble state of mind by receiving not more than ten stripes." The workhouse was expected to be self-supporting, with two-thirds going to pay expenses of the inmates and their families, and the other third meant to cover the overseer's salary and expenses.[162]

DEBTORS

Debtors received differential treatment, since they were more apt to represent a higher social status. Gaolkeepers, sheriffs, and courts tried their best to keep debtors apart from felons inside prison walls. *York County*

Old Gaol, York, Maine, exterior: Built in 1719, it is the oldest English public building in the English colonies still in use, though no longer as a prison. For over one hundred years, it served the entire Province of Maine and then became the York County Prison until 1860. In the late nineteenth century, it became a school, then in 1900 was opened as a museum. The Old Gaol is currently one of the Museums of Old York and open to the public. PHOTO TAKEN PRIOR TO 1900, COURTESY MUSEUMS OF OLD YORK

Records reveal that in 1746, the court ordered Sheriff Plaisted "to make proper partitions to the Gaol in York strong and sufficient to separate criminals from debtors."

Debtors who could provide bonds (which might be a watch or gold ring rather than hard cash) were permitted to attend Sabbathday services and given *"liberty of the yard"* within specific boundaries (although, as records show, many simply kept on walking). They were usually allowed to bring furnishings from home to make their cells as comfortable as possible in order to entertain family and friends. Debtors could seldom earn enough money to pay back what they owed while incarcerated, so their confinement was more effective as personal humiliation. Yet the debtor remained in jail

Old Gaol, York, Maine, interior cell or dungeon: The original stone cell was added to and structurally improved until 1806, when the edifice likely took its present form. PHOTO TAKEN C. 1952, COURTESY MUSEUMS OF OLD YORK

until he managed to put up security or his creditor dropped his demands. A creditor who had a debtor jailed was expected to cover all costs of that prisoner's food and other needs throughout the period of imprisonment.

There were other sorts of debt besides simply owing somebody money. Men accused of nonpayment of taxes to town or county might be bound out as indentured servants for three years, or until they worked off the amount owed. Tax collectors were jailed when they could not balance their books or were unable to collect taxes due from persons within their jurisdiction.

During the Provincial Period from 1692 through 1775, it became increasingly common to keep lawbreakers in prison as punishment. For example, anyone who neglected to pay the fine for selling strong liquors without the required license could expect to be locked up without bail for twenty days, or to spend three hours in the stocks. *Massachusetts Provincial Records* also included a penalty "for selling or exchanging with any Indian, strong beer, cyder, wine, rum, brandy, clothing or any other thing" was three months in jail. Customs officers who accepted bribes went to prison for six months, the same period of detention required for "dueling with a dangerous weapon. For assaulting, or offering any insolence or violence to any woman, in the fields, streets, or lanes," the term was thirty days in the house of correction, or a whipping.

CONNECTICUT'S UNIQUE NEWGATE PRISON

Named after the notorious London prison, Newgate in Simsbury, Connecticut (now East Granby), was first opened in 1705, replacing what is considered to have been the first copper mine in this country. When mining for copper proved unprofitable, the Connecticut colony converted it to a prison to house burglars, forgers, counterfeiters, and horse thieves. Kept in chains and iron fetters, and wearing metal bands around their necks that were fastened to a beam overhead, prisoners were kept busy making nails, barrels, and shoes.

A burglar named John Hinson was Newgate's first inmate in 1773, but managed to escape only eighteen days later. At night, the prisoners were kept in total darkness in an underground cavern, seventy feet below the earth's surface. Throughout the American Revolution, Tories and Loyalists were incarcerated in this incredibly damp and gloomy former mine, along with common criminals. Finally, deemed too costly to maintain and too easy to escape from, as well as what was finally deemed an inhumane environment, Newgate Prison was closed in 1827. Now a museum and historic site, it remains significant as an early experiment in rehabilitating perpetrators through tough living conditions and useful work.

PART X

The Case of Patience Samson Boston, the Penitent Prisoner

PATIENCE BOSTON WAS INCARCERATED IN YORK GAOL FOR MORE THAN a year for her deviant behavior, crime, trial, and execution. The Case of Patience Samson Boston, the Penitent Prisoner[163] contains many elements previously discussed in this book, including daily life in prison and the responsibilities of the gaoler and his family. The confession of this condemned Native American woman follows the predictable pattern of gallows literature, beginning with her sins of disobedience to adult authority, swearing, Sabbath-breaking, and the "dangers of drink," a path that eventually led to the capital crime for which the prisoner is about to be put to death. Patience Boston's offenses also included fornication and adultery. She explains the terror she felt when forced to undergo the *Ordeal by Blood* test. Like Rebecca Eames nearly fifty years before, Patience Boston also contemplated suicide. And like the condemned witch, Abigail Faulkner, she was able to plead her belly and receive a stay of execution.

The hanging of Patience Boston demonstrates how executions were considered *Publick Spectacles,* as recorded by eyewitnesses from that day in 1685 when James Morgan addressed the enormous crowd from his spot upon the scaffold. From that confessed killer's execution to pirates swinging from the gallows in the mid-eighteenth-century, ministers were in attendance. Those clerical fathers and sons, the Mathers and the Moodys, as well as many other ministers, visited accused prisoners wherever they were incarcerated, seeking confessions and schooling them toward redemption. After the Reverend Increase Mather ushered James Morgan's story into print, such detailed biographies of condemned criminals, warnings to the living, and gallows sermons became traditional and widely circulated lessons for the living.

On July 24, 1735, there was great excitement in York as hundreds gathered to witness the town's first execution in a decade. Patience Boston, the Indian princess from Cape Cod, was marked to hang, "for not having the fear of God before her eyes . . . being instigated by the Devil at Falmouth on or about July 9, 1734, she did push or throw eight-year-old Benjamin Trot into a well of water 16 feet deep," or so the judge said, delivering the verdict against her. She "did feloniously kill and murder him, contrary to the Peace, Crown and Dignity of our Lord the King . . . Upon which indictment the said Patience being arraigned at the Bar, pleaded guilty. It is therefore considered and ordered by the Supreme Court of Judicature that this said Patience Indian shall suffer the Pains of Death."

Business was at a halt this day, with every shop and market stall closed to allow every York citizen, as well as countless out-of-town visitors, to witness this *Publick Spectacle*. The big event had been advertised well in advance, allowing everyone to alter plans in order to attend. As was customary at all New England executions, vendors would be hawking food, and souvenirs would be sold.

Part of the appeal of the public event planned for the execution of Patience Boston was the prospect of a thrilling, sensational confession to be made by the convicted murderer before the sentence was carried out. The malefactor was expected to deliver a meaningful speech, owning up to the crime for which she would soon die, and offering valuable instructions to the living. Those on the brink of death were believed to possess special wisdom, and folks flocked to hangings to hear condemned criminals describe their personal roads to ruin. Parents were convinced their children would receive valuable moral benefits by listening to the sorry tale of one about to be "turned off" for a lifetime of evil deeds, beginning with disobedience to one's parents. Every execution provided a host of teachable moments.

For over a year, the Reverend Samuel Moody, York's fire-and-brimstone minister, and his son, the Reverend Joseph Moody, had been paying frequent visits to the Indian woman incarcerated in the dungeon of York Prison, tirelessly coaching her toward repentance. She had gotten to know the inside of York Prison and the gaoler there very well over the course of her unusually long incarceration—long, because she was pregnant at the time of her conviction, and her sentence was postponed until after the delivery. At first the clerics had referred to this Indian princess as "A Monster of wickedness," then as the "The Penitent Prisoner." Now on the day of her death, this twenty-three-year-old evildoer was expected to provide a detailed biography recounting her slide into sin, culminating with the murder of her master's grandson.

Born December 26, 1711, at Menomey (now Eastham) on Cape Cod, Patience Samson's father had been a chief and a "Praying Indian." As baptized Christians, the family regularly attended the Indian Church at Nauset. When Patience was three, her mother died and her father placed her with a white family as a servant.

She admitted to the two Moody ministers that even as a child, she "became rebellious, already following a sinful course . . . playing on the Sabbath, telling lies, and do[ing] other Wickedness." She even let the family cow loose in the cornfield, and at the age of twelve, set fire to the house three times. Her mistress chastised her "continually with Reproofs, Instructions, Counsels and seasonable Corrections," and warned Patience she "should come to the Gallows and some untimely End, if she did not speedily reform."

Patience was fifteen when her mistress, "who was a mother to me, died . . . On her death bed she charged me to mind her Counsel and to refrain from evil Words, shun bad Company, keep the Sabbath strictly, never tell any more Lies, and keep myself from the Sin of Uncleanness . . ." Yet, Patience remained

a wicked and rebellious Servant. . . . not only Profane, but set upon Mischief. I went out Nights, and followed lewd Practices, till I was freed from my Master, after which I thought myself happy [because] I had nobody to Command me. I might do as I pleased, and I grew

*worse and worse, and fell into the Sin of Stealing, and all with little
or no Remorse of Conscience . . . Then I was married to a Negro and
because his Master would have it so, bound myself a Slave to him as
long as we both should live.*

Thus, in marrying this slave, who was a seafaring man, the Indian teenager became Patience Boston, doomed to slavery for the rest of her life.

*After this I was drawn in to the Love of strong Drink by some Indi-
ans and used to abuse my Husband in Words and Actions, being mad
and furious in my Drink, speaking dreadful Words, and wishing bad
Wishes to my self and others. After I found I was with Child, I had
thoughts of murdering it, and whilst I was big I ran away from the
Master, my Husband being absent on a Whaling Voyage. I drank hard,
and broke the Marriage Covenant, being wicked above Measure . . .
I was delivered of a Child, which I had hurt in my Rambling, so that
both its Arms were broken, and it died in a few Weeks. I now think
I was Guilty of its Death . . . I went on Drinking, Lying, Swearing,
and Quarreling with my Husband . . .*

*I had Murder in my Heart toward my Second, as well as my first
Child; and so after that Child was born, attempted something that
way when I perceived its crying, and its taking up my Time to tend
it. And when at the end of two Months, it pleased God to take away
the Child by sudden Death in the Cradle beside us, which terrified me
not a little. In less than a Month, getting mad with strong Drink, I
quarreled with my Husband and to vex him, told him I had murdered
our Child . . . My Husband said he must go to the Justice, and inform
against me. I told him, I would go with him, and accuse myself before
the Justice, which I did.*

*Perceiving that I was in Drink, the magistrate put me off till the
next Morning: But I got more Drink on purpose to harden me in the
Lies I had framed against myself; and being sent for, I still affirmed I
had killed my Child. But the Justice not finding me sober, put off a full
Examination until afternoon. Accordingly, toward night he came to*

my Master's [home] and hearing his Voice, I presently ran to my Bottle, and drank more Rum; and again, said that I was guilty of murdering the Child, and so, was sent to Prison, where I was in a distressed Condition, not so much for my wicked Heart or wicked Life as for fear of Death and Hell, not being fit to go into another World.

I resolved not to tell any more Lies; for I knew if I went out of the World with a Lie in my Mouth, my Punishment from the Hand of God would be the greater. I had little or no Hope of escaping Punishment from the Hand of Man. I had three Times accused myself before the single Justice who sent me to Prison, and afterwards before three Justices together, all which witnessing against me on my Trial. I expected no other but to be Condemned and Executed. Yet, the verdict of the Barnstable Court upon me was not guilty.

Evident throughout this document, published in 1738, is the Native American woman's hunger for freedom. Though she spoke of her husband as a good man and even recalled how she loved to have him read to her, Patience Boston resented belonging to anyone. Her husband was frequently far away on lengthy whaling voyages, and Patience was not about to give up her drinking and carousing to sit home, awaiting his return.

"I committed Adultery and Fornication often . . ." Patience admitted, and when Goodman Boston or their slavemaster had enough of this wayward wife, she found herself sold to a sea captain and sailing off to Casco Bay, a place she'd never been, though she'd "heard it told Indians had more freedom in Maine." This master soon sold her to another man named Benjamin Trot. Trot mistreated Patience so that she seriously considered poisoning him, but she "did not know how to obtain poison to put in his victuals."

Trot was extremely fond of the eight-year-old grandson who was his namesake, lived in his household, and was often put in Patience's care. At her trial for the murder of Trot's grandson, for which she was convicted and sentenced to hang, she confessed to his "horrid willful Murder . . . I did last Fall bind my self by a wicked Oath that I would kill that Child, though I seemed to love him, and he me." She claimed that she took the boy into the woods, *designing to knock him on the Head, and got a great Stick for the Purpose; but as I was going to lift it up, I felt a trembling or a sense of God's Eye upon me, so had not the Powers to strike. I went to the Well and threw the Pole in, so I might have an Excuse to draw the Boy to the Well. I asked his help to get up the Pole that I might push him in, which having done, I took a longer Pole, and thrust him down under the Water, till he was drowned. When I saw he was dead, I lifted up my Hands with my Eyes toward Heaven, speaking after this Manner: Now, am I guilty of Murder, indeed?*

It could never be proved that she had actually murdered the boy, since there were no eyewitnesses to his death. Perhaps he fell into the well and drowned, and she was unable to save him with that pole. Did she confess to this crime because of guilt over the earlier demise of her own first child, and the crib death of her second? Ordeal by Blood did not reveal her as a murderer, although the authorities put her through that archaic legal attempt to convict. Hers is a tale of guilt, for in her own conscience, she becomes the murderer she believed herself to be at the time of the crib death of the baby she bore Whaler Boston.

Patience had never been able to accept the verdict of "*innocent*" pronounced on her by the Barnstable Court. Because there were no witnesses, the truth of what actually happened to the boy can never be known. Yet, Patience Boston confessed to his murder before three Superior Court judges, who traveled Down East from Boston. In order to accommodate the curious crowds, her trial was conducted in a local tavern.

The *Confession of Patience Boston* continues with her description of undergoing the dreaded Ordeal by Touch.

I went forthwith to inform the Authority, and when the jury examined the Body, I was ordered to touch it! This terrified me, lest the boy's Blood should come forth to be a Witness against me. I then resolved in my Heart to be a Witness against myself, and never deny Guilt; so that God would not suffer the Child to bleed. Then I laid my Hand on his Face, but no Blood appeared . . .

My Case seemed desperate . . . I was angry with the Prison Keeper for restraining me from my self-murdering Desires. If I could have found a Way to put an End to my Life, I should surely have done it. I wished for a Knife, or a String, since my Garters and Coat-String had been taken from me. I wished I could have gone to the River, which I saw through the Dungeon Grates, to have Drowned myself.

Pregnant for the third time when arrested, the law permitted Patience to *"plead her belly,"* with time to deliver and nurse her newborn in prison prior to her execution. The son was born in York Gaol's dank dungeon on March 9, 1735. He was baptized *Philemon,* after a slave in the Bible.

York's two ministers, Samuel Moody and Joseph Moody, eventually succeeded in bringing about Patience Boston's "remarkable conversion." Clergymen from Berwick and Falmouth, as well as several New Hampshire towns, also traveled to York Prison to counsel the Native American prisoner. The religious conversion that all the clerics had worked so diligently to bring about happened so suddenly that Goodwife Young, the gaoler's wife, had to run and fetch Father Moody out of bed in the parsonage in the middle of the night.

Puritans believed there was no greater joy in heaven than the joy over a redeemed sinner. Nor should anyone be sent out of this world without preparation to greet his or her Maker. Thus, clergymen considered it their duty to visit the condemned in prison, where they strove diligently to bring about each convict's remorse and religious conversion. Ministers meticulously recorded the malefactor's every word for future publication. They were also well aware that gallows literature and illustrated broadsides containing the dying speeches of criminals were surefire best sellers.

Patience said she experienced

a Glimmering of Hope, and a Day or two after Light and Joy so sweet and good that I can no more express it than I can make known the desperate Sorrow and Anguish that went before . . . I went to Bed one Night, full of Trouble. . . . It was long before I could get any sleep as before, but lay awake whole nights meditating on nothing but Terror.

Falling asleep at length, I slept I suppose till after Midnight, then awaked in a more calm and easy Frame than I had been for a Week, when I used sometime to cry out at my first Waking, that I was going to Hell! But now . . . all my Thoughts seemed to run upon Believing.

Following conversion, Patience "took great Delight in reading good Books, especially the *Bible* and the sermons of Increase Mather." She helped the gaoler's wife with household chores, and was permitted to attend services at the meetinghouse, where she found "Joy and Delight of Soul, beyond what I ever had at any merry Meeting for Drinking or lewd Practices . . . I returned to Prison in my Chains of Iron; yet more comfortable than I could have been with a Chain of Gold in my former imprisoned State of Soul. The Prison Keeper regularly came to me bringing counsel and comfort."

According to the Moody ministers, after conversion, Patience told them: "Now, sin seems the most hateful Thing in the World to me. I loathed myself for Sin, and for my dishonoring God, more than ever I loathed a Toad or a Rattle Snake." Patience claimed to be "much affected by a condemned group of pirates in Boston, especially when the day for their executions arrived, which the elder Moody minister [first cousin to Judge Samuel Sewall] attended." The prisoner, Patience, "having heard they were too little sensible of their own Conditions: . . . I would have been willing to take the place of one of those Pirates, if any Exchange might be made, he taking my Place, to have more Time to prepare for Death . . . Then my poor Child was taken with a fever," Patience lamented, "dangerously ill, and I wondered whether I was willing to part with it. My own Death would be easier if my Child was gone before . . . When God was pleased to restore it to health, I was truly thankful, and thought God might graciously allow the child to continue with me as a Comfort. I even had hope of escaping the Gallows to enjoy my Child . . ."

Patience Boston eventually "grew reconciled to death," according to her ministers, "though she would find it difficult to part with her infant son." Yet, the next life promised by the two Moodys now sounded so much better than this one to her. Perhaps there, she would finally know true freedom. The sheriff and the two ministers walked beside Patience Boston the mile from York Gaol to Stage Neck, offering her courage and hope all along the way. Militiamen pounded drums, and ahead of the little procession was the cart carrying her empty coffin. "Are you not afraid, Patience?" Joseph Moody asked.

"Not at all," she replied, though later, the Moodys would write that the prisoner nearly fainted when she came in sight of the scaffold and saw more than a hundred spectators, including many in boats and canoes below.

"Are you ready to embark on the Ocean of Eternity?"

"I am ready to make the journey," Patience Boston said.

The gallows was fixed in a valley with hills on both sides, offering all spectators an advantageous prospect. It was an upright post with a beam extended and braced beneath. Below was a narrow platform six or seven feet off the ground and reached by a ladder. This condemned prisoner had been well coached. She had memorized the lines that the ministers had taught her to speak.

"I pray for all those gathered here to see and be warned by my example." Patience sat in the cart next to her coffin, reading aloud what she and the two Moodys had penned together over many months. Addressing the crowd directly, she prayed for the ministers "helpful and kind; for the judges of the court who gave me fair trial . . . for the man who will execute me . . . I pray." (She had requested that her executioner not be the town's Common Whipper, or anyone doing the deed "just for the money.") Patience then called upon all young people present, to "wage a war against sin."

Eyewitnesses later claimed that "[s]he spoke very penitently and stepped off the cart without hesitation, approaching the gallows without hesitation . . ."

Several times the Moodys asked Patience whether "her Faith held out, and she professed that it did." Drums rolled as the prisoner climbed the ladder and a black cloth was draped over her head. The hangman also wore a black hood.

In the detailed document of Patience Boston's beginning and end, the Moodys wrote that "after the Rope was about her Neck, I asked her whether she did not believe that her faith which had helped her along so near her End, could not help her along the few Steps that yet remained? She (evidently with a Smile, which several others besides myself took notice of), answered, 'Yes.'"

After her face was covered, the elder minister asked her whether she "remembered what she designed to say?" "Yes," she answered. "Lord Jesus receive my Spirit."

As soon as the "malefactor was turned off," swinging lifelessly from the rope, loud cheers rose from the crowd, and everyone clapped with enthusiasm. Not only were hangings cathartic for the entire community, but they were also the most dramatic theater presentations possible. And Patience Samson Boston's life story and early death provided an unusually satisfying and memorable crowd-pleaser.

Following Patience Boston's execution, Jeremiah Moulton, the local sheriff, adopted her infant, Philemon. Moulton had the reputation of being one of New England's fiercest Indian fighters. He had hated Native Americans since the age of four, when he had witnessed the death of both his parents in York's 1692 Candlemas Day Massacre. Baby Philemon, sickly since his birth inside the prison dungeon, survived only ten months.

Early-eighteenth-century execution as public spectacle: "Hanged by the neck until the body be dead." The condemned man rode to the scaffold in the cart beside his empty coffin. Astride his horse, the sheriff issued the order to "Turn the malefactor off." EARLY-EIGHTEENTH-CENTURY BROADSIDE, AUTHOR'S COLLECTION

Afterword: From Ridicule to Reform

Meetinghouse confessions, public floggings, and locking lawbreakers in stocks and pillories with placards posted above their heads, announcing their specific crimes, were humiliating, to be sure. Yet these punishments seemed to have little or no impact upon misbehavior, murder, and sexual deviance. Cropped ears, permanent facial scars from branding irons, and letters sewn on clothing did not serve to deter forgers, thieves, or adulterers. Colonial punishments had been designed to frighten offenders and encourage everyone within the community to toe the line, but as New England's population grew, the number and types of crimes only increased.

Courts and justices eventually came to realize that public humiliation and corporal punishment had done little over time to curb criminal behavior. Laws from Old England brought to the New World and restructured using the Holy Bible as a legal guide seemed hopelessly outdated to most people by the mid-eighteenth century, when religion no longer governed daily life. Over time, the political power of the Puritan clergy declined, and ministers lost their former influence over colonial culture. Eventually, all Protestant religious sects were legally accepted throughout New England, and believers were free to build their own churches and worship as they wished.

The Age of Enlightenment that was transforming European thought could not help but have an effect on this side of the Atlantic, and these changes were reflected in how the colonies came to deal with crime and punishment. Whereas Puritan Calvinists viewed mankind as innately depraved—that is, born into original sin and prone to evil by nature—eighteenth-century philosophers such as John Locke, author of *An Essay Concerning Human Understanding* (1690), saw mankind as essentially good.

The Old Testament prescription, "An eye for an eye, a tooth for a tooth," gradually lost favor. Bodily mutilation and flogging came to be considered cruel and inhumane, if not downright barbaric. Public hangings, except for pirate executions, became less-popular events as society sought new solutions for dealing with deviants.

An essay entitled *On Crimes and Punishments,* by Italian reformer and jurist Cesare Beccaria, published in 1764, had a profound and transforming impact upon the American penal system and point of view. Beccaria wrote that the purpose of punishment should not be revenge or humiliation, but should always aim at reforming the offender. He believed harsh treatments served only to create more problems than they alleviated, and that the "purpose of punishment is not to torment a sensible being nor to undo a crime, but to prevent the criminal from doing further injury to society and to prevent others from committing the same offense."

Beccaria envisioned prisons as educational institutions, and urged humane treatment for all. He believed that severe punishments only serve to make lawbreakers repeat the same offenses they are designed to prevent, so that criminals are driven to commit additional crimes to avoid further punishment. The teachings of Cesare Beccaria had such influence in this country that by 1800, the majority of American states had amended their criminal codes to limit the death penalty to but a few crimes, and were consciously and actively engaged in penal reform.

Ironically, it was the Quakers, that religious sect whose members had been so mistreated by previous magistrates and ministers, who first demonstrated that with humane treatment, criminals might be rehabilitated and returned to society. Their conviction that every individual was capable of social and moral improvement was incompatible with penal codes that regularly employed whipping posts and assigned bodily mutilation. The Society of Friends taught that the reformation of every criminal should be the ultimate goal of any good society. In William Penn's Pennsylvania, where murder was the only hanging offense, the codes of the Pennsylvania Experiment enacted between 1682 and 1718 became widely recognized as a model of enlightenment. Prisons were transformed from holding places where deviants were locked away while awaiting trial, in order to keep the rest of the community safe, into facilities where offenders were housed for a prescribed amount of time to offer every convict the opportunity to reflect upon the crime committed. The idea developed that during this period of isolation from general society, the prisoner would come to understand the need to alter his or her behavior, eventually returning to

The clergy accompanied the condemned to the scaffold, urging the malefactors to "Repent! Repent!," for "[T]here is no joy in heaven as great as a redeemed sinner." MID-EIGHTEENTH-CENTURY GRAPHIC FROM A BROADSIDE, AUTHOR'S COLLECTION

the community as reformed individuals eager to function as law-abiding members of society. As these convicts reconsidered their offenses, they would realize the need for change, and through their own consciences, would be inspired to improve their behavior. Incarceration would encourage lawbreakers to come to terms with their predicaments, experience remorse, and thus, be transformed into useful and worthy citizens.[164]

Prison architecture reflected this new approach to penology. New buildings were designed to separate both men and women and felons from those who had merely committed misdemeanors. Prison work was increasingly considered a highly positive psychological tool, because it offered those who were incarcerated discipline and purpose that demonstrated the value of productive labor. The idea that work was the most useful tool against idleness and sin was a view still widely held by most eighteenth-century New Englanders.

After the American Revolution, it seemed that the mores and methods of the seventeenth century were necessarily left far behind by a New Nation founded upon the ideals of freedom. Sweeping social changes signaled the end of the Colonial Way and issued in the era of the New Republic. In 1787, the same year that the Philadelphia Society for Alleviating the Miseries of Public Prisons, was founded by the Society of Friends, Dr. Benjamin Rush (1746-1813) of Pennsylvania, a signer of the Declaration of Independence and founder of the Pennsylvania Prison Society, wrote eloquently regarding positive changes in the philosophy and practice of crime and punishment:

> *The Reformation of a criminal can never be affected by public punishment . . . Experience proves that public punishments have increased propensities to crimes. A man who has lost his self-respect at a whipping post, has nothing valuable to lose in society. Pain has begotten insensibility to the whip; and shame to infamy. Added to his old habits of vice, he probably feels a spirit of revenge against the whole community whose laws have inflicted this punishment upon him, and hence, he is stimulated to add to the number and enormity of his outrage upon society.*[165]

Endnotes

1. Koehler, Lyle. *A Search for Power: The "Weaker Sex" in Seventeenth-Century New England.* Urbana, Chicago, London: University of Illinois Press, 1980, p. 47.
2. Powers, Edwin. *Crime and Punishment in Early Massachusetts, 1620–1692: A Documentary History.* Boston: Beacon Press, 1966, p. 58.
3. Ibid., p. 86.
4. Clark, George L. *A History of Connecticut: Its People and Institutions.* New York: G. P. Putnam's Sons, 1914, pp. 18–19.
5. Archer, Richard. *Fissures in the Rock: New England in the Seventeenth Century.* Lebanon, NH: University Press of New England, 2001, p. 104.
6. Clark, p. 443.
7. Earle, Alice Morse. *Curious Punishments of Days Gone By.* New York: MacMillan, 1898, p. 128. http://sitekreator.com/my.history/the_woodenhorse.html/.
8. Jones, Ann. *Women Who Kill.* New York: Holt, Rinehart & Winston, 1980, pp. 57–58.
9. Vaughan, Alden T. *New England Frontier: Puritans and Indians: 1620–1675.* Boston: Little, Brown & Company, 1965, p. 22.
10. Ibid., pp. 346–347.
11. Ernst, George. *New England Miniature: A History of York, Maine.* Freeport, ME: Bond Wheelwright Company, 1961, p. 152.
12. Willis, William. *The History of Portland, from its First Settlement.* Part I. Portland, ME: Day, Fraser Company, 1831, pp. 86–87.
13. Powers, pp. 288–89.
14. Lepore, Jill. *The Name of War: King Philip's War and the Origins of American Identity.* New York: Alfred A. Knopf, 1998, pp. 21–25.
15. Taylor, Dale. *The Writer's Guide to Everyday Life in Colonial America.* Cincinnati, OH: Writer's Digest Books, 1997, p. 10.
16. Clark, p. 444.
17. Haines Mofford, Juliet. "And Firm Thine Ancient Vow," *The History of North Parish Church of North Andover, 1645–1974.* Lawrence, MA: Naiman Press, 1975, pp. 22–23.
18. Lewis, Alonzo, and James R. Newhall. *History of Lynn, Essex County, MA, Including Lynnfield, Saugus, Swampscott & Nahant.* Boston: John L. Shorey, 1865, p. 209.
19. Godbeer, Richard. *Sexual Revolution in Early America.* Baltimore & London: John Hopkins Press, 2002, p. 90; Powers, pp. 175–76.
20. Chapin, Bradley. *Criminal Justice in Colonial America, 1606–1660.* Athens: University of Georgia Press, 1983, p. 139.
21. Hawke, David Freeman. *Everyday Life in Early America.* New York: Harper & Row, 1988, pp. 113–14.
22. Godbeer, *Sexual Revolution in Early America,* pp. 30–33.
23. Wall, Helena. *Fierce Communion: Family and Community in Early America.* Cambridge, MA: Harvard University Press, 1990, pp. 104–105; f. n. 212–213.

24. Mather, Reverend Cotton. *Ornaments for the Daughters of Zion.* Boston: 1692.

25. *Plymouth Court Records,* March 1655.

26. Willis, William. *History of Portland, from 1632 to 1864, with a Notice of Previous Settlement, Colonial Grants & Changes of Government in Maine.* Portland, ME: Bailey & Noyes, 1865, p. 169.

27. Koehler, pp. 209–10.

28. Ibid., p. 138; f.n. pp. 66–67; Essex County Records, VIII, pp. 272, 273; Ulrich, Laurel, *Good Wives,* p. 188.

29. Thompson, Roger. *Sex in Middlesex: Popular Mores in a Massachusetts County, 1649–1699.* Amherst, MA: University of MA Massachusetts Press, 1986, pp. 116–17; f. n. 14, p. 224.

30. Wall, p. 105.

31. *Ipswich Quarterly Court Records,* April 19, 1675.

32. *General Court of Trials,* Newport County, p. 20, f.n. 99.

33. "Testimony of Mary Freeman and her daughter-in-law, Hannah Freeman." Eastham, 30th day of March 1734 from the manuscript Record Book of Samuel Tyler, A Clerk of the Superior Court of Judicature, May 4, 1734.

34. *Boston News-Letter,* July 19–26, 1733.

35. Ibid., June 6–13, 1734.

36. Hansen, Chadwick. *Witchcraft at Salem.* New York: George Braziller / New American Library, 1969, p. 95.

37. Dayton, Cornelia Hughes. *Women Before the Bar: Gender, Law, and Society in Connecticut, 1639–1789.* Durham: University of North Carolina Press, 1995, p. 138.

38. Clark, p. 91.

39. Haskins, George Lee. *Law and Authority in Early Massachusetts: A Study in Tradition and Design.* New York: Macmillan, 1960, p. 81.

40. Hawke, p. 89.

41. Koehler, p. 45.

42. Powers, p. 418.

43. Weisman, Richard. *Witchcraft, Magic and Religion in Seventeenth-Century Massachusetts.* Amherst: University of Massachusetts Press, 1984, pp. 80–91.

44. Benton, Josiah Henry. *Warning Out in New England, 1656–1817.* Boston: W. B. Clarke, 1911 (entire book as general background source).

45. *Essex County Quarterly Court Records,* Ipswich, April 1679.

46. *Ipswich Quarterly Court Records,* April 1679.

47. Bailey, Sarah Loring. *Historical Sketches of Andover, MA, Comprising the Present Towns of North Andover and Andover, MA.* Boston: Houghton, Mifflin & Riverside Press, Cambridge, 1880, pp. 70–71.

48. *Salem Quarterly Court Records,* June 1662.

49. Bailey, pp. 68–69.

50. *Essex County Court Records,* June 1674; Godbeer, pp. 23–25.

51. Hosmer, James Kendall, ed. *History of New England from 1630 to 1649: Journals of John Winthrop (Massachusetts Historical Society; Original Narratives of Early American History).* New York: Charles Scribner's Sons, 1908, p. 64.

52. *General Court Records,* Boston, June 1641.

53. Koehler, pp. 269–70.

54. Chu, Jonathan M. *Neighbors, Friends, or Madmen: The Puritan Adjustment to Quakerism in Seventeenth-Century Massachusetts Bay.* Westport, CT & London: Greenwood Press, 1985, pp. 93,106; Powers, pp. 322–24.

55. Ibid., p. 116 ff.

56. *Essex County Court Records 1662,* #5.

57. *Essex County Quarterly Court of Sessions,* May 5, 1663.

58. Chu, p. 126 ff.

59. Powers, p. 358.

60. Ibid., pp. 338–47; Drake, Samuel Adams. *A Book of New England Legends and Folklore in Prose and Poetry.* Boston: Roberts Brothers, 1888, pp. 36–45.

61. Powers, pp. 344–45.

62. Koehler, pp. 315–16.

63. Thatcher Ulrich, Laurel Thatcher. *Good Wives: The Lives of Northern New England Women, 1650–1750.* New York: Alfred Knopf, 1982, p. 254–55, f.n. 11.

64. Godbeer, *Sexual Revolution in Early America,* pp. 20–21.

65. Thompson, *Sex in Middlesex,* p. 89.

66. *Plymouth Court Records 1639,* Vol. I, p. 127.

67. Sanborn, Melinde Lutz. *Lost Babes: Fornication Abstracts from Court Records,* Essex County Courts, Massachusetts, 1692 to 1754, n. p.

68. *Essex Country Court Records,* September 28; January 21, 1742.

69. *Court of General Sessions,* Essex County, September 27, 1692.

70. *Essex County Court Records,* March 22, 1704/5.

71. *Essex County Court Records,* March 28, 1710.

72. Wall, p. 71.

73. *Plymouth Court Records,* 1639.

74. Dayton, p. 166.

75. Wall, pp. 69–70.

76. *York County Court Records,* Vol. I, 1636–1671.

77. *Maine Province and Court Records,* September 8, 1640.

78. *Plymouth Court Records,* 1657.

79. Godbeer, *Sexual Revolution in Early America,* pp. 110–11.

80. Ibid., pp. 44–49.

81. Deetz, James, and Patricia Scott Deetz. *The Times of Their Lives: Life, Love, and Death in Plymouth Colony.* New York: W. H. Freeman & Co., 2000, pp. 139–41.

82. Ibid., pp. 135–36.

83. *Boston Court Records,* Massachusetts Bay, April 2, 1674.

84. *New Haven Colony Records,* Vol. I: pp. 62–69, 70–73; Vol. II: pp. 132–33, 440–43.

85. Godbeer, *Sexual Revolution in Early America,* pp. 111–12.

86. *Massachusetts Bay Colony Records,* June 14, 1642.

87. Lewis and Newhall, pp. 151–52.

88. Dayton, pp. 275–77.

89. *Massachusetts Superior Court of Judicature,* 1686–1700, pp. 49–50.

90. *Plymouth Court Records,* 1648.

91. *Essex County Court Records,* Vol. II, 10.

92. Ibid., April 1686.

93. *Essex County Court Records,* Vol. IX, p. 93.

94. *Suffolk County Court Records,* Early Files, #2636.

95. *Records & Files of the Quarterly Courts of Essex County, MA,* 1675-78, Vol. VI. (Salem, MA: Essex Institute, 1917) pp. 139, 141, 212–13.

96. Examination of Elizabeth Emerson, *Essex County Court Records,* Vol. IX, May 11, 1691; *Suffolk Court Records, Early Files,* #2636; Ulrich, Laurel Thatcher, pp. 197–201.

97. Jones, p. 45; Powers, p. 307; Hull, N. E. H. *Female Felons: Women and Serious Crime in Colonial Massachusetts.* Chicago & Urbana: University of Illinois Press, 1987, pp. 27–28.

98. Koehler, p. 268.

99. Dow, George Francis. *Everyday Life in the Massachusetts Bay Colony.* Boston: Society for the Preservation of New England Antiquities, 1935, pp. 212–13; *Records and Files of the Quarterly Courts of Essex County, Massachusetts,* Vol. I, 265; Demos, *Entertaining Satan: Witchcraft and the Culture of Early New England.* Oxford, England & New York: Oxford University Press, 1982, pp. 61–62.

100. Demos, John, ed. "A Sinner Cast Out," in *Remarkable Providences,* 1600–1760. New York: George Braziller, 1972, pp. 222–39; Cott, Nancy F. "Church Trial of Mistress Ann Hibbens," in *Root of Bitterness: Documents of the Social History of American Women.* New York: E. P. Dutton, 1972, pp. 47–58; Drake, Samuel Adams "Case of Mistress Ann Hibbens, 1656," in *A Book of New England Legends and Folk Lore in Prose and Poetry.* Boston: Roberts Brothers, 1888, pp. 28–35.

101. Demos, *Entertaining Satan: Witchcraft and the Culture of Early New England.* p. 341.

102. Ibid., pp. 176–77, 345–46.

103. Demos, *Remarkable Providences,* p. 349.

104. Tomlinson, Richard G. B. *Witchcraft Trials of Connecticut: The First Comprehensive Documented History.* Hartford, CT: Bond Press, 1978, p. 35; Clark p. 149.

105. Ibid., pp. 7–8.

106. *Connecticut Court of Assistants: Trials of Katharan Harrison,* Hartford, October 12, 1668, May 11, May 25, 1669; Tomlinson, pp. 43–50.

107. Tomlinson, pp. 55–60; Demos, John. *Entertaining Satan,* p. 92.

108. Demos, *Entertaining Satan,* pp. 355–57.

109. Clark, pp. 152–53; Demos, *Entertaining Satan,* pp. 183, 185.

110. Koehler, p. 388.

111. Weisman, p. 83.

112. Demos, *Entertaining Satan,* p. 522, f.n. 22.

113. Norton, Mary Beth. *In the Devil's Snare: The Salem Witchcraft Crisis of 1692.* New York: Alfred A. Knopf, 2002, p. 41.

114. Rosenthal, Bernard. *The Salem Story: Reading the Witch Trials of 1692.* Cambridge, England & New York: Cambridge University Press, 1993.

115. Rosenthal, Bernard. ed. *Records of the Salem Witch Hunt.* Cambridge, MA: Cambridge University Press, 2009; "Tryal of Bridget Bishop, alias Oliver, June 2, 1692," Mather, Cotton. *Wonders of the Invisible World,* in Burr, George Lincoln, ed. *Narratives of the Witchcraft Cases, 1648–1706 (Original Narratives of Early American History).* New York: Charles Scribner's & Sons, 1914, pp. 223–29; Boyer, Paul, and Stephen Nissenbaum, eds. "Bridget Bishop," *The Salem Witchcraft Papers: Verbatim Transcripts of the Legal Documents of the Salem Witchcraft Outbreak of 1692,* Vol. I. New York: Da Capo Press, 1977, pp. 36–53. (1692 witchcraft cases are on-line, organized alphabetically: http://etext.virginia.edu/salem/witchcraft/texts/transcripts.html).

116. Brattle, Thomas. Letter, October 3, 1692, in Burr, George Lincoln, ed. *Narratives of the Witchcraft Cases, 1648–1706 (Original Narratives of Early American History).* New York: Charles Scribner's & Sons, 1914, pp. 169–90.

117. "Captain Cary's Account," from Robert Calef's *More Wonders of the Invisible World* (London, 1700), in Burr, *Narratives of the Witchcraft Cases, 1648–1706,* pp. 349–52.

118. John Alden's "Account," Calef's *More Wonders of the Invisible World,* in Burr, pp. 352–55.

119. "Testimony of Allen Toothaker" from "Examination of Martha Carrier" in Boyer and Nissenbaum, Vol. I.; Mather, Cotton. *Wonders of the Invisible World,* in Burr, pp. 241–44.

120. "Examination of Mary Toothaker," Boyer and Nissenbaum, Vol. III, pp. 767–70.

121. Thompson, *Sex in Middlesex,* pp. 133–35.

122. *Billerica Selectmen's Records,* March 12, 1682/3.

123. "Coroner's Report," *Suffolk County Court Records,* Vol. 32, #2690; "Roger Toothaker" in Boyer and Nissenbaum, Vol. III.

124. "Examinations of Mary Lacey Jr. and Mary Foster Lacey" in Boyer and Nissenbaum, Vol. II, pp. 519–533 and 513–517. http://etext.virginia.edu/salem/witchcraft/texts/transcripts.html.

125. Bailey, p. 237.

126. Konig, David T. *Law and Society in Puritan Massachusetts: Essex County, 1629–1692.* Chapel Hill: University of North Carolina Press, 1979, pp. 141–42.

127. *Essex County Court Records,* September 1686, pp. 601–2.

128. Cotton Mather, "Tryal of G. B. at a Court of Oyer & Terminer," *The Wonders of the Invisible World,* 1693, in Burr, pp. 215–22; Boyer & Nissenbaum, Salem Witchcraft Papers, Vol. I. or http://etext.virginia.edu/salem/witchcraft/texts/transcripts.html.

129. Sibley, John Langdon. *Biographical Sketches of the Graduates of Harvard University in Cambridge, MA,* Vol. II. Cambridge, England: Cambridge University Press, 1873 and Boston: John Wilson & Son, 1885, pp. 325–26; 329–54; "George Burroughs" in Boyer and Nissenbaum, Vol. I, p. 216.

130. Charles Burroughs, *MSS Attainer. Massachusetts Archives,* Vol. 135, #136.

131. Boyer and Nissenbaum. Vol. II, "Examinations: Ann Foster," pp. 341–44; "Mary Lacy Senior," pp. 513–17 and "Mary Lacey, Junior," pp. 519–33, July, 1692.

132. Mofford, Juliet Haines. "Andover's First Murder" *Andover, MA: Historical Selections from Four Centuries.* Andover: Merrimack Valley Preservation Press, 2004, pp. 25–26.

133. "Examination of Rebecca Blake Eames," Boyer & Nissenbaum, Vol. II, pp. 279-85.

134. "Examination of William Barker, Sr.," in Boyer and Nissenbaum, Vol. I, p. 63–69.
135. Mofford, Juliet H., *Cry Witch! The Salem Witchcraft Trials 1692*. Carlisle, MA: Discovery Enterprises, 1995, pp. 55–57; *Massachusetts Resolves of 1957*, Chapter 145.
136. *Andover Selectmen's Manuscript Records*, May 7, 1661.
137. Vaughan, p. 199.
138. Powers, pp. 190–91, 417.
139. Ibid., p. 170.
140. *Ipswich Court Records*, Salem Quarterly Court, September 27, 1666.
141. Judd, Sylvester. *History of Hadley, Including the Early History of Hatfield, South Hadley, Amherst & Granby*. Northampton, MA: Botwood, Metcalf & Co., 1863, p. 261.
142. Hull, p. 51; Powers, p. 294.
143. Powers, pp. 306; 416–17.
144. Dow, George Francis, and John Henry Edmonds. *Pirates of the New England Coast, 1630–1730*. Salem, MA: Marine Research Society, 1923, p. 316.
145. *New England Courant*, July 22, 1723; Dow and Edmonds, p. 308.
146. "An Account of the Pirates & Divers of Their Speeches," Boston, 1723.
147. Dow and Edmonds, pp. 20, 308.
148. Hosmer, ed., *Journals of John Winthrop*, pp. 95–96.
149. Dow and Edmonds, pp. 73–74.
150. Ibid., pp. 81–82, 377.
151. Ritchie, Robert C. *Captain Kidd and the War Against the Pirates*. Cambridge, MA & London, England: Harvard University Press, 1986, pp. 209–10.
152. Snow, Edward Rowe. *Pirates and Buccaneers of the Atlantic Coast*. Boston, MA: Yankee Publishing Company, 1944, p. 47.
153. Ibid., p. 184.
154. Dow and Edmonds, pp. 325; 335–40.
155. Powers, p. 226.
156. Clark, p. 438.
157. Powers, p. 230.
158. Hull, p. 76.
159. Powers, pp. 228–29.
160. Ernst, p. 151.
161. *York County Commissioners' Records*, Vol. 2, 1774, p. 368.
162. Clark, p. 426.
163. Moody, Samuel and Joseph, Ministers at York, *The Faithful Narrative of the Wicked Life & Remarkable Conversion of Patience Boston, Alias Samson, Who Was Executed at York, July 24, 1735*. Boston: Kneeland & Greene, 1738 (Early American Imprints, Series I Evans #4245, http://xroads_virginia.edu/~mao5/peltier/conversion/boston.html.
164. Erikson, Kai T. *Wayward Puritans: A Study in the Sociology of Deviance*. New York, London, Sydney: John Wiley & Sons, 1966, p. 199.
165. Rush, Benjamin. *Essays: Literary, Moral & Philosophical*. Philadelphia, PA: Thomas & William Bradford, 1798.

Bibliography

For a listing of the many early New England court designations throughout the various colonies, see the valuable reference book by legal historian, Diane Rapaport titled, *New England Court Records: A Research Guide for Genealogists and Historians* (Quill Pen Press, 2006).

"An Account of the Pirates and Divers of Their Speeches." Boston, 1723.

Anderson, Virginia DeJohn. *New England's Generation: The Great Migration and the Formation of Society and Culture in the Seventeenth Century.* Cambridge, England: Cambridge University Press, 1992.

Andover Selectmen's Manuscript Records, Andover, MA.

Archer, Richard. *Fissures in the Rock: New England in the Seventeenth Century.* Lebanon, NH: University Press of New England, 2001.

Arraignment, Tryal, and Condemnation of Captain John Quelch, for sundry piracies, robberies, and murder . . . found guilty at Court House in Boston, June 13, 1704. London: Benjamin Bragg, 1705.

Bailey, Sarah Loring. *Historical Sketches of Andover, MA, comprising the Present Towns of Andover and North Andover.* Boston: Houghton Mifflin (Cambridge, MA: Riverside Press, 1880).

Bartlett, John Russell, ed. *Records of the Colony of Rhode Island & Providence Plantations in New England, 1636–1706,* 3 vols. Providence, RI: A. C. Greene, 1857.

Benton, Josiah Henry. *Warning Out in New England, 1656–1817.* Boston: W. B. Clarke, 1911.

Billerica Selectmen's Manuscript Records, Billerica, MA.

Boyer, Paul, and Stephen Nissenbaum, eds. *The Salem Witchcraft Papers: Verbatim Transcripts of the Legal Documents of the Salem Witchcraft Outbreak of 1692,* Vols. 1–3. New York: Da Capo Press, 1977.

Bradford, William. *Mounts Relation: A Journal of the Pilgrims at Plymouth.* Originally published in 1622 by John Bellamie, London, as "A Relation or Journal of the Beginnings and Proceedings of the English Plantation Settled at Plymouth in New England, by certain English adventurers both merchants and others." Bedford, MA: Applewood, 1963.

———. *Of Plymouth Plantation: 1620–1647.* New York: Random House, 1981.

Burns, Henry. *Origins and Development of Jails in America.* Urbana, IL: Southern Illinois University Center for the Study of Crime, 1971.

Burr, George Lincoln, ed. *Narratives of the Witchcraft Cases: 1648–1706* (Original Narratives of Early American History). New York: Charles Scribner's Sons, 1914. Reprint: New York: Barnes & Noble, 1946.

Calef, Robert. *More Wonders of the Invisible World.* Boston, MA: Printed by the author, 1700.

Chapin, Bradley. *Criminal Justice in Colonial America, 1606–1660.* Athens: University of Georgia Press, 1983.

Chapin, Howard Millar. *Documentary History of Rhode Island.* Providence, RI: Preston & Rounds Company, 1916.

Chu, Jonathan M. *Neighbors, Friends, or Madmen: The Puritan Adjustment to Quakerism in Seventeenth-Century Massachusetts Bay* (Contributions to the Study of Religion). Westport, CT & London: Greenwood Press, 1985.

Clapp, David Jr. *Memoirs of Roger Clap, 1640.* Boston, 1844.

Clark, George Larkin. *A History of Connecticut: Its People and Institutions.* New York & London: G. P. Putnam's Sons, 1914.

Cohen, Daniel A. *Pillars of Salt, Monuments of Grace: New England Crime Literature and the Origins of American Popular Culture.* Oxford, England & New York: Oxford University Press, 1993.

Connecticut Archives: Crimes & Misdemeanors, 1st Series (1662–1789). Hartford: Connecticut State Library, n.d.

Connecticut Court of Assistants, Hartford. October 12, 1668, May 11, May 25, 1669.

Cott, Nancy F. *Root of Bitterness: Documents of the Social History of American Women.* New York: E. P. Dutton, 1972.

Dayton, Cornelia Hughes. *Women Before the Bar: Gender, Law, and Society in Connecticut, 1639–1789.* Durham: University of North Carolina Press, 1995.

Deetz, James, and Patricia Scott Deetz. *The Times of Their Lives: Life, Love, and Death in Plymouth Colony.* New York: W. H. Freeman & Company, 2000.

Demos, John Putnam. *A Little Commonwealth: Family Life in Plymouth Colony.* Oxford, England & New York: Oxford University Press, 1982.

———. *Entertaining Satan: Witchcraft and the Culture of Early New England.* Oxford, England & New York: Oxford University Press, 1982.

———, ed. *Remarkable Providences, 1600–1760.* New York: George Braziller, 1972.

Dow, George Francis. *Everyday Life in the Massachusetts Bay Colony.* Boston: Society for the Preservation of New England Antiquities, 1935.

Dow, George Francis, and John Henry Edmonds. *The Pirates of the New England Coast, 1630–1730.* Salem, MA: Marine Research Society, 1923.

Drake, Samuel Adams. *A Book of New England Legends and Folklore in Prose and Poetry.* Boston: Roberts Brothers, 1888.

Earle, Alice Morse. *Curious Punishments of Bygone Days.* New York: Macmillan, 1898.

———. *The Sabbath in Puritan New England.* New York: Macmillan, 1897.

Erikson, Kai T. *Wayward Puritans: A Study in the Sociology of Deviance.* New York, London, Sydney: John Wiley & Sons, 1966.

Ernst, George. *New England Miniature: A History of York, Maine.* Freeport, ME: Bond Wheelwright, 1961.

Essex County Quarterly Court of Sessions Records, (9 volumes). Salem, MA, 1911–1978.

Essex County Court Records, (10 volumes). Salem, MA.

Fiske, Jane Fletcher. *Gleanings from Newport Court Files, 1659–1783.* Boxford, MA: Privately printed by author, 1998.

———. *Rhode Island General Court of Trials, 1671–1704.* Boxford, MA: Privately printed by author, 1998.

Foulds, Diane E. *Death in Salem: The Private Lives Behind the 1692 Witch Hunt.* Guilford, CT: Globe Pequot Press, 2010.

General Court of Trials, Newport County, RI.

General Court Records. Boston, MA.

Godbeer, Richard. *The Devil's Dominion: Magic and Religion in Early New England.* Cambridge, England: Cambridge University Press, 1992.

———. *Sexual Revolution in Early America.* Baltimore & London: Johns Hopkins University Press, 2002.

Hall, David D. *Worlds of Wonder, Days of Judgment: Popular Religious Belief in Early New England.* Cambridge, MA: Harvard University Press, 1989.

Hall, David D., John Murrin, and Thad Tate, eds. *Saints & Revolutionaries: Essays on Early American History.* New York: W. W. Norton, 1984.

Hansen, Chadwick. *Witchcraft at Salem.* New York: George Braziller Inc. / New American Library, 1969.

Haskins, George Lee. *Law and Authority in Early Massachusetts: A Study in Tradition and Design.* New York: Macmillan, 1960.

Hawke, David Freeman. *Everyday Life in Early America.* New York: Harper & Row, 1988.

Hill, Frances. *The Salem Witch Trials Reader.* Cambridge, MA: Da Capo Press, 2000.

Hosmer, James Kendall, ed. *History of New England from 1630 to 1649: Journals of John Winthrop* (Massachusetts Historical Society: Original Narratives of Early American History). New York: Charles Scribner's Sons, 1908.

Hull, N. E. H. *Female Felons: Women and Serious Crime in Colonial Massachusetts.* Urbana & Chicago: University of Illinois Press, 1987.

Ipswich Quarterly Court Records. Essex County, MA.

Johnson, Captain Charles. *A General History of the Robberies and Murders of the Most Notorious Pirates* (London, 1724). Reprint, Guilford, CT: The Lyons Press, with Introduction by David Cordingly, 1998.

Jones, Ann. *Women Who Kill.* New York: Holt, Rinehart & Winston, 1980.

Judd, Sylvester. *History of Hadley, Including the Early History of Hatfield, South Hadley, Amherst & Granby.* Northampton, MA: Botwood, Metcalf & Co., 1863.

Kawashima, Yasuhide. *Puritan Justice and the Indian: White Man's Law in Massachusetts, 1630–1763.* Middletown, CT: Wesleyan University Press, 1986.

Knight, Janice. *Orthodoxies in Massachusetts: Rereading American Puritanism.* Cambridge, MA: Harvard University Press, 1994.

Koehler, Lyle. *A Search for Power: The "Weaker Sex" in Seventeenth-Century New England.* Urbana, Chicago, London: University of Illinois Press, 1980.

Konig, David Thomas. *Law and Society in Puritan Massachusetts, Essex County, 1629–1692* (Studies in Legal History). Chapel Hill: University of North Carolina Press, 1979.

Kramer, Heinrich, and Jakob Sprenger. *Malleus Maleficarum, or The Hammer of Witches.* Originally published 1484; approved by Papal Bull of Innocent VIII in 1486. Reprint, New York: Dover, 1971.

La Plante, Eve. *The Life and Repentance of Samuel Sewall, Salem Witch Judge*. New York: HarperCollins, 2007.

Lepore, Jill. *The Name of War: King Philip's War and the Origins of American Identity*. New York: Alfred A. Knopf, 1998.

Lewis, Alonzo, and James R. Newhall. *History of Lynn, Essex County, MA: Including Lynnfield, Saugus, Swampscott & Nahant*. Boston: John L. Shorey, 1865.

Maine Province and Court Records. Portland, ME.

Massachusetts Resolves. Boston, MA, 1957.

Massachusetts Superior Court of Judicature Records. Boston, MA.

Mather, Reverend Cotton. *Magnalia Christi Americana*. London: Thomas Parkhurst, 1702.

———. *Ornaments for the Daughters of Zion*. Boston: privately printed by author, 1692.

———. *Pillars of Salt; Monuments of Grace: The History of Some Criminals Executed in This Land, for Capital Crimes, with Some of Their Dying Speeches, Collected and Published for the Warning of Such as Live in Destructive Courses of Ungodliness*. Boston: Printed by B. Green and J. Aden for Samuel Phillips, 1699.

———. *Vial Poured Out Upon the Sea: A remarkable relation of certain pirates brought unto a tragical and untimely end: some conferences with them, after their condemnation; their behaviour at their execution; and a sermon preached on that occasion*. Boston: T. Fleet, for N. Belknap, 1726.

McManus, Edgar J. *Law and Liberty in Early New England: Criminal Justice and Due Process, 1620–1692*. Amherst: University of Massachusetts Press, 1993.

Middlesex County Court Records, 1649-1699. 6 vols. Office of the Clerk of the Courts. Cambridge: printed by Office of the Court, n. d.

Miller, John C. *The First Frontier: Life in Colonial America*. New York: Dell, 1966.

Mofford, Juliet Haines. "And Firm Thine Ancient Vow," *The History of North Parish Church of North Andover, 1645–1974*. Lawrence, MA: Naiman Press, 1975.

———. *Cry Witch! The Salem Witchcraft Trials of 1692* (Perspectives on History). Carlisle, MA: Discovery Enterprises, Ltd., 1995.

———. *Andover, Massachusetts: Historical Selections from Four Centuries*. Andover: Merrimack Valley Preservation Press, 2004.

Moody, the Reverends Samuel & Joseph. "The Faithful Narrative of the Wicked Life & Remarkable Conversion of Patience Boston, Alias Samson, Who Was Executed at York, July 24, 1735." Boston: Kneeland & Greene, 1738. (Early American Imprints, Series I, Evans #4245; http://xroads_virginia.edu/~mao5/peltier/conversion/boston.html).

Morgan, Edmund S. *The Puritan Family: Religious and Domestic Relations in Seventeenth Century New England*. New York: Harper & Row, 1944, 1966.

Morrison, Samuel Eliot and Zechariah Chafee, eds. *Records of the Suffolk County Court 1671-1680*. Boston: Colonial Society of MA, 1933.

Noble, J., and J. F. Cronin, eds. *Records of the Court of Assistants of the Colony of Massachusetts Bay*. Boston, 1901-1928.

Norton, Mary Beth. *In the Devil's Snare: The Salem Witchcraft Crisis of 1692*. New York: Alfred A. Knopf, 2002.

Oberholzer, Emil Jr. *Delinquent Saints: Disciplinary Actions in the Early Congregational Churches of Massachusetts.* New York: Columbia University Press, 1956.

Page, Elwin Lawrence. *Judicial Beginnings of New Hampshire, 1640-1700.* Concord: New Hampshire Historical Society, 1959.

Plymouth Court Records. Plymouth, MA.

Powers, Edwin. *Crime and Punishment in Early Massachusetts, 1620–1692: A Documentary History.* Boston: Beacon Press, 1966.

Quincy, Joseph, Jr. *Reports of Cases Argued & Adjudged in the Superior Court of Judicature of the Province of Massachusetts Bay, 1761–1772.* Boston: Little Brown, 1865. Reprint, New York: Russell & Russell, 1969.

Rapaport, Diane. *The Naked Quaker: True Crimes and Controversies from the Courts of Colonial New England.* Beverly, MA: Commonwealth Editions, 2007.

————. *New England Court Records: A Research Guide for Genealogists and Historians.* Burlington, MA: Quill Pen Press, 2006.

Records of the Inferior Court of Common Pleas of Essex County, 1690-1782. 13 vols. Office of the Clerk of the Courts, Essex County Court House, Salem, MA. n.d.

Reis, Elizabeth. *Damned Women: Sinners and Witches in Puritan New England.* Ithaca and London: Cornell University Press, 1997.

Ritchie, Robert C. *Captain Kidd and the War Against the Pirates.* Cambridge, MA & London, England: Harvard University Press, 1986.

Rosenthal, Bernard, ed. *Records of the Salem Witch Hunt.* Cambridge, England: Cambridge University Press, 2009.

————. *Salem Story: Reading the Witch Trials of 1692.* Cambridge, England & New York: Cambridge University Press, 1993.

Salem Quarterly Court Records. Salem, Essex County, MA.

Salem Witch Trials Documentary Archive online (University of Virginia, Professor Benjamin Ray & team), http://etext.lib.virginia.edu/salem/witchcraft.

Sanborn, Melinde Lutz. *Lost Babes: Fornication Abstracts from Court Records,* Essex County Courts, Massachusetts, 1692–1754. Derry, NH: Printed by author, 1992; (www.ancestryandgenealogy.com/freedataancforn.asp).

Sewall, Samuel, Thomas M. Halsey, ed. *The Diary of Samuel Sewall, 1674–1729 (Newly Edited from the Manuscripts at Massachusetts Historical Society).* New York: Farrar, Strauss & Giroux, 1973.

Shepard, Odell. *Connecticut: Past and Present.* New York: Alfred A. Knopf, 1939.

Shurtleff, Nathaniel B., and David Pulsifer, eds. *Records of the Colony of New Plymouth in New England,* 12 vols. Boston: William White & AMS Press, 1861; Reprinted, NY, 1968. (www.histarch.uluc.educ/plymouth/laws1.html).

Sibley, John Langdon. *Biographical Sketches of the Graduates of Harvard University in Cambridge, MA,* Vol. II. Cambridge, England: Cambridge University Press, 1873; Boston: John Wilson & Son, 1885.

Simons, D. Brenton. *Witches, Rakes, and Rogues: True Stories of Scam, Scandal, Murder and Mayhem in Colonial Boston.* Beverly, MA: Commonwealth Editions, 2009.

Sinnott, Edmund W. *Meeting House and Church in Early New England.* New York: McGraw Hill, 1963.

Snow, Edward Rowe. *Pirates and Buccaneers of the Atlantic Coast.* Boston: Yankee Publishing Company, 1944.

Suffolk County Court Records. Boston, MA.

Taylor, Dale. *The Writer's Guide to Everyday Life in Colonial America.* Cincinnati, OH: Writer's Digest Books, 1997.

Taylor, John M. *The Witchcraft Delusion in Colonial Connecticut, 1647–1697.* New York: Random House, 1995.

Thompson, Roger. *Cambridge Cameos: Stories of Life in Seventeenth-Century New England.* Boston: New England Historical & Genealogical Society, 2005.

———. *Sex in Middlesex: Popular Mores in a Massachusetts County, 1649–1699.* Amherst: University of Massachusetts Press, 1986.

Tomlinson, Richard G. *Witchcraft Trials of Connecticut: The First Comprehensive Documented History.* Hartford, CT: Bond Press, 1978.

Tryals of Sixteen Persons for Piracy, Four of which were found Guilty . . . At a Special Court of Admiralty for the Tryal of Pirates, Held at Boston within the Province of the Massachusetts Bay in New England, on Monday the Fourth Day of July, 1726 . . . Boston: Joseph Edwards, Printer, 1726.

Trumbull, J. Hammond, and Charles J. Hoadly, eds. *The Public Records of the Colony of Connecticut, 1636–1776,* 15 vols. Hartford, CT: 1850–1890. Higginson, 1994.

Ulrich, Laurel Thatcher. *Good Wives: Image and Reality in the Lives of Women in Northern New England, 1650–1750.* New York: Alfred A. Knopf, 1982.

Vaughan, Alden T. *New England Frontier: Puritans and Indians, 1620–1675.* Boston: Little, Brown & Company, 1965.

Wall, Helena M. *Fierce Communion: Family and Community in Early America,* Cambridge, MA: Harvard University Press, 1990.

Weisman, Richard. *Witchcraft, Magic and Religion in Seventeenth-Century Massachusetts.* Amherst: University of Massachusetts Press, 1984.

Williamson, Joseph. *Capital Trials in Maine before the Separation.* Portland, ME: Maine Historical Society, 1890.

Willis, William. *History of the Law, the Courts, and the Lawyers of Maine.* Portland, ME: Bailey & Noyes, 1863.

———. *History of Portland, from 1632 to 1864, with a Notice of Previous Settlement, Colonial Grants & Changes of Government in Maine.* Portland, ME: Bailey & Noyes, 1865

Winslow, Ola Elizabeth. *Meetinghouse Hill, 1630–1783.* New York: Macmillan, 1952.

York County Commissioners' Records. Portland, Maine.

York County Court Records, 1636-1775, including Records of the Court of Common Pleas, 1730-1773. Original documents on microfilm.

Index

Italicized page references indicate illustrations.

A

abuse
  child, 98–99
  domestic, 6, *28*, 29–36
  verbal, 24–27, 34–35, 45–46, 50–53, 55, 58, 61
adultery
  bastard birthing due to, 14–15, 80
  biblical interpretation of, 81
  cases of, 31, 82–85
  definition, 81
  fornication *vs.*, 75
  as grounds for divorce, 36, 37
  indictment statistics, 83
  justification of, 85
  legislation regarding, 82
  letter symbolism as public ridicule for, 81, 82, 83, 84, 86
  neighbor surveillance on, 20
  punishments for, 10, 20, 82, 83, 85, 86
African Americans, 13, 43, 79, 86, 94, 167
alcohol, 42–43, 44, 52–53, 195. *See also* drinking and drunkenness
Alden, John, Jr., 124–26
animals, 5, 50–51, 89–90, 90, 103, 160, 165–66
Antinomian Controversy, 68
Appeal, Right of, 6
apprentices, 24, 39, 43, 50, 51, 75
arson, 56, 165–67
assault, 5, 6, 19, 22, 32, 44, 195

B

bachelors, 39–40
banishment, 11, 58, 59, 62, 64, 68, 88, 91, 138, 163
banns, 75
baptism, 78, 94, 138
Barker, William, Sr., 150–53, *153*
bastard birthing, 10, 77–81, 95, 96–101, 168
Beccaria, Cesare, 207
bestiality, 89–91
Bible, 2, 5–6, 9, 14, 74, 81, 86, 87, 89, 102, 103
Bishop, Bridget Oliver, 34–36, 119–20
Black Jack, 167
blasphemy, 8, 31, 58–59, 61, 66–67, 85, 152
Boston, Patience, 191, 196–205
Bradford, William, 3, 4, 54, 89, 89–90
branding, 31, 64, 67, 83, 88, 91, 94, 162–64
brawling, 24–27, 34, 35, 88, 95
breaking and entering, 164–65
broadsides, 47, *179*, 202, *205, 208*
Bull, Dixey, 170–72
burglary, 31, 162, 164
burning at stake, 103
Burroughs, George, 104, 133–41, *135, 141*, 146, 151

C

Calef, Robert, 120, 125, 140
Calvinists, 3, 21
carnal copulation. *See* fornication
cart-whipping, 11, 64, 66, 67, 72–73, 81
Cary, Nathaniel and Elizabeth, 120–24

Acknowledgments

My deepest appreciation to Eldridge H. Pendleton, former executive director of the Old Gaol Museum and Old York Historical Society (renamed The Museums of Old York, Maine). It was he who first led me down this path of crime. Who could know then what the National Endowment of Humanities Youth Projects Grant we wrote together would lead to, or how, through tenacious research, those *"Young Historians"* could re-create the life and imprisonment of an Indian woman hanged for murder in 1735? Thanks to historian and scholar Laurel Thatcher Ulrich, for calling the attention of staff and students to the capital cases of Elizabeth Emerson and Patience Boston.

Thanks to my fellow writer-friend, Diane Foulds, for shared historical passions and for her ongoing encouragement, enthusiasm, and expertise.

To Lauren, Lindsay, and Eric, for their patience in explaining digital matters and offering valuable computer and photography advice when I became overwhelmed by technological gremlins. For your love and support, as well as your professionalism, thanks always!

Above all, my thanks to Tad, whose enduring friendship and unconditional love has never failed to fill my life with fun, the mutual love of learning, and the support and confidence to meet all of life's challenges.

ABOUT THE AUTHOR

Juliet Haines Mofford has been exploring the seventeenth century and investigating early court records since 1981, when hired as the first director of education and research at the Old Gaol Museum in York, Maine. A graduate of Tufts University, she continued academic studies in art history at Goethe Universitat in Frankfurt, Germany, and Boston University. She taught American culture and language in Japan, Spain, and the West Indies, and was a reference librarian before becoming a professional museum educator. She has published eleven books, two of which received national awards from the American Association for State and Local History. Her articles have appeared in more than twenty magazines and newspapers. She has scripted and produced eight historical plays for community organizations and schools. She and her husband, an English professor, live in coastal Maine, and are the parents of three adult children.